To my good friend
John Conner
from one of his greatest admirers.
Lawrence Willet
1-31-63

Listen to Leaders in

BUSINESS

Listen to Leaders SERIES:

Listen to Leaders in BUSINESS

IN PREPARATION:

Listen to Leaders in LAW
Listen to Leaders in MEDICINE

Listen to Leaders in

BUSINESS

Edited by

ALBERT LOVE AND

JAMES SAXON CHILDERS

TUPPER AND LOVE / *Atlanta*

HOLT, RINEHART AND WINSTON / *New York · Chicago · San Francisco*

Designer: Ernst Reichl

85336–0113

Printed in the United States of America

Contents

Listen to Leaders in
BUSINESS

How This Series of Books
Came About

ONE SUNDAY AFTERNOON, a group of college students were sitting around talking and the talk drifted to what they wanted to do with their lives, the careers they wanted. Some wanted to be lawyers, but admitted they didn't know much about the law. Some were interested in medicine. Others spoke of business. They kept saying they wished they could talk with the "big men" in business, in law, medicine, and other professions.

We two older men—who have turned out to be the editors of this series of books—happened to be hearing all this and we decided that here was where we came in. The students wanted to be in touch with the top men (and hundreds of thousands of other young people want this same privilege), and so we decided we would see what could be done about it.

Since they had asked for top men, and since we had the whole series in mind, we thought of various men to write for all the books—business, law, medicine, and those other books that will come—and we began the undertaking by one of us going to see Mr. Justice Felix Frankfurter. He thought it a great idea, wonderful for the young people of the nation to have these men tell their experiences, answer questions, and give the advice and guidance that is so much wanted. Here was *really* something worth while. But a book! He was continuously busy on the Supreme Court—for this was before his retirement—and he had no possible time to write a book or any part of a book.

This was the way it was with everyone. None of the men or women we visited for any of these books could take time from work as a Justice of the Supreme Court or a lawyer with a demanding practice; as Chairman of the Board or President of some huge corporation; as a surgeon, a psychiatrist, or a doctor directing the work of some great hospital staff. Yet, each did take the time to write for young people, telling about business and the professions, telling how to make a career in whatever direction a young person wants to go.

In doing what they set out to do, to write their experiences and to advise and teach young people, these men and women have done a great deal more than that. As they related facts, both of the past and of the present, they unintentionally, unknowingly perhaps, disclosed their own philosophies of business, of law, of medicine, and so on. They not only shared their experiences but also their beliefs in an open and uncommon way. The books, therefore, are far more than books for young people only. They are of professional use to businessmen, to lawyers, doctors; they are of personal use and value to anyone.

To thank these writers is impossible. What they have done puts them beyond the province of thanks, and establishes only the obligation of the editors and of the readers.

Each of the authors has written his chapter in his own way, in his own style; they have not all exchanged chapters to compare them. For this reason, there are marked diversities—at times, abrupt diversities—of thinking and writing. And yet, you will see that a few basic beliefs seem to run through a number of the chapters, but this is because these beliefs are common to the various writers and not because they were devised for agreement in this book. Actually, there are a number of disagreements, some of them important, and this is because each writer is talking for himself about what he himself has learned, what he believes. It is finally true, however, and unmistakably true, that what they say, when put altogether, can wisely suggest to a person how to make a career, or to improve a career, and build a worth-while life for himself.

—A.L. and J.S.C.

_1_ *Business:*

AN INTRODUCTION

BY HENRY FORD II

CHAIRMAN OF THE BOARD

Ford Motor Company

HENRY FORD II

Born: 1917, Detroit, Michigan

Hotchkiss School
Yale University

Lieutenant (j.g.) United States Navy, 1941
  Released to direct War Production of Ford Motor Company, 1943

Ford Motor Company, 1940
  Vice-president, 1943
  Executive Vice-president, 1944–45
  President and Chief Executive Officer, 1945
  Chairman of the Board, 1960

Alternate United States Delegate to the United Nations General Assembly, 1953
Member President's Advisory Committee on Labor-Management Policy
Member Business Council (Formerly Business Advisory Council of the United States Department of Commerce)

Trustee: The Ford Foundation

Director: General Foods Corporation

THERE IS NO sure-fire formula for business success. Indeed, there is a sizable element of luck involved—and no one can tell anyone how to be lucky. Still, a young man trying to decide on a career needs help. And some of the most practical help he can get when he is in this period of decision—or indecision—comes from experienced men in the different career fields he is considering.

In the hope that it will be helpful to young people at this point in their lives, I am glad to contribute what I can of one industrialist's experience. There is a good chance that some of this experience will be useful to you, that it will provide partial answers to specific questions you might ask me if we were talking informally in my office in Dearborn.

My point of view will be that of an executive in a large manufacturing corporation, because that is where my experience lies and because the corporation encompasses almost all forms of business activity. In addition, this point of view will help make an otherwise impossibly big subject manageable.

Think for a moment how big a subject business is. Business includes the Main Street store where you greet the owner by his first name, the industrial complex that designs and builds your car, the bank that protects your savings and helps you with investments. It is the publishing house that prints your books and the studio that cuts your records. It is a board room, an office, and a laboratory. It is a giant press stamping out metal forms at high speed, an ocean-going ship unloading cargo at a dock, an oil well pumping away in the Rio Grande Valley, and a trailer truck rolling across the prairie.

The business world is all of these things and a great deal more.

Above all, of course, it is people—people who, with their minds and talents and energies, are dedicated to the enormously difficult but enormously rewarding task of keeping this country the most abundant, the most prosperous in the world.

Even suggesting the business world's complexity and variety, its powerful forces and challenges, its vividness and excitement is quite a job. I would like to start on it by focusing on some of the questions and answers that are apt to be of concern to the young man investigating business as a possible career. He is worth all of the attention and consideration established businessmen can give him. In the very near future now, he and others like him will bear the responsibility for the continuing and increasing success of our economic system—or for its decline and failure.

What opportunities does business offer the young man of today? There are great opportunities in business, particularly with the larger established companies that have been providing goods and services for many years. I don't mean to imply that the day of the lone entrepreneur is over. His day will never be over. In just the last decade or so, a surprising number of relatively young men have—almost singlehandedly—built new companies into amazing successes. And, in doing so, they have created impressive fortunes for themselves.

James Ryder, who once could afford only a $30 down payment on a $130 used Model-A Ford truck to start a one-man hauling operation, is now president of Ryder System. Today, his company leases out great numbers of trucks and cars, as well as various other kinds of equipment. According to a series of newspaper articles that appeared about a year ago, Mr. Ryder's assets at that time totaled more than $11 million.

James Ling—whose motto is, in his words, "Originate your own business deals"—scraped together $3,000 to go into business as an electrical contractor. Today, at thirty-seven years of age, he is president of Ling-Temco Vought, which makes aero-space products. The company has assets of about $150 million, and Mr. Ling's personal fortune—according to the same newspaper series —is in excess of $10 million.

Just eight years ago, Charles "Tex" Thornton founded Litton Industries to make computers, business machines, and electronic components. In the beginning, the company's stock sold at about $10 a share. Litton, too, has grown fast. Today—after a remarkable twenty-five mergers and allowing for a two-to-one stock split —the company's stock is worth about $160 a share. Mr. Thornton, incidentally, was one of ten outstanding young Air Force officers who joined Ford Motor Company after World War II. In time, a number of them chose to strike out on their own. Of the majority who remained, one—Robert S. McNamara—rose to the presidency of our company, and then was called by President Kennedy to serve as Secretary of Defense.

You may be tinkering with an idea that you hope will create a new business. If so, more power to you. If you feel you can start your own small business and operate it imaginatively and aggressively, then by all means take that route. Small businesses can be challenging and highly profitable to their owners, and they make an enormous contribution to this nation's economy.

Most of the time, however, a young man enters business not as an owner but as an employee. He may have training in a specific field or he may have a general education and learn special skills on the job. In either case, the business world, being tremendously varied itself, offers him all kinds of opportunities. Jobs are waiting for lawyers, accountants, mathematicians, scientists, engineers, commercial artists, market researchers, and other people with specialized training, as well as for liberal arts graduates of high intelligence and scholastic performance.

I shall have more to say about these jobs later. But what I would like to do for the moment is to encourage you to think *beyond* your special field. Any special training will be of value to the company that hires you, indeed, it may be the primary qualification that gets you your first job. But your development of skills beyond your college major and beyond your area of study in graduate school will be of even greater value to the company. For management talent is in short supply, and that means job opportunities all up and down the line.

I have emphasized college and graduate study. I realize, of course, that there are many young people who have no college training, yet have ambitions in business. I am glad to say to them that they, too, will find open doors. In business, as elsewhere, there are always opportunities for anyone who has intelligence and talent and drive. The young man with such qualities—whether he chooses to develop them inside the formal educational structure or outside it through practical firsthand experience—can go far. But I would be unfair and misleading if I did not point out that a college education is usually a first requirement of any young man being considered for a possible position in management. Indeed, many men now in management did not stop with a bachelor's degree from college, but went on to take postgraduate degrees. They knew, and today's young men should know, that the requirements of management are demanding and are becoming even more so.

Evidence of the shortage of management talent lies all about us. Take a look at the "positions available" page of the *Wall Street Journal* any Monday morning. You will find little material to help you get your first job, but you will find plenty of material to indicate how many different management fields are open and how high you can set your sights. Or consider the mushroom growth of the management placement agencies. The agencies themselves have become big business.

Another evidence of the shortage of management talent—and this one is highly pertinent to your present circumstances—is to be found in the growth of college recruitment programs. More and more companies are coming to realize that they must have recruitment programs—and good ones—or operate under an increasingly serious competitive disadvantage. A recent study of five hundred and fifty-nine of the thousand largest corporations in the country analyzed fourteen thousand executive positions. According to the study, the median age of upper-management executives is fifty-seven.

This, and the anticipated rapid expansion of the national economy, indicate that in the years ahead there is going to be an even higher premium on management talent than there is now, and, necessarily, an even greater demand for young men in management positions.

Every employer, when considering a possible job applicant, must answer the question: "Would this applicant, if hired, be an asset to my company?" Finding the answer to that one is not easy, simply because human beings are not easy. But, relative to business, we know many of the qualities that make a good man a good man. Here—in capsule form—are the main ones, roughly in the order of ascending importance.

Proficiency is required of every man in his field, and your college training is the company's economic justification for hiring you. But it would be well for you to remember that when an employer thinks about an applicant's college training, he thinks about more than a major in one field. He thinks about the applicant's reading speed and comprehension, his ability to write the English language, and his knowledge of the principles of mathematics. These form the hard logical base not only of a successful education but of a successful career as well. Naturally, the better prepared you are in accounting or public relations, engineering or market research, product design or law, the better are your chances of matching the description of the job that is open. Never forget, however, that specialized training alone is not enough. It may get you that first job; but if it is all you have to offer an employer, it may also bury you in that first job.

A good man will show his social competence—though "social competence" may be a kind of unsatisfactory term that always means too many things. Perhaps I can clarify it somewhat by pointing out that the social skills a young man learns while in school will serve him well in a large corporation. The ability to co-operate with others in purposeful activity, congeniality, knowing how to follow and lead—all of these personal traits are important in school, and they are important in a company. This is not to suggest that an employer is going to be automatically impressed by a long list of extracurricular activities. Your chairmanship of the dance committee speaks highly for you. But as far as an employer is concerned, your chairmanships in the professional and honorary societies speak more highly and more to the point. They indicate that you possess the kinds of skills highly prized in a company.

We must consider, too, the matter of analytical power. You have exercised analytical power in the classroom to the extent that you gathered evidence, interpreted it, and drew logical conclusions. You will also exercise it in business, but there will be a difference—a big one. When you apply the scientific method to a problem in a classroom, most often you don't apply all of it. In a mathematics class, for example, a teacher *gives* you the problem, and you work out the solution to it. In business, you often have to *find* the problem before you can even start thinking about the solution. The point I wish to emphasize is this: in business, recognizing the problem is just as important as knowing the method that will solve it.

Curiosity is an advantage, a very great advantage. An employer is always on the lookout for questing minds. Many people with specialized training and the ability to reason can deal easily with accepted facts. Fewer people are blessed with the kind of curiosity that breaks up familiar patterns and starts fresh thoughts. This is the very source of innovation: the less costly manufacturing technique, the quicker accounting system, the more effective sales plan, the better design.

Now for an essential—integrity is an essential. This is the quality that gives meaning to all the rest. You must have it first of all for yourself, of course, for without it no person is whole. But individual integrity also makes for group integrity—and this is essential to a company. It is the guidance-and-control system that directs company performance. And by its performance over the long haul a company lives or dies.

Notice that the qualities sought by employers are the concern and the result not so much of specialized education as of liberal education. Notice also that they are the kind of qualities that will stand you in good stead, regardless of the kind of company you join. They are "transferable"—a favorite term of Theodore O. Yntema, Vice-president of Ford Motor Company and Chairman of our Finance Committee.

Mr. Yntema has been deeply interested in liberal education since his own days as an undergraduate in a small liberal arts college, so interested, in fact, that he went on to take not one, but two masters degrees—one in chemistry and one in business—and a doctorate in economics. He taught at the University of Chicago for twenty-five years, and also served during that period as a business consultant and as research director of the Committee for Economic Development. He came to Ford in 1950 and has been a full-time—and very successful—businessman ever since.

From his experience as a professor and as an executive, Mr. Yntema has come to believe that the liberally educated man not only has a sense of values thoughtfully evolved, a body of classified and ordered knowledge, and the capacity for finding satisfaction in work and play and the good things of life, but also has a collection of basic abilities and skills that are widely useful and transferable from one field of work to another.

"Many men," he has stated, "prepare for one career but shift with little or no handicap to another. Executives move from one kind of job to another, often with greater success than if they stick to one specialty. I have seen a number of persons who were successful in teaching and research move easily to success in business. Consultants tackle problems with which they have little prior acquaintance and solve them readily. In my own experience, I have been amazed at the transferability of abilities and skills as I have shifted from one career to another and from one job to another. What impresses me is how the various jobs have so many requirements in common, and how easy it is in most instances to pick up the special knowledge in a particular field."

What are these transferable abilities and skills as Mr. Yntema sees them? I have alluded to some of them above. The scientific method, for example, in its basic characteristics, remains largely the same from field to field and can be universally applied. And here are some additional ones that will be essential or highly useful to you. No matter what kind of a career you choose, you will get along best if you know how to maintain sound relationships with people, communicate clearly and listen carefully, organize your own activities and those of others, work hard and like it, and memorize faces, names, and facts important to your job. The liberally educated man with these abilities and skills is prepared to fill almost any position with credit.

Every young person is obviously interested in employing his talents fully, but how are they best to be put to work in a large company? Young people don't want to spend endless years in some sort of apprenticeship that requires only partial and routine application of what they know. They want to stretch out. In most companies, an able and industrious young man can expect to be performing responsible jobs in a relatively short time. I would go farther and say that there are certain jobs that require the touch of youth. I have a great deal of respect for experience; but experience can always benefit by a large infusion of young talent, especially on a job involving a break with tradition and a new approach.

The best example I can think of has to do with an interesting problem from Ford's recent history. It illustrates how a great many talents can be channeled to achieve a specific end. And on this particular job, young men were not just useful—they were *essential*. The problem was to bring to the automobile market at the right time an economy vehicle that responded best to the changing tastes of the motoring public. Our solution to the problem was the Falcon car.

We made the final decision to place an entry in the compact-car sector of the market in March of 1957. And to develop this entry, we assembled a task force of young engineers, young stylists, and young product planners. They had in common free-roving minds and a willingness to try new ideas. The oldest members of the team were no more than forty years. And the youngest—well, the ink on their diplomas was hardly dry. We told them that the car must weigh so much, cost so much, and offer so many specific features. This meant that they would not take off from a traditional design. Instead, they would establish an ideal design toward which we would move. And they would have free rein to attack all of the problems involved without regard to tradition. We got splendid results. We got ideas and brilliant design developments in two years that normally would have taken a decade.

Hundreds of young people poured their talents into the car. Market researchers, for example, carried out extensive studies to determine what economy-car features were most in demand. With the data from these studies, we were able to maintain a running description of a car designed, so to speak, by the very people who would buy it. And in the light of these expressed consumer desires, the product planners continually resolved the conflicts that arose between engineering objectives and financial requirements. They built and kept current a "paper car."

All the while, imaginative and enthusiastic young engineers and stylists were spending endless hours discussing changes for a radiator design, a steering knuckle, a brake drum, or a body contour. They were meeting deadlines to do literally hundreds of things that had not been done before. They whipped the weight problem, for example, largely by designing a new, light-weight engine. This in turn allowed weight savings in the trans-mission, drive shaft, supporting members, brakes, wheels, and tires. And they whipped the cost problem with what, to my knowledge, was the most ambitious design simplification program ever undertaken in the industry.

I have not by any means exhausted the list of talents—both young and mature—that went into the building of the new com-pact car. But perhaps I have said enough to make this point clear: any large company needs great numbers of talented men with aggressiveness, with the ability to spot problems and search systematically for solutions, and with a sense of responsibility for the resources entrusted to them.

There is a place in a large company for the full exercise of your talents. Bear in mind that creating a new compact car was only one of the projects going on at Ford during the period I have been discussing. At the same time, we were bringing out and promoting our already established car lines. And with other research and development programs, we were strengthening the company for the future, preparing it years in advance for situa-tions about which we could only guess. Imagine yourself in any similar large company, put that company into the great tidal flows of the national and international economies, and you begin to get some idea of the opportunities you will have to use your training and talent.

It is worth adding that there are 1,750 different kinds of salaried jobs—1,750 job *categories*—at Ford, including many that you might not expect to find in a large corporation, for example, X-ray technicians and dieticians, investigators and motion-picture directors, real-estate men and claims adjusters, librarians and translators, teachers and artists.

You may have some concern that life in a large company will stunt your growth as an individual, that such a company will make impractical demands on you as a person. It is an intelligent concern. It shows that you place high value on one of the most important of all human possessions: independence. But generally speaking, it is an unwarranted concern. Most companies—far from being hostile and restrictive—have a friendly, open environment that encourages the development of the individual.

This is in the very nature of things, perhaps more so in business organizations than in, say, military or government organizations. Talent, and especially young talent, is absolutely necessary to keep a company strong and competitive. And there is such a tremendous demand for talent that it must be noted, must be encouraged, and must be used in the most responsible positions possible. Otherwise, a company is guilty of improper use of its resources. In all fairness, I must admit that there are instances where poor supervision temporarily blocks the development of a talent. But these instances are the exceptions, not the rule.

Again, you may fear that you will be required to conform to some overpowering corporate system that intimidates the individual. This kind of pressure, of course, exists to some degree in all organizations. In some, it exists to a ridiculous degree. However, I am happy to say that in the Ford Motor Company, as well as in most other American companies, the prevailing feeling is that a man's family life, his social ties, his political beliefs, his religious convictions—all are his own business. Most companies are interested in performance, not conformance.

This is not to say that a young man who comes into a large company and *looks* for the protective coloration of conformity cannot find it. He can. All he has to do is perform exactly and without imagination the tasks he is asked to perform, shun additional responsibilities of all kinds, and keep silent except possibly to discuss a change in the weather—and no one will ever notice him. Nor will he ever rise above his routine tasks to a managerial position. Certainly, he misses the point of managing—and I am not at all sure that he doesn't miss the point of living.

In a company, as in other kinds of organizations—including the family, school, church, and government—there are certain rules that must be observed by everyone. This is not conformity. It is common sense. Efficiency dictates such rules, and without them no organization could stay organized, much less fulfill its functions. If, for example, you as a student attended a class only every fourth time it met, turned in assignments on whim, and otherwise ignored routine requirements, you would compromise the larger purposes of the class: to disseminate specific knowledge to as many students as possible and to encourage constructive curiosity.

By the same token, if you as a young man in a company came to work irregularly, observed your own instead of the company's deadlines, and generally indulged in irrelevancies, you would compromise the larger purposes of the company: to produce quality goods or services at minimum cost and on schedule.

You might also remember this about efficiency. Doing routine tasks well and quickly gets them out of the way, saves time, frees you to do other things in less-traveled ways. And the time you spend ranging after new ideas can be as vital to the company's well-being as it is to your individual well-being. For this reason, if for no other, most company managers are not going to let you get into a rut unnecessarily.

In a large company, you will find you have practically unlimited opportunities for individual growth. When an individual joins a large company, he gains access to many resources that would otherwise be unavailable to him. Intelligent use of these resources—and they include funds, the most advanced technological equipment, and the counsel of experts in many fields—enables one man to extend his reach, to multiply himself.

Even though you believe that you have some idea of American business, its size and accomplishments and potentials, I think that you might be surprised at the tremendous number and diversity of opportunities for individuals in the larger companies today. At Ford, for example, we are concerned not only with our primary business of producing and selling cars and trucks, tractors and farm implements, parts and accessories; but also with electronics, communications, rocketry, advanced weapons technology, and space-guidance systems. One of our projects is a "300-pound talking ball" that is destined to streak a quarter of a million miles into space, land on the surface of the moon, and automatically radio lunar data back to earth. We are also studying the possibility of a "space train" which, as visualized now, will have three sections: up front, a command post; in the middle, a propulsion unit for orbital corrections; and back in caboose position, a detachable living or laboratory car for maneuvering in space.

When you realize that just one company can be engaged in these diverse activities, along with many others that I have not mentioned, then you begin to get some idea of the *extent* of American business as a whole. I have written about our company simply because I know it best, and I have mentioned only those projects and undertakings which I believe to be of interest to you. But there are any number of other companies in America engaged in imaginative and multiple activities. This, along with the explorative temper of the times in which we live, means that there are not only opportunities for an individual to find a place to start, but also almost unlimited opportunities in which to grow.

It should be fully understood that the demands made on the young man in business will be strenuous. Events are moving at great speed. We are advancing rapidly in the old and experienced fields, and we are actually impatient of the earth and yearning to hurtle into space. An individual, as well as a company, *must* move fast today. The Stone Age lasted fifty thousand years. The Steam Age has continued for about two hundred years, although its whistles are growing fainter by the day. But in our immediate time, there are several swift and fascinating ages existing simultaneously: the machine, air, electronic, atomic, and space ages.

This is the time of momentous scientific discoveries and long technological leaps forward. We are making great progress in treating mental illness. There is a chance that we will find a complete cure for cancer in the Sixties. This decade may see the test-tube creation of a living cell. The 1½-million-pound-thrust rocket engine, the Saturn S-1, is already a reality. Far more powerful booster rockets are being designed, and in a few years they will help fulfill President Kennedy's pledge that an American will walk on the moon in this decade. Beyond this event—in the 1970's—lie manned flights to Mars and Venus. And toward the end of the century, scientists expect to have a spacecraft at the very edge of our solar system and perhaps outside it.

It is not enough for me to indicate that a large modern company in our time is complex and fast-moving and also to admonish you to grow with the times in order to keep up with what is happening. "Grow in what way?" you ask—and quite properly. Let me try to suggest the general direction of growth.

Every company is markedly different from any other. But no matter what company he may be in, a young man is always faced with the job of bringing a tremendous number of variables under control. Hunches won't do. Intuition won't do. Simple rules-of-thumb won't do. These things may help, yes, and we have all used them at one time or another. But what it really takes to achieve order and steady progress is system, and the young man must learn to master that system. The extension of his mastery over it—regardless of the level at which he works—is one measure of his growth.

As he formulates the principles that enable him to meet rapidly shifting conditions, the young man nowadays has help that has not always been available to businessmen. Lightning communications, for example, regularly put information from around the world at his finger tips. Highly trained specialists tell him not only what is happening in the world but also, oftener than not, something of what will happen. And if the experts get bogged down, they can now run alternative courses of action through electronic computers and get quick, accurate answers that used to be available only after weeks or months or even years of strenuous work.

Learning the value and use of all of these aids contributes to the growth of a young man. But the greatest help of all to him, as he seeks control of the variables that confront him, is his own mind. It is the element that keeps his system from becoming too rigid. It provides the flexibility that enables him to move in fast or to try a different direction to accommodate discoveries in his field of specialization or rapid social and economic shifts that affect his company. It is important, therefore, that his mind be full, that it be stored with knowledge, not just during the formal educational period, but afterward, too, through experience and independent reading. Language and marketing, literature and capital, philosophy and taxation, psychology and manufacturing—the more the young man in business knows of these and other branches of human knowledge, the more effective his work will be and the faster he will grow.

I have spent a lot of time explaining how much a career in business will demand of you. It will demand plenty. If anything, I am guilty of understatement. Business is not, technically speaking, a profession. Except in certain special cases, it requires no *prescribed* education and no license, as do medicine, law, and teaching. But business—once you rise above routine tasks—is as demanding as any profession. It has to be. Here, in America, we have the strongest, most abundant economy in the world, and it can be kept that way only by dedicated, tough-minded men capable of carrying great responsibility.

But if business demands much of its people, it also returns much, financially and otherwise. There is very little of a specific nature that I can tell you about the financial rewards of business. For one thing, detailed salary schedules are competitive information that is seldom published. For another, salaries vary widely, depending on such things as the type of business, the demand for its products or services, and its geographical location. I can say this much: business salaries are generally very attractive, and most often they are supplemented with various benefits that are well worth your close attention. A young man going into business —if he is qualified and if he works hard—can reasonably hope to achieve quite a high standard of living in a few years. And there exists always, of course, the chance for even greater prosperity.

Salary is important, but I would like to make one further point about it. Don't allow yourself to become preoccupied with salary. Focus your attention not so much on what you take out of your job in the form of a pay check as on what you put into your job in the form of imagination, thought, and energy. Albert Einstein, shortly before his death, had this to say to a young man, "Do not strive for success—strive to be a person of greater value." If you follow this advice, most often your advancements and pay checks will take care of themselves.

Concentrating on doing your work imaginatively and well will also free you to become a pro in one of the biggest, most exciting games that human beings engage in. It is a game that requires your total professional involvement and a considerable share of your personal involvement. Commitment to your work will make the game fun for you. And it ought to be fun, since if you choose a business career, you will very likely be playing it for the rest of your professional life.

The game is global. If you look around your home town, for example, you will likely find an automobile made in Germany, a transistor radio made in Japan, and a shirt made in Hong Kong. These products are from far away, but they are competing right here; they are having tremendous influence right here.

The game is also for keeps. Competition has a very keen edge. If you don't do your job well, another man will. If your company as a whole doesn't do its job well, another company will. Slackness, inefficiency, lack of foresight—these are the weaknesses that put a man or a company out of the game. And this is as it should be. Surely, such traits should not be tolerated, much less rewarded. Getting the work of the world done is too important.

If the penalty for failure is always there, so is the reward for success: the zest, the excitement you feel when sales jump. Sales figures—assuming a satisfactory level of profits, of course—are a kind of scoring system for the game. They tell you how you are doing. And when they are up, you know you are doing all right. You know that by cutting the cost, coming up with the new design, finding the new manufacturing technique, changing the advertising approach, forecasting the market shift, you and your associates are matching or beating the performance of your competitors.

Standing up to a wide variety of challenges, responding to and using the new ideas being generated at a rapid rate by our fast-moving technology, having a share in dynamic group action that leads to measurable success, and in general helping direct the powerful economic forces of this country—these generate excitement enough for any man. But a man doesn't work for excitement alone, any more than he works for money alone. He needs to know that what he is doing is worth-while, not only to himself but to others as well—in material ways and in larger ways, too.

Business is engaged in a constant world-wide search for ways to keep this country and its people prosperous. And our economy, under the direction of business, has created unprecedented abundance for 180 million Americans. In one sense, the tens of thousands of goods and services produced by business are "materialistic." But when, in their production and consumption, they mean more security, more freedom from drudgery, more leisure, more independence, and more sheer fun; are they only materialistic? Obviously not.

Business is also a partner with government in broadening the whole economic base that generates revenues for necessary government services and for national defense. And it is a tremendous and benevolent social force that helps provide and administer such programs as unemployment benefits, hospitalization insurance, life insurance, retirement plans, and pensions. These, I would say, are substantial contributions to the spiritual well-being of this nation.

These, for what they are worth, are a few impressions held by one businessman. I hope they prove helpful. There are few decisions in life more important than the one you make when you choose your career. It charts the first course of a long voyage. You would do well to remember, however, that the decision you make does not bind you for life. Determine now—well ahead of the actual events that your future holds—never to allow this first career decision to lock you up. As you move into your working life, you will have additional opportunities—and some of them will come at odd times and in strange guises—to make career decisions. Be prepared to make them. And start preparing now by acquiring a truly liberal education, with all of the skills and abilities that this implies.

As for the decision that now may be close at hand, take plenty of time for thought. Talk with your family, your friends, your teachers, and men in the fields that interest you. Then take a long, hard look at your talents and personal desires, and judge for yourself where they can best be placed to take you farthest and keep you happiest.

2   *Your Education–*
AND A CAREER IN
BUSINESS

BY WILLIS J. WINN

DEAN, WHARTON SCHOOL OF FINANCE AND COMMERCE
University of Pennsylvania

WILLIS J. WINN

Born: 1917, Plattsburg, Missouri

Central College: A.B., 1939
University of Pennsylvania: M.A., 1940; Ph.D., 1951
Central College: LL.D., 1959

Member of the faculty:
  University of Pennsylvania, 1941–
  Professor of Finance, 1957–
Dean: Wharton School of Finance and Commerce, 1958–
Vice-provost: University of Pennsylvania, 1958–

Member: American Economic Association
  American Finance Association
  Royal Economic Society

Director: National Bureau of Economic Research, Inc.
  National Association of Business Economists
  American Association of Collegiate Schools of Business
  Federal Reserve Bank of Philadelphia

Author: Book, articles, monographs in the field of money and banking, finance and investments

IN EXAMINING the careers of the authors of the several chapters of this book, one is immediately impressed by the diversity of the backgrounds of these men and by the wide variety of education, training, and experience which have led them to their present posts. However, one can sense in all of them their enthusiasm for their jobs and their belief in what they are saying in each of these chapters. They may attribute different reasons for the achievements, but there is an unmistakable common element present in each instance: *each knew those things he needed to know when that knowledge was needed.*

The things that one needs to know today, and will need to know tomorrow for a successful career in business, are growing at an almost frightening rate. New resources are discovered every day. Energy is available in almost immeasurable quantities. Production techniques are undergoing revolutionary changes. Automation may be a savior or a scourge. Channels and methods of distribution are in a state of flux, and the theories and practices of organization and control are being drastically revised. Not only are the fields of knowledge in the business area undergoing dramatic change, but more emphasis is also being placed upon understanding the contribution that other forces are lending to the solution of business problems. It is becoming certain, for example, that business problems cannot be isolated from local, national, and international influences, or from social and political developments.

While changes in the natural sciences during the past twenty years have captured the imagination of all, the changes which have taken place in the field of business are almost as dramatic, though they are less widely recognized and appreciated. The evolution in the worlds of science and of business undoubtedly will continue at an accelerated pace, but the sound of the explosion of the hydrogen bomb pales in relation to the sounds of the explosion of knowledge which is occurring in all fields. We are truly in the forefront of a Knowledge Revolution. Consequently, if you are to know what one needs to know to keep pace with this age, you must take advantage of every possible educational opportunity and recognize quite early that education is a continuing lifelong process.

All too often we think of education only in terms of formal schooling, but some of the most effective education comes from our own observations, experiences, reading, and study. These methods are becoming even more important, as we struggle to keep abreast of current developments in our mushrooming fields of knowledge. The sooner we master the skills of education, the more we can learn outside the arena of formal education. Furthermore, self-education is immediately available to anyone.

However, despite the convenience and the value of self-education, it is obvious that the established educational pattern is to be preferred. The method of formal education can be a great economizer in the learning process, avoiding waste and duplication and forcing us to concentrate an important part of our energies on the cultivation and stimulation of our minds. It hastens the development of our skills in communication, expands and sharpens our analytical powers, quickens our adaptability to changing environments, increases our understanding in a wide variety of fields, and develops the lifelong habits of study and inquiry.

The variety of formal educational opportunities available to those aspiring to careers in business is almost limitless. I would like to establish now, early in this chapter, that for those who crave to take advantage of these opportunities, provided their desires are strong enough, they can overcome almost all the commonly discussed obstacles to a formal education. There is no reason why they should be blocked from their education by any of the ordinary causes; neither by overcrowded schools, high costs, inadequate personal background, or insufficient time. Formal education at the college or university level is, of course, an expensive commodity; but, fortunately, few of those who seek it are asked to pay its full cost. It is available, therefore, to anyone who seriously desires it and is qualified to receive it.

The importance of such education is being increasingly recognized, and each year we see that formal education is more and more a common and weighty screening device for initial employment opportunities. With the possibility in the years ahead that the population in the eighteen- to twenty-four-year bracket will increase more rapidly than the normal increase in employment, the significance of this screening device is emphasized.

As this becomes clear, as it becomes more certain that employment in a wide variety of fields is increasingly dependent upon formal educational requirements, you may ask what kind of education, and how much, do I need for a career in business? Should I enter a business school or a liberal arts college? Should I plan to spend two, four, six, or eight years at the college or graduate levels? What about on-the-job training or a short, highly specialized commercial or vocational course? Should I pick a large or small, a rural or an urban, local or national institution? Is part-time or full-time study to be preferred? Should I take my military service before completing my formal education or take it later?

Suppose we begin by considering the major choices facing the secondary school graduate at the end of his senior year. For the boy or girl, these are the common choices: a job, more education, or a combination of both. Besides these choices, the young man may consider military service, and, in rarer instances, so may the woman graduate. The girl may also consider marriage; so may the boy, but his plans still must include the choice of job, education, or service, while the wife may become a homemaker, which can, of course, be a full-time job in itself.

Before beginning our discussion of job and/or education, suppose we look at the question of the service obligation. The student graduating from high school who is not certain about what he wants to do, having no "burning desire" to go on to college and with no job readily available in his interest area, may well think about the service. There, he can learn more about himself, get started in a trade, prepare himself through reading for a formal education later, and gain the maturity to make a wiser decision about his future when he leaves the service.

However, the service is no panacea for indecisiveness. It will not automatically answer the question: "What shall I do with my life?" And one can pick up some very bad habits in the service. Furthermore, anyone taking his service before his education, has a major problem: will I *ever* get to college? The last year of high school provides the momentum for college work, especially in mathematics and languages, where a break can spell disaster. Those wanting college education, and who are qualified for it, would be wise to go on and get it, taking their stint in the service sometime later.

The further you go in formal education, the higher your *initial* salary is likely to be; also, the broader base you have on which to build a business career. This educational base, or background, often becomes the differential in competition for employment and for promotion.

Here, though, let me raise an important warning. Despite my emphasis on formal education, I do not mean to suggest that it will assure success. Personality, ambition, opportunity, judgment, tact, initiative, and a host of factors are also significant. Nor does the lack of education deny success; it simply can be the telling difference when all other factors are equal.

For some, a high-school diploma will mark the termination of formal education; but they need not feel that *all* education for them is thereby ended. On-the-job training and experience can provide channels for continuing improvement. Likewise, there is time in the evenings or on week ends for study, either alone, in afternoon or evening classes, or by correspondence. This can give at least an introduction to higher education, and help assess aptitudes and interests. It also serves to establish habits of work and self-discipline and helps in numerous ways to gain business recognition and responsibility.

Part-time study, however, is not to be compared with a full

academic program. Part-time students have neither so much time nor so much energy as full-time students. Nevertheless, a good student, with drive and determination to get an education, can benefit greatly from skillfully planned programs of this kind. It is impressive how many current leaders in business got their education in part-time study while working at full-time jobs.

Some students, after graduation from high school, will continue their education in technical or vocational schools. These programs place heavy emphasis on the development of particular skills: secretarial, sales, bookkeeping, office management. They provide young men and women with skills essential for initial employment in specific jobs, but they do not give the broad training in the arts and sciences which prepare a person for a variety of work or for some of the more extensive responsibilities of business executives.

Furthermore, these restricted courses prevent many students from discovering latent interests or talents, because they are not challenged by new ideas or exposed to new disciplines. This concentration of work in specialized vocational areas may, therefore, be looked on as another weakness of these programs. If the deficiencies or gaps caused by specialization are recognized in time, the young man or woman may overcome them by supplemental work or by self-education; but the problem is to recognize them, and the bigger problem is to do something about them.

Some high-school graduates go on to a two-year junior college. The curricula in such institutions range from almost complete vocational emphasis to the equivalent of two years of liberal arts. There is a tendency, however, for work in the junior colleges more and more to reflect vocational training.

A student who enters a junior college with even a slight idea of continuing his education later, going on for a baccalaureate degree, should avoid specialization and keep vocational course work to a minimum. This will facilitate a transfer of credits to a senior college, and will permit him to take advantage of the academic strength of the higher institution. It may also lessen his problems in complying with graduation requirements.

There is nothing so frustrating to a transfer student as the discovery that he has already completed most of the work for his major or that he must now take an inordinate amount of one or two subjects in order to qualify for his degree. If a transfer is planned from a junior to a senior institution, the student should consult the senior college early about what courses he should take.

Many secondary school graduates will embark immediately on a four-year program leading to a baccalaureate degree. For those who are interested in a career in business, there will again be the familiar pattern of choice. Should they go to a liberal arts college? Should they go to an institution with strong business leanings?

It is not the *kind* of institution that is important, but the *individual* college or university. Some liberal arts colleges permit more courses in business than some business schools. A student should select the institution that appeals to him, rather than be concerned about its academic classification.

Wherever he goes, he will be confronted again with choice. What courses should he take? Should he begin at once to specialize in business studies? Should he postpone specialization until he has become familiar with other areas of study: the liberal arts, the sciences, and so on?

At the beginning of his college training, a student is well advised to select individual teachers and courses rather than moving into some general area of study. An accounting course can be a very narrow, mechanistic exercise or an exciting experience in logic and philosophy. The same is true of courses in history, literature, mathematics. In seeking to acquire wisdom, and to learn good study habits, it is always better in early college years to find the good teachers and the good courses, selecting them above any specialty.

The benefits of delaying specialization are recognized by some institutions in that they concentrate their business courses in the latter part of their academic program.

One should know, however, that at other institutions business and non-business courses are taken concurrently through the entire four-year period.

A student should keep this difference in mind in selecting the institution which suits him best.

Increasingly, college students are attending graduate schools of business. This thought is even creeping into the plans of forward-looking juniors and seniors in secondary schools.

This growing desire for graduate education in business comes from varied reasons. With some students, it is the realization of the need for greater maturity before entering the business world. It may be spurred by recognizing the initial job advantage for those with graduate degrees and the probability that this advantage will increase. Some students realize the weakness of the business curriculum in their undergraduate college and postpone their studies in this area. Others, disappointed in their undergraduate program, want to try again in graduate school. Still others go into graduate study merely to widen their academic areas of study. Finally, it is true that a certain degree of fadism has influenced the trend toward graduate business education.

What preparation is needed for this study? Graduate schools of *one* year in business administration usually expect their candidates to have had basic courses in business, as well as a good foundation in economic theory. Conversely, schools with *two*-year programs usually prefer non-business students, wanting to give them the background that they wish them to have.

At some undergraduate institutions, students are given such a heavy dosage of business courses that they should seriously debate continuing their studies in this area. Certainly, they should not look on graduate work as a necessary or automatic extension of their formal education. Repetition and overlap would be endless, and stimulation lacking. Moreover, there is the danger that they would suffer in their business careers from such over-specialization in their studies.

Some of the more progressive undergraduate schools of business administration are recognizing this danger, and they are concentrating their programs around new courses in both the liberal arts and business. By controlling the balance of work between the two, these schools prepare students to assume positions of importance in business, giving them the broader background that is useful in competing with their liberal arts brothers. Also, if graduates of such schools desire to continue in advanced work, they usually can be admitted to any of the graduate schools of business, those with either one or two-year programs.

Whatever the undergraduate program of any candidate, it is helpful in graduate work to have had a course or two in economics and in some business area. The benefit is not only in background, but for insight into business education. It is disturbing whenever a graduate student withdraws, disillusioned after a month's work, with the remark: "This is not what I thought business administration was like." It is not only disturbing but it is a waste; such exploration should have been made before matriculation.

It should be understood that admission to graduate school is not automatic for those achieving the baccalaureate degree. The screening process, so familiar to secondary school students seeking admission to college, must be faced again. The mesh of this screen, however, is much finer. Graduate aptitude examinations and undergraduate records of scholastic and extracurricular activities are reviewed most carefully by admission offices. Candidates with work or military experience are regarded as priority candidates in a majority of schools, even though their academic credentials and test scores may leave something to be desired. These candidates, however, are older, more settled and serious, and often they are making a greater sacrifice to continue their education. One cannot change an inferior college record, but military service and work experience can go far to compensate for it. This has been shown a good many times in the academic records of graduate students.

If a student plans graduate work in business administration or, as it is becoming more frequently known, management training, he should know that there are good and mediocre graduate schools, and he should learn to recognize the difference. Some give a watered-down version of an adequate high-school commercial program and still have the effrontery to award a master's degree. Others operate in a vacuum, without contact with the business world for which the student is being prepared. Fortunately, these are few. Most graduate schools are extremely conscientious, even though their programs and approaches may vary widely.

None of these schools, just as no individual, has found the magic formula for the making of a successful businessman. When we do find it, our graduate curricula will all be similar and each school will mold everyone to fit the formula. It is doubtful that such a tailoring job will become a pattern in our lifetime, and we can, therefore, continue the exciting job of revamping courses, revitalizing programs, adding and subtracting projects, and generally trying to do our best to prepare the business student of today to be the business leader of tomorrow.

Any student who is continuing his education, either in undergraduate or postgraduate study, will be confronted with two important questions: To what school do I want to go? Can I get in?

The answer to the second question will be influenced considerably by the screening I have mentioned, used by almost all schools and based on achievement, aptitude, and objective tests; on school records, as measured by grades and class standings; on any combination of these or any other demonstrable indication of ability. It should be realized that each institution will always be seeking students of similar abilities, for the effectiveness of the educational process is increased whenever those receiving instruction are of more or less uniform capacity. This also assures that the majority of students will be working at the maximum of their ability.

When admission officers are beguiled into admitting students whose past records and achievements are substandard, the result rarely proves to be a blessing. Often, heartaches and disappointments result from the recognition, some months later, of academic inadequacy. In perhaps more than ninety per cent of such cases, the students do not have the ability or the background, or they lack both. Unable to meet the requirements of the school, they have to be dropped.

A student should not depend entirely on an institution to determine if he is fitted for admission. He himself should find out about standards, and apply for admission only where he is qualified. It can be a serious mistake to be too far out of step with the group. If the pace is too advanced for his abilities, it can lead to a short educational experience which may later prove a handicap in his business career, as well as causing frustration and the development of feelings of inferiority.

The opposite of this is also true, for if his abilities are too superior to the group in which he is placed, he may develop poor work habits or become too confident. Another disadvantage is that he may find the work boring and lose interest in it.

In the screening of college applicants, in reviewing the progress of thousands of undergraduate and graduate students, in analyzing the achievements of business leaders, one fact can never be overlooked. It is a simple and primary fact, far too little considered by most students: the overwhelming importance of the famous three "R's."

For a person going into business, the ability and the desire to read rapidly and extensively is essential. Such reading is required in his work, in keeping up with the records and reports that constantly come to his desk. Ability in reading is required in understanding the explosion of knowledge in our time and maintaining his position as a person of intelligence, worthy of respect and capable of advancement.

In regard to writing, the student who believes that he can rely on a secretary, or some staff member, for his lack of ability to use words or to put words together or even to spell them is not at all realistic. The proper placing of a comma can make or break a sales campaign, can alienate a customer or offend a director, can block promotion and place a strain between an executive and his boss. Writing, as every businessman has found out and will quickly tell you, is always important in business, no matter what that business may be.

Finally, something of whatever is needed for success in a mathematical program appears to be needed, at least to a degree, in business. This may not necessarily be mathematics itself; it may be the ability to think logically and in quantitative terms.

In deciding about your education, seek the aid of the professionals in the field: your guidance counselors and teachers. Their advice will be particularly valuable because it is based on personal knowledge of you and your capabilities. They know about schools and admission standards. They know about the changing educational requirements for employment, and this is important to you.

Talk with students at institutions that interest you, especially juniors and seniors. From them, you will learn about the institution itself and also about the strength and weaknesses of its programs.

Write to the admission office for a catalogue and for brochures describing the school and life on its campus. Let me urge you to read them carefully, with reference to course offerings, admission and graduation requirements, costs, types of financial aid. Besides learning facts about the curriculum, the buildings, the laboratories, you will gain an insight into the philosophy of the institution.

Finally, let me suggest that you visit more than one campus. Go inside the buildings, particularly the library; talk with students and faculty, as well as the admission officers.

The success or failure of a course, a college, a postgraduate school, depends largely on teachers. A good teacher can make a course come alive, endowing it with qualities that make it memorable. A poor teacher can give the same course and make it dull, destroying its meaning.

The use of faculty time is a much-debated question in academic circles, and you should have some idea of what is involved here. Can a good research man be a good teacher? Active participation in research assures that the faculty member is conversant with new developments in his specialty. It also increases the likelihood that he will pass on to his students a sense of inquiry and an an analytical approach applicable to a host of problems. At the same time, he cannot give as fully of himself and his energies to his students and their problems as the full-time teacher can.

Other teachers, not particularly concerned with research, have skills in synthesizing and summarizing knowledge and ideas and in directing the activities of their students. Yet, do not be misled by this, for the mere act of devoting one's entire time to teaching does not guarantee that one is a good teacher.

A little investigation on your part will indicate how the balance falls in regard to individual teachers at your school, though you probably will not get a unanimous opinion concerning them. I believe, though, that a good teacher is recognized on a campus, and I think that you stand a better chance of being inspired by a teacher who has inspired others.

The size of classes and methods of instruction vary from school to school and even within a school. Individual attention is important for some students and in some courses, but small classes and personal instruction are expensive. Also, some faculty members are just as effective in large classes. Each student must assess his own requirements, for he may be completely at ease and a success in one class, yet restless and even a failure in another.

You may be thinking by now that I am writing chiefly about education in general and not specifically about business education, and in a way you are right. My concern is not only for your business education, but for your *education*.

I am the dean of a business school, but I would not have your schooling restricted to business and its administration. Your future in business will be affected by your general education and limited by your lack of it. A general education and a business education can go along together, and neither one, to achieve its real purpose, should preclude the other. Furthermore, the same standards should apply to all schools and to all faculties, whatever the over-all study or specialization may be.

A choice that confronts some students is between a large and a small institution. To which should he go?

A large institution can offer a wider variety of courses and extracurricular activities. It can offer the teachings of a greater number of specialists on its faculty. However, it is difficult for teachers in large institutions to maintain personal relationships with a class, and even more difficult for them to work with an appreciable number of individual students.

Another choice for some students is between a rural and an urban institution.

The rural institution is perhaps more spacious and with a more pleasant physical environment. There is usually a higher degree of cohesiveness among students and faculty. Conversely, the urban institution can use the cultural and business organizations of the community, making for a broader program in its teaching and extracurricular activities. The urban setting may result in some loss of group esprit de corps, but it can add a great deal of reality to a collegiate experience.

In selecting a college or a business school, a student should be aware of pitfalls. Do not be unduly impressed by the physical attributes of any school. We all enjoy attractive environment and the contribution that surroundings can make to the use of one's time, but superior environment cannot substitute for academic excellence. Packaging plays an important role in modern merchandizing, but the quality of the product is more important than the package in which it comes.

Consider carefully the catalogues and other promotional material sent out by colleges. I have just read a catalogue with a superb description of a new program. It stresses an approach to business education based on some of the new quantitative tools of analysis. This sounds fine and one can be enthusiastic about it. There is one hitch. In another section of the catalogue, one finds that the basic mathematics course, an essential element in the program, is not scheduled until the student's final semester of his college career!

A second source of confusion in catalogues can be titles and descriptions of courses. In several catalogues, these descriptions may be quite similar, though the differences can be very real. The quality of the faculty, and of the students, can be determining ingredients in a course; but these qualities cannot be conveyed in course descriptions. Here again, the student must find out for himself, both about the institution as a whole and what goes on in the classrooms.

Evaluate the talk you hear about each school and college. Generally, it is about as accurate as tips on horse racing and the stock market. It may originate in a well-intended manner, but the originator can be misinformed, overly enthusiastic, careless, or just plain irresponsible. Never overlook a comment about a school, but never accept it without evaluating it.

A student probably never will find the Elysian fields of the academic world; but he can search with greatest care, asking, listening, judging, until he finds the institution which he believes suits him best and will be most beneficial to him.

In the planning of his education, any student will be confronted with many decisions. This, too, is a part of his training, for the making of decisions is essential to any man whose career is business.

_3_ *You as a*

BANKER

BY S. CLARK BEISE

PRESIDENT
Bank of America

S. CLARK BEISE

Born: 1898, Windom, Minnesota

Windom High School
University of Minnesota: B.S., 1922
St. Mary's College: LL.D., 1960 (Honorary)

Minneapolis Trust Company, 1922–24
Office of Comptroller of the Currency, Washington: National Bank Examiner, 1924–27
Peoples National Bank, Jackson, Michigan, 1927–33
National Bank Examiner, Washington, 1933–36
Bank of America National Trust and Savings Association, 1936–
    Executive Vice-president, 1945–51
    Senior Vice-president and Chairman of the Managing Committee, 1951–54
    President, 1954–

American Institute of Banking
American Bankers Association:
    Committee on Government Borrowing
    Centennial Commission
Association of Reserve City Bankers:
    Board of Directors
    Committee on Federal Relations
    Trustee of Banking Research Fund
San Francisco Clearing House Association
Banca d'America e d'Italia (Milan):
    Board of Directors
Department of Commerce, Business Advisory Council:
    Committee on Taxation
Stanford Research Institute:
    Board of Directors
    Director, International Committee
    Finance Committee
San Francisco Symphony Association:
    Board of Governors
International Progress in Management:
    Board of Advisors
American National Red Cross:
    Golden Gate Chapter, Director
United Community Fund (San Francisco)
World Affairs Council of Northern California
Italian-American Chamber of Commerce of the Pacific Coast:
    Advisory Board
Committee for Economic Development
National Industrial Conference Board

A STRAIGHT LINE is the shortest distance between two points"—and while this is an old geometric postulate, I believe it is one you might well apply in charting the course of your career, for it can help you avoid much frustration and disappointment, as well as wasted years.

You stand at one point today. From here, you will set out for the second point: your ultimate goal in life. It is important that you decide upon and keep this second point in mind in everything you do from now on. Glean from each new experience and each bit of learning the elements and information which will aid you in your career.

Your ultimate goal will be, of course, success. But success in what field? To help you make your decision, this chapter will present a picture of the contemporary banking industry. It is my hope that the information which follows will enable young people to better assess the challenge and opportunity open to them today in banking.

First, let's return for a moment to the subject of success. What are some of the requisites for success in any field?

Your natural aptitudes—the things you enjoy doing and do well—should be the key factor in helping you decide in which field you will have the best chance for success. You will spend a great deal of your life working at your career; eight hours a day, or forty hours a week, will be the bare minimum. To attain any level of success, you will have to spend many more hours with your work than is required, not necessarily sitting at your desk, but carrying your job with you in your mind, thinking about new approaches to problems, developing new ideas to improve your own performance and that of others about you, and learning more about your field. In order that you may live with your work constructively, it is vital that you truly enjoy your profession and find it stimulating.

One striking example of the value of this attitude was the founder of Bank of America, A. P. Giannini. He once said of his work: "A lot of people you and I know get through their jobs every day so they can get out to something else. Their jobs are a more or less disagreeable necessity to their lives; they get through them as best they can so as to go to what they like better. Some of them are thinking of home and dinner, others want to get up to the club, get out in the car, play some game. Well, this is my game. I get more fun out of doing just what I'm doing here than anything else I know."

And it was obvious to all of us who knew "A. P." that he meant it. Only a man who ate, slept, and lived his work could have accomplished what he did in the forty-five years from the founding of this bank until his death.

Finding true pleasure in your work, then, is the cornerstone of success. But there are other qualifications with which you build from this foundation.

The second requisite is technical competence: education and experience in the mechanics of your field. This comes naturally, if you find your work interesting and challenging—willingness to learn and improve is one of the elements sought by administrators who select young people to be moved into more responsible positions.

Then, as your competence grows and your experience broadens, you must acquire administrative ability: the ability to direct and work through others to get the job done. Many competent young people who fail to develop the essential tools of leadership are bypassed in the promotional process. And no matter how stimulating they have found their work in the past, the knowledge that they have come to a dead end in their careers dulls their interest and sense of fulfillment.

I remember one young fellow, in particular, who some years

ago came to our bank highly recommended from his college. He was intelligent and apt, he took hold of his work and became proficient at it, and we watched him carefully to determine the right moment to move him upward and to learn in which area he showed the greatest interest and skill. We asked his superior to try him in new and more responsible work, to have him make decisions, to watch his relations with his fellow workers, looking particularly for leadership ability. But we were badly disappointed. He showed little inclination to extend himself into new areas of responsibility or to develop new skills. His attitude toward his co-employees was, "You do your work; I'll do mine." We felt perhaps he did not find his work challenging enough or that there was a personality conflict in his department, so we tried him in other posts; but in each one he showed interest only in performing his assigned duties satisfactorily. Today, he holds a position only slightly above that for which he was hired.

Perhaps this man is satisfied with his progress, but I doubt it. It must be disheartening for him to watch the rise of other employees; some have become his superiors, others have bypassed him and gone into new areas. His ability in his particular job is equal to, sometimes better than, many of theirs. But they have tried harder to learn and grow.

Finally, as you continue to expand your knowledge and administrative ability, you approach the executive level. It is at this point you must broaden your scope of interests and demonstrate your competence to those outside your own organization; that is, you must become known for your ability by the people in your industry and in your community.

These are the aims you must hold in mind as you cast about for the life's work which best suits you. I cannot overemphasize the importance of retaining this long-range picture. Recruiters for industry and other personnel people comment that many job applicants fail to seriously consider the *future* of a position which is offered to them. They want success, and the glamour which attaches to apparent success, immediately, and they fail to give adequate consideration to whether or not there is opportunity to grow and advance.

I can't say that my first few jobs in banking were the most exciting in the world. While I was in high school, I had the opportunity to work in banks in my home town in Minnesota. Later, I worked in Minneapolis banks while I was attending the University of Minnesota School of Business. By the time I graduated, I knew that I wanted banking to be my career; I could see that it was a growing and changing field with a challenging future, and I wanted to participate in that future.

And so, I entered the banking profession in earnest. I received my practical grounding in the techniques and skills of banking in Midwestern banks and with the National Bank Examiner's office in Minneapolis. I came to San Francisco in 1933 to work for the Twelfth Federal Reserve District, and it was here that I began to learn about a new kind of bank and a new kind of banker: the bank was the largest and most successful branch banking system in the United States, Bank of America National Trust and Savings Association; the banker was its founder, A. P. Giannini. His philosophy, drive, and personality impressed me deeply, and in 1936 I joined his staff as a vice-president.

But my greatest sense of satisfaction does not come from the post I hold or the title I bear. My own real satisfaction comes from having participated in the banking industry's most exciting era of change and modernization, and from having played a role in the growth and success of one of the most dynamic organizations in the world. But remember, this niche wasn't available to me immediately after I completed my academic training. There were fourteen years when I devoted my efforts to learning all I could about banks and the banking industry, before I joined Bank of America. Willingness to accept such a period of "internship" is vital to every career, and it requires—I repeat here for emphasis—that you truly like your work and have faith in your profession.

Jobs which offer immediate glamour and excitement too often grow routine and dull after a time, when the employee begins to realize that he is not being offered the training or experience to advance into a more challenging position. At this point, after a number of valuable years have been wasted, he finds he must begin again to build a career solidly based on training, experience, and proven competence.

If the reader feels he is ready to build this kind of a career for himself now, then there is a place for him in banking.

Modern banking is a highly technical, complex, and dramatic industry. It has come a long way from the day in which banks simply provided a safe depository for funds and exchange facilities for business. Banks have turned their attention toward service—service to business, industry, government, the community, and, more significantly, service to the individual.

Our society and economy have grown more and more prosperous and complex in the past fifty years. In order to share the benefits of prosperity and to meet the needs resulting from this complexity, banking has had to become an up-to-date, competitive industry. New services are constantly being developed; they are merchandised in the same way as is a new product of industry. Automation and mechanization have relieved bank personnel of most of the burdensome detail work once associated with banking and have spurred efficiency, freeing bank employees' time for more challenging tasks.

The modern bank is as far removed from the austere turn-of-the-century bank as the latest sports car is from the horse and buggy. New ideas and techniques are being adapted to banking every year, and they have been so successful that the industry has grown more and more receptive to innovations. Even the building in which the modern bank operates is different. Few banks are constructing the imposing Greek temples once thought to convey an aura of security and conservatism. Today's bank often is housed in a pleasant, contemporary structure which symbolizes its role as a progressive, well-integrated adjunct to the community it serves. Growing numbers of able, skilled young people are needed in this new banking industry, to help it fulfill its modern role, to provide the spark of new ideas, and to follow them through to their acceptance and conclusion.

Today, the banker who looks at present and prospective customers only in terms of balance sheets and financial statements is an anachronism. While there may be a few of these im-

personal, turn-of-the-century bankers about today, most contemporary bankers look upon their customers as individuals who
have hopes and dreams and goals. Today's banker knows that at
one time or another in the course of life, nearly everyone—young
and old, rich and poor—seeks the advice and assistance of his
banker. The banker, in turn, likes the people with whom he deals
and enjoys helping them.

These are two very important qualifications for a banker today.
A great deal of his satisfaction must come from helping others
build, because this is the nature of his business. Young married
people seek his counsel in buying and furnishing their first home,
in purchasing a new car, in making financial plans for their
family's education. Businessmen ask his advice on how to make
more efficient use of capital, how best to expand production,
how to open new markets for their products. People in their
middle years bring him their life savings and ask his help in
making investments and estate plans, which will give them
income and security in their later years and which will assure
that the benefits of their life's work will be passed on most
equitably to their heirs. This is the essence of the modern
banker's work, and, as in any work, he must honestly enjoy it in
order to succeed.

There is one quality I have not mentioned before, but which
is implicit in any up-to-date list of the qualities needed for
success in banking. It is extremely important for any business
or professional man, but especially for a banker, to be articulate.
Some people are naturally gifted in this respect, but the majority
of us must acquire it and must work constantly to perfect it. In
banking, it is important because of the complicated nature of
various operations which must be explained to our customers.
People are suspicious of what they do not understand, but once
procedures and the reasons behind them are explained clearly
and logically, they usually accept them. Bankers deal with
people who come from all sorts of backgrounds and who have
various types of training; the ability to clearly communicate
information with which you are extremely familiar to those who
have no concept of your operation is an art which must not be

underestimated. Unless a banker masters this art, he cannot adequately explain the value of a service to the customer who needs it. In other words, he is not serving the public as well as he might.

I must point out here that my frame of reference—and, I fear, my prejudice—lies in branch banking. This is the area where I found the greatest opportunity and where I built my career, and it has been a source of inspiration and challenge to me that my organization, Bank of America, was the originator of the modern concept of banking and remains a pioneer in many areas of service to the individual.

Permit me to tell you something of why the bank was founded and how it grew, so that you will have a better understanding of my point of view.

There is a popular misconception that A. P. Giannini, the founder of Bank of America, was an immigrant fruit peddler. Granted, this version is more in line with the Horatio Alger success stories once beloved by all Americans, but the real facts are hardly less dramatic.

A. P. was born in San Jose, California, the son of a young couple who migrated from near Genoa, Italy. His father ran a small hotel, but died when A. P. was seven years old. His mother remarried Lorenzo Scatena, who became a successful produce merchant in San Francisco within a few years, and A. P.'s first job was with the Scatena firm. His dynamic personality and innate business sense were immediate assets in the produce business, and by the time he was nineteen, he was made a partner in the firm.

In 1901, at the age of thirty-one, he retired, and sold his interest in the firm to its employees. When his father-in-law died the following year, he became executor of his estate, and took his seat as a leading director and stockholder in a San Francisco savings-and-loan firm. He quickly became impatient with the conservative methods of financing which were practiced in that era, and suggested the firm make its services available to more of the small businessmen in the Italian North Beach section of San Francisco by actively soliciting their accounts.

Frustrated in this aim by the more cautious members of the board, he announced he would found his own bank for the small businessman.

On October 17, 1904, he did just that. Bank of Italy was opened to serve the residents and businessmen of North Beach, many of whom barely spoke English and had never had a bank account before. They had been overwhelmed by the awesome appearance of established banks of the day and, as immigrants or first-generation Americans, had little by way of collateral to offer. A. P. considered the ability and ambition of honest men the finest collateral available. And he actively solicited these accounts. He explained his ideas on this then-unorthodox practice to a friend: "If business is worth having, it is worth going after."

The little bank grew steadily. Not only North Beach residents, but owners of other small firms in the city came to regard A. P. as their champion in the financial world. But it was the earthquake of April 18, 1906, and the ensuing fire that set the stage for the future tremendous growth of the Bank of Italy.

Although the building which housed his bank was destroyed, A. P. had managed to get the bank's gold, cash, and records safely to his home in San Mateo. California's governor declared a bank holiday on April 19th, to prevent a run on the San Francisco institutions; some of them were closed for more than a month, others opened only for very limited transactions.

But by April 22nd, the Bank of Italy had set up temporary quarters in two locations to cash checks for limited amounts, accept deposits, and make loans to rebuild the homes and firms of all those who would promise to help put San Francisco back on its feet. When a customer would ask A. P. for a loan, he would lend him half the amount sought and urge him to raise the other half on his own. This was a needed lift to the morale and incentive of his borrowers. They literally "beat the bushes" to raise their half of the money. Gold and hoarded cash were brought from hiding places by friends and neighbors and went toward both reconstruction and deposits in the little bank. A. P. also went along the wharf making loans to ship captains and urging them to "go North and get lumber."

The results of his activities were impressive. North Beach

was far ahead of the rest of San Francisco in rebuilding, and the growth of the Bank of Italy after the fire was phenomenal. It was this demonstration of the value of helping the individual and the small businessman that decided A. P.'s future; he wanted to stay in banking and take his concept of banking to as many people as possible. But he could only serve a limited number of people in one location. California is a huge and diversified state, and, in 1906, it had hardly begun to flex its muscles.

In 1907, Woodrow Wilson, then president of Princeton University, spoke at the meeting of the American Bankers Association in Denver, Colorado. The bank panic of 1907 had illustrated clearly that the banking industry in the United States was disorganized and chaotic, and served well only the few citizens who were fortunate enough to dwell near the nation's financial centers. Wilson suggested branch banking as a remedy which would "put the resources of the rich banks of the country at the disposal of whole countrysides to whose merchants and farmers only a restricted and local credit is now open. . . ."

This idea had been gaining in popularity in the United States, and it aroused A. P.'s interest. He took a trip through Canada, studying the successful Canadian system of branch banking, and decided that this was the answer he was seeking to the question of how to bring the services of his bank to all the people of California.

In August, 1907, the first branch of Bank of Italy was opened in San Francisco's Mission Street. The Mission District had not been touched by the fire, and its firms and residential areas were booming.

On January 1, 1910, the first out-of-town branch was opened in San Jose, California, heart of the rich Santa Clara Valley. In an article in the San Jose *Mercury and Herald,* A. P.'s brother, Dr. A. H. Giannini, outlined what was to be the operating philosophy behind all of Bank of Italy's branches when he said that this new branch "does not mean that San Jose coin will be taken away to San Francisco, but that San Francisco coin will be brought into San Jose."

By putting this principle into practice throughout his lifetime, A. P. made the resources of Bank of Italy, later Bank of

America, available to the smallest businessman in the most remote area of the state. In 1935, President Franklin D. Roosevelt said, "In my opinion, A. P. Giannini has done more to build California through his great bank and his personal efforts than any other Californian."

Bank of America has continued to operate by these same principles, laid down for it by A. P. before his death in 1949. Today, the bank has more than seven hundred branches in California, in addition to branches and representative offices located around the world. And nearly every one of these branches provides the entire range of our seventy banking services to its customers. Behind our smallest branch in a wilderness area of California stands the total resources and knowledge of Bank of America.

This concept of service to the individual is no longer unique. It is accepted by every successful corporation and financial institution in the land, for all have come to realize that their success or failure depends largely upon their ability to serve. In banking, this has a broader application than in most industries. Every bank should be prepared and willing to serve the total financial needs of every individual who comes into its lobby. The businessman who comes to seek a commercial loan might also need financing for his home, his furniture, his appliances, his auto, or his family's education. Conversely, the homeowner might also need the services of the bank in building or strengthening his business. The depositor might be helped by a convenient checking account, or a safe-deposit box, the bank's trust and estate planning facilities, or might conserve his savings and interest by taking out a small loan to meet costs created by sickness or other unexpected situations. The bank is the one financial authority to which every citizen has ready access; it should be prepared to meet this responsibility as completely as possible by providing a variety of financial and counseling services for all the individual's needs.

Now, let's consider some basic questions you will have about banking. Your first question doubtless will be: What can banking offer me?

Banking is a growth industry that itself grows as the economy expands. In 1900, there were about ten thousand banks in the United States, with deposits of less than $9 billion. Today, there are more than fourteen thousand banks and some eight thousand five hundred branch offices, with about $250 billion on deposit. Americans use these bank facilities to write more than thirteen billion checks per year, amounting to almost $2½ trillion.

Against this background of growth, here is what the banking industry can offer you:

First, opportunity—In almost no other industry is the route upward open to so many young people; nor is there any other industry in which one thousand chief executive officers are needed each year, as is the case in banking. Some twenty per cent of all bank positions are of a supervisory or official nature. Each year, an estimated five thousand positions of this type open up in the nation's banks. Advancement in banking is rapid for those with ability and ambition, because these positions must be filled. There are many cases where bank officers have stayed on the job past their retirement age because there were no qualified successors to fill their positions.

Second is the matter of salary. It has long been said, and believed, that banking is a low-paying industry. This is no longer true, for as more skills and specialties have been required to improve and modernize banking, salaries have increased accordingly. Starting salaries in banking often are not high, but at the end of a few years, the able individual will earn about the same or more than workers of comparable age, education, and ability in other industries. A survey of a hundred and twenty-four banks made in 1957 indicated that forty-two which had deposits of between $200 million and $500 million expected to start college graduates at an average salary of $341 monthly. Thirty banks which had deposits of more than $500 million expected to pay college graduates an average starting salary of $373. In a hundred and four large- and medium-sized corporations that year, the average starting salary for college graduates was expected to be $382.

However, during the same year, a survey was made of banks

and other industries to determine the average salary they were paying people who had graduated from college ten years before. In banks with deposits of over $200 million, these people were earning an average of $863 per month; in larger corporations, comparable individuals were earning an average of $768 monthly.

In addition, banks generally offer more comprehensive fringe benefits than other industries. A recent survey by the United States Chamber of Commerce showed that bank employees received an average of $31.70 in non-wage payments for each $100 in salary. This was the highest figure for any industry, and was almost one-third greater than the average for all industries.

Third—now we must consider training. Because of the wide range of official and supervisory positions in banking and the great responsibility incumbent upon those who hold these jobs, training and supplementary education is extremely important. Most banks recognize this and many large institutions have their own internal program of training and development. In addition, the banking industry, along with some colleges and universities, has developed educational programs at the local, regional, and national level, to enable young people to learn the business thoroughly and to advance more rapidly. The American Institute of Banking is the educational section of the American Bankers Association. It has chapters in most localities and sponsors a wide range of courses for bank personnel. Other banking courses are offered by the Stonier Graduate School of Banking, in cooperation with Rutgers University, the School of Banking of the University of Wisconsin, the School of Banking of the South at Louisiana State University, the Pacific Banking School in Seattle, the School of Financial Public Relations at Northwestern University, and the International Banking Summer School at Oxford University, England. These courses usually are sponsored jointly by the educational institutions involved and various banking associations, and most of the students attending are sent by their banks as a part of their career training.

Fourth—prestige. Because of the traditional ethical standards of the banking industry, bankers are looked upon as representatives of honesty, integrity, sound thought and practice in both business circles and in their local communities. This prestige and the respect attached to banking is an important reward which cannot be overlooked as an attribute of success.

Fifth, we come to a consideration of stability and security. Banking has the highest career-security record of any industry. Banks deal in a commodity that never becomes outmoded: money. Because the money which banks handle belongs to others, it must be used wisely and conservatively. The usefulness and conservatism of banks, along with the fact that banking is the most closely regulated and heavily insured of any private industry, mean that it is slower to reflect swings in the economy and that the effects of these swings are not as drastic as in other industries or in the economy as a whole. These factors, coupled with the banking industry's generous programs of insurance and other fringe benefits for employees, give bank personnel maximum job security.

Sixth, has to do with location. Every town of any size in the United States has one or more banks. Since the industry has fairly standardized procedures and regulations throughout the country, a young person properly trained for employment in one bank is virtually trained for all. He can seek a banking opportunity in almost any city he chooses.

Here is where a branch banking system offers another advantage, for an officer has the opportunity to advance his career in a number of branches in various types of communities. In this way, he not only increases the scope of his knowledge, but is also in a fine position to determine the type of community he would find most pleasant as a permanent location in which to live. At the same time, he has at his disposal all the specialized banking, training, and informational facilities of a large bank.

Seventh, there is opportunity for service and responsibility. Bankers play an important part in the growth and development of the communities in which they operate and of their state and nation. Banks invest a large amount of funds each year in public or quasi-public bonds for construction or development of schools, highways, bridges, parks, and other public facilities needed to maintain our nation's high standard of living. In addition, millions of individuals and families look to their banker for advice and assistance in financial matters. Bankers, thus, are called upon to make decisions each day upon which the lives of individuals in their communities and the welfare of the communities themselves hinge.

And, eighth, there is, of course, variety. Nearly every type of skill, interest, and talent has a place in banking. In smaller banks, each officer must wear many hats, for he must have the competence and knowledge to make decisions in a wide variety of complex financial matters. In large banks and branch systems, this adaptability grows in importance as an officer progresses higher on the ladder of advancement, but the initial opportunity to specialize exists. It usually is assumed that the experience needed to broaden one's background will come naturally with time and supplemental training.

This brings us to another question you will ask when deciding upon your career: How can my particular talents and abilities be applied to this field?

Banking is a profession where there is need for a wide range of special aptitudes and interests. It no longer is just a business for accountants, although an interest in finance and business generally still is important. Young people interested in learning about finance, budgeting, and how to help others acquire the goods or security they want and need will find lending, as well as other bank services, fertile areas in which to fulfill these interests (and here I shall simply list the various points in order to keep them clearly separate):

First: Through consumer lending, banks help people attain a better way of life. Each week, a bank officer helps dozens of customers budget their incomes and acquire more necessities and comforts for themselves and their families by educating them in the basic principles of money-handling.

Second: Career-seekers with an interest in the inner mechanics of business, large and small, can find an outlet in corporate or commercial finance. Knowledge and counsel in this field is needed to enable industries of all sizes and types to build and grow. Within this framework, a variety of special interests—from electronics to transportation to the arts—is valuable.

Third: Those with an interest in agricultural economics are needed particularly in branch banking systems or in independent rural banks. With knowledge and experience in this field, a bank lending officer can help farmers increase the size, productivity, and efficiency of their lands through better equipment and horticultural practices.

Fourth: If foreign lands intrigue you, you may find your niche in one of the many large banks which need specialists for international finance. These officers have the satisfaction of participating in the efforts of underdeveloped countries to grow, modernize, and prosper. At home, they introduce local firms to the potentialities of foreign trade and enable them to open new markets for their products overseas.

Fifth: Trust service is an important facility of most modern banks. The variety of interests which find an outlet within this area is, again, wide. Trust officers work with large firms to establish employee-benefit or profit-sharing plans, and with individuals and families to plan for future financial needs or their estates.

Sixth: If your interest lies in finance and investment, most large banking headquarters need specialists to study and invest profitably the funds entrusted to them by depositors, estates, trusts, and other sources.

There also are many opportunities in banking for those who have a peripheral interest in business and finance, but whose primary talents lie in other areas (and here I think it wise for me to list my points again):

First: Those who enjoy dealing with people and helping them to grow in ability and learn are needed in personnel, training, and other administrative capacities. Selecting the proper person for the job and training him to accept new responsibilities assumes great importance in banking, where so many positions are of a supervisory or official nature. Helping able young people along in their careers can be a most rewarding career in itself.

Second: young men with a law background will find that all large banks have legal staffs, where valuable experience can be gained in all phases of corporate law.

Third: economics is a good basic interest for all bankers. But for those who are absorbed in the economic process, most large banks have staffs of economists who devote their time to the study and interpretation of national, regional, and/or local economic trends.

Fourth: marketing specialists have become valued additions to the staffs of most large banks. The industry has learned that it is important to offer more and better services to its customers and employs specialists in marketing to create, adapt, and merchandise new ideas for bank use. In branch banking, marketing experts are, in addition, employed to evaluate prospective locations for new branches.

Fifth: electronics is a bright new field as applied to banking. Here is where the laborious detail work long associated with the industry is being eliminated and where new standardized procedures are simplifying banking processes for the benefit of both employee and customer. The future of electronics and automation in banking is most challenging.

Sixth: and finally, there is a place in banking for people with creative talents. As the industry has become more and more conscious of its image and its efficiency, there has developed a need for writers, editors, and audio-visual specialists to work in publicity, public relations, advertising, and training capacities. These specialists prepare various types of material for publication or other graphic presentation outside the banks, and create and prepare manuals and aids for internal training and informational purposes.

This brings us to the third question you might ask: What educational background and special knowledge will help me in my banking career?

There are opportunities for the high-school graduate in banking. While he would be likely to start at the messenger or clerk level, a demonstration of ambition, ability, and willingness to learn by taking advantage of educational and training facilities will open opportunities for advancement. In any case, as the employee acquires more useful knowledge and skills—whether through a higher degree of formal education or through attainment of self-imposed goals—the path upward becomes easier. This process continues as long as the employee shows willingness to further increase his proficiency and ability in the field.

All other factors being equal, most large banks and branch systems prefer a college degree for admission to executive training programs and are interested in graduates with either a business or liberal arts background. Training in economics, accounting, commercial law, political science, finance, and statistics are particularly desirable for prospective bankers. However, for those who wish to combine a special field with banking, such as law or electronics, a background in banking operations can be acquired through the American Institute of Banking or other training courses after employment.

In a small city or rural bank, the basic economics background again is valuable, and the smaller the bank, the broader the background needed. In a rural bank, a knowledge of agricultural economics is most helpful. Special interests and skills, such as law or writing ability, often are useful in small banks, but usually must be combined with, if not subordinated to, banking duties.

The advantages of careers in the various types of banks differ, and each reader must decide for himself which is most suitable to his drives, tastes, and interests. In a large bank, there is the opportunity to specialize. For the ambitious and competent, tremendous challenge is offered by stimulating competition with other able young people.

The small bank and, I must add, the branch bank offer greater personal prestige for the banker in his own community. He is friend and advisor to his fellow residents and businessmen. Although absence of an executive-training program in a small bank may mean the employee must provide his own motivation and seek his own opportunities for learning, those with ability can often rise faster to key positions and gain broader experience than in a large bank. The officer of a small bank also will have greater personal impact upon his institution than his counterpart in a larger bank, and can influence the bank's policies, philosophy, public image, and even its physical appearance more significantly.

I believe the branch bank combines the best of both systems. It is true that for those interested in pure banking experience, there is tremendous opportunity to gain a wide range of experience by working in branches in various locations. Thus, a young officer can develop each of his abilities and interests to a high degree by transferring to branches with different community characteristics. He can attain a high level of autonomy and prestige in the particular branch in which he operates, yet can call upon his organization's specialists to advise him upon situations outside his area of competence. The ambitious officer has the choice of striving for the highest possible branch position or moving into the administrative departments. He can even combine the two types of careers.

This, then, is banking today. Like most other modern industries it is open to all who are interested, able, and willing to work and learn.

Those of you who now are about to embark upon your careers are very fortunate. Never before in history have young men and women had so great an opportunity to follow their own talents, skills, and preferences in shaping their futures as they have in modern America. Never before have so many had the opportunity to acquire the education needed for the career they want. And never before have so many varied and challenging types of work been open to young people.

Once more, I emphasize the importance of choosing your career early and pursuing a well-organized, integrated course to its attainment—the straight line of which I initially spoke. The decision and the successful fulfillment of it is up to you.

4 *You as a* BROKER

BY GEORGE U. HARRIS
and **HENRY U. HARRIS**

PARTNERS

Harris, Upham & Company

55

GEORGE U. HARRIS

Born: 1898, Chicago, Illinois

St. Mark's School: 1917

United States Army: 1917
  General Headquarters: Chaumont and Nancy
  Graduated from French Artillery School: Saumur
  Field Artillery: Argonne Front
  Army of Occupation, Germany: 1918–19

Member: Chicago Board of Trade: 1919
  Active trading in wheat pit
Member: New York Stock Exchange: 1924–
Former Governor New York Stock Exchange
  Member: Business Conduct and other committees
Active on floor of Exchange until late 1930's
Assumed administrative duties Harris, Upham & Co., late 1930's
Partner: Harris, Upham & Co. (and its predecessor firm), 1924–

Director (at various times):
  The Empire Trust Company
  Tuxedo National Bank
  Lima Locomotive Works, Inc.
  Warren Foundry & Pipe Corporation

HENRY U. HARRIS

Born: 1900, Chicago, Illinois

Fay School
St. Mark's School
Harvard: A.B., 1923

Governor: New York Stock Exchange, 1941–47
Governor: Association Stock Exchange Firms, 1937–38
Director: American Steel Foundries, 1928–54
Director: Economic Club of New York, 1940–44
Director:
  Chemical Bank New York Trust Company
  Great American Insurance Company
  American National Fire Insurance Company
  Southern Pacific Company
  Texaco, Inc.
  Stone & Webster, Inc.
President and Director: Oceanarium, Inc.
Partner: Harris, Upham & Co.
President: Alumni Association, St. Mark's School, 1945–47
Trustee and president: Fay School
Trustee: Community Hospital, Glen Cove, New York, 1932–56
Member: Advisory Board, Boy Scouts of America, Nassau County, New York
Mayor: Village of Brookville, Long Island, 1940–52

IT IS with great pleasure that we look back over our past forty years in the brokerage business. In this span of time we have witnessed much progress, many improvements, and a growing interest and understanding by the American people in the investment of savings in sound and seasoned equities. It is with a good deal of satisfaction also that we have seen how thousands—yes, millions of men and women in this country—have benefited by investing in the economic growth under our free enterprise system.

As many know, the very heart and soul of the security business is centered in and around the New York Stock Exchange, its members, and member firms. This great institution was founded on May 17, 1792, when a couple of dozen New York businessmen began meeting daily under a buttonwood tree in lower Manhattan at what is now known as 68 Wall Street. These merchants and auctioneers agreed to trade only with each other, during specified hours, and to charge a commission on shares bought and sold for outsiders. The very next year this new association moved indoors into the Tontine Coffee House at the northwest corner of Wall and William streets. Members were seated at the daily meeting; hence, the term "seat" came to indicate membership in the trading association.

Some twenty-five years later, the New York Stock Exchange Board, as it was known by then, adopted its first formal constitution. It provided that among the president's duties, he was to call out the names of stocks, fix commissions, and set fines. Trading began at 11:30 each morning. As each stock was called, the brokers who wanted to trade would make their bids and offers. After all transactions in a given stock had been completed, the president called the next one on the list, and so on.

Gradually, as the nation's economy expanded and developed, the number of securities on the list kept increasing, and the number of daily transactions multiplied enormously. For example, on March 16, 1830, the total number of shares traded on the floor was thirty-one. Today, the daily volume runs, on the average, between 3,500,000 and 4,500,000 shares.

To handle this volume more efficiently, the call market was replaced, in 1871, by a continuous auction market, which made it possible for brokers to trade in any listed security at any time during business hours. This continuous auction is essentially the same procedure that prevails on the New York Stock Exchange today.

In this procedure, the responsibility of the broker is to act as the middleman between buyers and sellers. Arranging for buyers and sellers to meet is as old as history and it has always been an element of most businesses. A common example that comes to mind is the real-estate broker who lists on his books those properties which he has for sale and who then seeks buyers for them. One might say, too, that a department store is a broker between a manufacturer and the consumer. There is little chance for a housewife to go directly to the manufacturer for her pots and pans; she must depend on a middleman to secure them, place them on display, and allow her to select the ones she wants.

This service of the broker, acting between buyer and seller, is essential in the security business, and a simple example will illustrate. An individual in Spokane, Washington, let us say, is the owner of one hundred shares of General Motors and wishes to convert these shares into ready cash to buy a house. It so happens that there is a man in Tallahassee, Florida, who thinks that General Motors is a good investment, and he would like to find someone to sell him one hundred shares.

Both individuals go to their stockbrokers in their respective cities, and, since General Motors is listed on the New York Stock Exchange, the two brokers wire their orders—one to sell, one to buy—to their offices in New York City. The orders are transmitted to the floor of the Exchange and in a very short time the man in Spokane has sold his stock and the fellow in Tallahassee has bought it. Without the brokers, and the vast organization at their disposal, the seller in Spokane would have had a hard time finding the individual all the way across the country in Tallahassee who wanted to buy one hundred shares of General Motors.

In this transaction, and in all others like it, the *selling* broker tries for the highest price possible. The *buying* broker wants to get the stock at the lowest price he can. Each is doing his best for his client, and the resulting sale is at the fairest price that can be arranged. In this way, each broker renders a service to his side at small cost.

Actually, the transaction is not between these two people only, not just this one buyer and this one seller. There are dozens, scores, possibly hundreds of people at any minute of the trading day who want to buy or sell General Motors stock. Some of them will be offering to *sell* the stock at the price they think they can get. Others will be offering to *buy* at the price they are willing to pay. These prices are being constantly adjusted—the seller coming down, the buyer coming up—until a sale is made. It is an auction, really; with the broker acting as the auctioneer and arranging the sale.

A full and public record is kept of each sale, showing the price, the time of the sale, the number of shares traded, and the name of the brokers. This record is open to inspection at any time.

The Exchange itself is open to visitors, and there are guides to explain what is going on. They show you the "floor" while trading is actually taking place, and they give a little talk, telling about the history of the stock market and how shares are bought and sold. They also make clear the broker's part in the transactions, and they are quick to answer any questions. A young person interested in this, and in a career as a stockbroker, should be certain to visit the Exchange and see for himself what goes on. He need have no introduction. He can just walk in off the street and he will be welcome.

At the end of 1960, there were some fifteen hundred issues of stock listed on the "Big Board," the New York Stock Exchange. They totaled 6.5 billion shares. Their worth was nearly $308 billion.

At the same time, there were nearly twelve hundred bond issues. Their market value was $108 billion.

Access to still other billions of shares could be had through the American Stock Exchange and other exchanges around the country.

There is also the Over-the-counter Market, which deals in some fifty-three thousand issues not listed on the major exchanges. (Over-the-counter stocks are not listed because the companies either are too small to meet the minimum sales and earnings requirements of the various exchanges, or because too much stock is held by the management to permit extensive trading, or because of various other technical reasons which might make the security ineligible for listing.)

In 1960, more than thirty-one hundred branch offices of the New York Stock Exchange operated around the country and abroad. This compares with six hundred and sixty-two branch offices forty years ago.

During these past forty years there have been many improvements provided by the New York Stock Exchange and by most of the registered exchanges in this country for the protection and convenience of the investing public. Here are some of them.

In order that investors in all parts of the United States may be on the same footing as investors living close to the Exchange, a country-wide network of *high-speed tickers* is provided. Every sale is printed almost instantaneously as it occurs on the "floor." Thus the sale of the hundred shares of General Motors referred to above appeared on the Spokane and Tallahassee tickers at the same instant as it appeared in New York.

Any news of national or world interest, whether financial, political, or of whatever significant nature, is immediately disseminated throughout the country by *news ticker*, so that any and all who are interested may have access to it at the same time.

Practically every city of any size in the United States is

connected by private teletype wires, called *long-leased wires*, with some member house of the New York Stock Exchange, so that the American public always will be kept informed.

Another development in recent years has been the installation of electric quotation boards, private cable services, and, more recently, electronic quotation services. Other *electronic equipment* also has been installed for the handling of the vast volume of paper work necessary in a modern-day brokerage office.

Now, where do "You as a Broker" come into this complex financial structure of today? Will you be a trader, the modern representative of the original "Buttonwood Tree" group? If so, you will require capital, plus a "seat." The current price of a seat is about $200,000.

Will you, perhaps, be a "floor" member, one of the men handling the actual brokerage transactions? If so, here again you will need capital or at least a number of years of experience as a floor clerk before you might be chosen by a member firm to handle its orders.

Even more than experience, a floor member needs a certain attribute or knack of "sensing the market," a gift which only a few have. Quite a number of floor brokers are men who have done it the hard way, rising without having had capital, but learning floor procedure by experience as clerks and then being fortunate enough to gain the confidence of their employers and become their "floor" members.

Here is the real "stock broker," in the purest sense of the term. Here is the man who executes the orders, who knows when to "hit the bid," to sell in a weakening market; or, in similar circumstances, to execute only a part of a "buy order," waiting in the hope of obtaining a lower price. He must use his judgment in sensing the general market, and he must know the activity and the volume of the stock that he is buying or selling.

There is another position, one of particular interest, that is undertaken by some men. The responsibility of maintaining liquid, active, and orderly markets is placed on the shoulders of the *specialist*, whose function is of great importance to the investing public.

The specialist system began at the New York Stock Exchange in 1879 quite by accident. A broker was immobilized by a broken leg, and, instead of wandering around the exchange floor to place his orders, he remained at the post where Western Union stock was traded. This put him in a position to keep a particular eye on the Western Union market, and he became a "specialist" in that stock. Before long, he began executing Western Union orders not only for himself but for other brokers. Thus, he became a "broker's broker," one of the jobs that the specialist still fulfills today some eight decades later.

As a broker's broker, the specialist, for a commission, accepts orders from other brokers who have customers wishing to buy or sell a stock at other than the immediate market price. They believe that the stock will go up, or they believe it will go down, and are willing to wait for it to act according to their beliefs. If, for example, Harris, Upham & Company has a customer who wishes to buy one hundred shares of General Electric, but not at the current market price, since he believes that the price will go lower, then the Harris, Upham broker leaves the order with the specialist in GE stock. The specialist enters the order in his GE "book," listing it beneath any previous orders he has received at that same price. Waiting at his GE post, constantly watching, he will know the instant that any GE stock is offered at the price he is looking for. If that day, or later, sellers of the stock offer it at the price he has listed in his book, he executes the order immediately and buys. He also buys for all other orders listed in his book at that same price, taking them in turn for as long as there is stock offered at that price.

The second responsibility of the specialist is of paramount importance. In maintaining an orderly market, it is his duty to keep each trade in any stock as close in price as possible to the trade before it. This is in the interest of "price continuity." A price of a stock advances, or falls, by an eighth, a quarter, a half, seldom by any wide difference between any two sales. This is because the specialist is not only buying and selling from orders listed in his book—orders that often vary by only an eighth, a quarter, or a half—but because he himself is also ready to take additional action in order to maintain price continuity and keep the market orderly.

If he receives orders that are widely separated, with an open gap between his buy orders and his sell orders, he himself may come into the gap with a bid or an offer of his own. He does this to reduce the gap, lessening the wide spread between buy and sell, and keeping prices in closer continuity. He does it, too, because he hopes, on the average, to make a profit. In his slowing of the market—keeping it from going too fast either up or down —his use to the investing public is obvious; but his motives are not purely altruistic, since he constantly figures on possible profit for himself. However, whether he makes a profit or not, he tends to stabilize the market, risking his own capital in the interest of an orderly market.

The record of the specialist in this regard is very good, for in 1961, of all shares traded by the Big Board's three hundred and fifty specialists, eighty-five per cent were either purchases in a declining market or sales in a rising market. The role of the specialist, and the part he plays, is one of the most interesting of any associated with the stock market, and he, by his stabilizing practices, has contributed in no small degree to the confidence in the New York Stock Exchange held by investors who accept it as the number one market of the world.

Perhaps, if you come into this industry as a career, you may not be a trader or a "floor" member; instead, you may be attracted by another phase of the brokerage business that has interested so many young men; the security analyst. About thirty years ago the New York Society of Security Analysts was founded. It has already established the significant status of the analyst in the eyes of brokerage firms, banks, insurance companies, and investment trusts.

The days of the "big" trader, the spectacular splurger, seem to be over, and he has given way to the investment manager of a large portfolio who wants to know all he can about a stock before he places an order. This trained and experienced investor now depends largely on the advice he gets from the security analysis department of his brokerage firm. He will place his orders with the firm that consistently gives him the best advice.

A senior analyst often brings in a good deal of business simply because it is widely known among the "investment fraternity" that in his field he is the best-informed man in the "Street." To reach such a position requires much time and experience, to say nothing of the additional basic training beyond that of college. Any young analyst must realize that he has a long way to go, but he can still look forward to a satisfying career. He can be of great assistance to the large institutions and to the sophisticated investor; he can also help the inexperienced. To keep the unknowing buyer away from ill-conceived investments, to guide him into prime securities, and to witness the growth of a small nest egg into a sizable fund can be a most worth-while experience.

None of the positions in the brokerage business that we have mentioned so far may attract the interest of some young men. They may be interested in "operations," a glamorized word for "back office" personnel. Like the iceberg whose size is only fractionally visible at the surface, a brokerage house needs a great number of back-office personnel.

These people must care for customers' accounts, posting each transaction to buy or sell, posting every receipt or delivery of stock certificates, every acceptance or pay-out of dividends, every conversion of rights or warrants into stock or into cash, every collection of bond interest.

Of course, not all accounts are so elaborate, because some investors are retail customers who place their orders and pay, or receive, cash upon completion of each transaction. There are many other customers, however, who keep their entire investment accounts with a brokerage house. With the number of such customers growing, and daily transactions steadily increasing, the volume of work in accounts and records has become so great that mechanical data processing is now almost universal in the financial industry. This, in itself, has required a new staff with new skills; men trained in this field have most extensive opportunities.

Mechanical equipment, however, has not done away with the need for the accountant, and opportunities for men skilled in accounting still continue, and, in fact, are constantly increasing.

It seems to us that the *real opportunity* for "You as a Broker" lies in becoming a registered representative, the modern counterpart of yesteryear's customers man. "Registered" in this sense means authorized by the Exchange to undertake public dealings in securities for a firm. The men you see at the outer desks in brokerage offices, talking with clients, advising them, executing their orders—these men usually are registered representatives.

The representative is now governed by many regulations, being required to pass examinations that are becoming more and more rigid and exacting. Also, he must meet heavy competition—at the end of 1961 there were just under twenty-eight thousand registered representatives with member firms of the New York Stock Exchange. About fifteen hundred of them, incidentally, were women. In our opinion, there is plenty of room and opportunity for more representatives in this growing economy of ours.

What about the future of a young man desiring a career in the security brokerage business as a registered representative? What qualifications are needed and what opportunities are offered? Why should anyone enter this industry and make it his life work?

Occasionally we hear of a young man who wants to come into the brokerage business because he imagines that he can report for work at 10:00 A.M. and quit at 3:30 in the afternoon, the actual trading hours for most Exchanges. Nothing could be more ridiculous. The brokerage business is a service business, and requires long hours and hard work, exactly as any other worthwhile endeavors.

Dismissing this young fellow quickly and turning to others who have no foolish ideas about sleeping late and quitting early, what is wanted in each of these young men?

In the first place, he must have absolute integrity. Then, he must be willing to work with no thought of time, and he must have a thorough desire to learn the business from A to Z. He must keep informed of financial and business news. He must read and

understand the annual reports of corporations. He must follow
the Federal Reserve and bank reports on money matters. He
must keep up with world affairs and affairs in Washington,
D.C.

All these factors have their influence on stock and bond prices
and they must be taken into account when advising investors.
For example, in the summer of 1929, when the stock market was
booming, the Andstadt Credit Bank failed in Austria. It was an
event of utmost importance, for it started a chain of events which
led to the market crash of that year. No matter how far away an
event may be, or how slight it may seem at the time, it needs
to be recognized and interpreted by men in the financial industry.

Must a young man desiring a career in the brokerage business
have a college degree? It helps, but it is not a requisite. It usually
means that he has attained a certain amount of self-discipline and
concentration, a broadening viewpoint, a desire and an ability to
get ahead; and college usually means additional friends. Yet, we
know of many men in our, and other, organizations who started
at the bottom of the ladder and worked themselves up to important positions with simply a high-school education.

One unmistakable requirement of the young man wanting a
career as a broker is flexibility. Flexibility is particularly needed
by the registered representative, for he must be able to see a
change of viewpoint whenever one occurs, and be able to revise
his opinion in the light of the changing conditions—and sometimes they change overnight. A revision of the tax law on depre-
ciation allowances may suddenly add new market appeal to a
business that has been overlooked. A government anti-trust action may cast an entirely new light on a whole industry.

A further need for flexibility in the representative is in his dealing with clients. Some will have their minds made up whenever
they telephone him, so that all he has to do is to take the order.
Others want advice from the Research Department. Still others
have no idea of what to buy, and will lean completely on him for
guidance.

He must be flexible, too, in knowing when not to "buck the tide" and when not to "go along with the crowd." If the market is in a definite downward trend, he must be able to advise his client to withhold his investment for the time being. He may do this despite his own beliefs as to the economic outlook, but here is where integrity as well as flexibility come in—and if the client can buy later at a cheaper price, he will indeed be grateful. There is no greater assurance of a representative's continued success than a satisfied customer. A wise representative always realizes that his own success depends on conscientiously keeping the interest of his client first.

What is the outlook for the brokerage business? Is it a growth industry?

Some revolutionary changes have taken place regarding the stock market in the past fifteen years. Shortly after the end of World War II, the Brookings Institution made a survey of the number of stockholders in the United States. The report disclosed that only six million people, less than five per cent of the population at that time, owned stock in U.S. companies. Today, the number has doubled to twelve million, and it is still increasing rapidly.

Why has this figure doubled in so short a time?

For one thing, the astronomical costs of winning World War II left this country with a vastly depreciated dollar, in terms of buying goods and services, when compared with pre-war levels. Furthermore, it became the obligation of the United States to take the place of war-weary England in policing the world, in giving financial aid to destitute countries, and, as we have seen more than once in recent years, in putting out "brush fire wars." This continual outpouring of capital on the part of our country has led to deficits in the national budget of varying amounts each year and has contributed to a further decline in the purchasing power of the dollar.

It is estimated that the 1962 dollar is worth about forty per cent of the pre-war value.

The result has been that many people wanted to offset this

"dollar devaluation," and they have done it by buying equities. They found that fixed-income securities, like bonds and preferred stocks, paid the same amount year in and year out, whereas the cost of bread, milk, shoes, and consumer goods in general, increased. The retired teacher, living on a fixed annual pension, was sorely handicapped in his or her standard of living, as were the thousands of dependents, beneficiaries, and others, who were living on the income from legal trusts. Nor could this income be increased, because, at this time, the trusts themselves were required by law to invest only in highest-grade securities whose incomes were fixed.

They could not invest in common stocks, even though to do so would give them the opportunity of sharing in the greater profits and increased dividends of well-managed companies which were able to adjust the prices of their goods and services. For example, petroleum stocks, with their high reserve of oil and natural gas, and paper stocks, with their vast holdings in timberland, offered a clear hedge against the deteriorating value of the dollar.

This condition finally brought about important changes in the law, and these changes allowed legal trusts, savings banks, and life-insurance companies to invest varying percentages of their funds in common stock. As a matter of fact, the step was imperative, because high-grade bonds were yielding less than three per cent, and the dollar was continuing to decline in value. Common stocks, on the other hand, were yielding nearly five per cent, and often were increasing dividends.

The decline in the value of the dollar, therefore, with all the results of inflation, has been an important influence on the stock market since World War II.

A second tremendously important influence has been the education of the public about stocks and the buying of stocks. The New York Stock Exchange deserves a great deal of credit for urging the public to "own a share of America." The American people have been carefully taught, and have come to understand, that common stock represents a share of some going business.

They have learned, too, that these shares are not reserved for the wealthy alone.

The need for this teaching can be indicated by an incident that occurred to the manager of one of our offices in West Virginia back in 1948. It seems that one day he joined a threesome of young men at the local golf club. These men were all junior officials employed at the local plant of one of our great industrial companies. After they had all teed off with good long drives, right down the middle, our manager remarked facetiously that he guessed he should buy some stock in their great industrial company, if these fellows could hit a golf ball that well. All three of them turned to him immediately and told him that the stock could not be bought by an outsider or even by them, that it was all owned by the management! This ignorance seemed almost incredible to our representative, because shares of the company were traded in daily on the New York Stock Exchange, often thousands of shares, and were bought and sold by people all over the country.

Ever since then, this manager of ours has devoted many hours toward educating people in understanding business, corporate finance, and common stock ownership. He has been intent on overcoming such ignorance, as was exemplified in these young men who held good jobs, had decent educations, and otherwise showed reasonable general knowledge. The New York Stock Exchange has been doing this same kind of education on a national basis, and the chances are that today no three young junior officials of a company would be so ignorant of that company's stock as they might have been back in 1948.

It is our belief, entirely apart from any thought of our own business, that such public knowledge of corporate finance and common stock ownership is of great individual and national benefit. The more stockholders we have, the more proof we have of our faith in our national economy, and this, surely, is a weapon against international communism.

The New York Stock Exchange has admirably educated the public about stocks, about American corporations, and the benefits of owning stock in them. On the other hand, the New York Society of Security Analysts has been doing a job, almost equally important, in educating these same corporations about stockholders and their significance in the American economy.

In the early 1930's, when the Society of Security Analysts was formed, many leading corporations merely issued an annual report, and took little care to give information to their stockholders about sales, costs, and other matters. Often, an analyst, seeking information which he should have had from corporate management, was barely treated civilly. Top management also brushed off invitations to luncheons of the Society of Security Analysts, where they could have told their corporate story to sophisticated and influential listeners.

So the analysts began their work of patiently pointing out to management that their policy was shortsighted, that they needed to discuss their business and report their progress to the analysts themselves, to financial writers, and, most of all, to their stockholders. This teaching gradually had its effect, and now the New York Society of Security Analysts has a waiting list of presidents, all of them anxious to tell about their companies. These companies also are now issuing quarterly reports and have opened their plants for inspection. They have at last awakened to the reality of the stockholder as an owner of the corporation, a person entitled to know what's going on.

Inflation and education, therefore, have had a very great influence on the stock market since World War II, but there has been another factor of extensive importance. This has been the coming into the market of "institutions," the great legal trusts, savings banks, insurance companies, and others.

Exorbitant income taxes and capital-gains taxes may have all but eliminated the big individual trader, but institutions have more than taken his place. As soon as the law was changed, as we have previously mentioned, and these institutions were allowed to come into the market, the trusts, banks, and insurance companies began to buy. The effect of this buying is indicated by a study of a single day in September, 1961, which showed that institutions and their intermediaries (banks and trust companies) accounted for 26.2 per cent of all shares purchased and sold on that day.

A recent article in one of our financial magazines, compiled and written by an authority on the subject, showed the extent of institutional buying in the stock market.

He found that forty-four per cent of corporate pension funds and profit-sharing plans were invested in equities: a total of $14 billion.

Of mutual funds, ninety per cent were invested in equities: also $14 billion. (This high percentage is understandable, because these funds are designed primarily to provide the small investor with a means of sharing in equities, while at the same time protecting himself through broad diversification.)

Other institutional investors, such as banks and trust companies, with a total investment of $57 billion, had placed $40 billion in common stock.

Insurance companies, other than life, had invested $9 billion out of their $30 billion in common stock.

Life insurance companies had invested $5 billion out of $120 billion.

Non-profit foundations had placed fifty per cent of their $12 billion in common stock.

Many others, such as colleges, religious organizations, foreign institutions, and mutual savings banks, had also invested a notable portion of their assets in common stock.

Furthermore, it is interesting and perhaps indicative to recognize that all this has developed within the past fifteen years. In fact, only within the past few years did American Telephone and Telegraph Company, with the largest of all pension funds, exceeding $3 billion, decide to place up to twenty per cent of its assets in common stock.

Here, then, are the recent factors that have influenced the stock market especially: inflation, education, and the purchases of institutions. They cause us to believe that change and betterment for the stock market will continue. They give us every right to feel optimistic about the growth of the industry.

Now what about personal earnings if you anticipate a career as a stock broker? How much can you expect to make in any one year as a registered representative associated with a New York Stock Exchange firm?

Well, to use two somewhat hackneyed expressions: "the sky is the limit" and "it all depends on you." Literally, though, this is true. There are no set salaries, such as in banks or industrial companies, where clerks earn so much, junior officers earn so much more, and where length of service may entitle one to higher pay. For the most part, a representative receives a percentage of what he produces.

Many firms have training programs, as do we, where a young man with good qualifications is paid a reasonable salary for a year or so in the expectation that he will eventually be able to live on his own commissions. There is no obligation to refund these allowances, nor any obligation on his part to stay with the firm or even continue in this field. But many of our registered representatives who have continued, after starting from scratch, have been able to earn one to two thousand dollars a month and to earn it within a reasonable time. Furthermore, these amounts are by no means the ceiling. An individual's take-home pay in this industry depends strictly on him and on his alertness and his willingness to devote himself to his work.

And it requires a lot of hard work. There are pleasures in it and enjoyable associations, but underneath there is hard work. It requires, too, an intelligent interpretation of the news, and, curiously, one also needs a certain amount of patience. To quote a famous financier of yesteryear: "The stock market will continue to fluctuate"; and sometimes it gets ahead of itself, discounting favorable swings in the economy too far in advance. When this happens, there may follow a period of liquidation when clients prefer to take their profits, and there may be a time of dullness when the public is momentarily disenchanted with common stocks. Bonds may seem relatively more attractive, at least for the short term. Or savings banks may have raised their rates to a higher level. These are the ups and downs of being associated with the stock market, and the periods of dullness are logical occurrences. At such times, a lower income is to be expected in a business without fixed salaries.

Aside from the monetary aspect, what are the rewards for being a registered representative, for being a stockbroker? At the beginning of this chapter, we referred to the forty years of service that we have enjoyed while providing our clients with that service in good times and bad. Our business is essentially a service business. The shares of Texaco that we suggest are no different from those proposed by our rivals across the street, but we must be alert in keeping our client posted on the progress of this company, whether it be good news or bad. There can be a great personal satisfaction in placing a client in the right stocks at the right time, in working out an investment program for a man's children or for a widow whose primary need is income.

The stock market is a dynamic entity, the pulse of the nation. It represents the *effect* of many happenings, and not, as some erroneously believe, acts as the cause. It is an exciting business to be in, and a constant challenge to predict and interpret its vagaries. To be a part of it, one must obviously believe in the Capitalist system, convinced that this system has been the reason for the highest standard of living for any people at any time in the history of the world. One must believe, too, that the fundamental basis for any successful business is the freedom of individual initiative and freedom from any frustrating restriction of government.

Many examples can be cited to prove what can be done in business and industry when man is free to use his brains and energy in the development of his ideas and undertakings. There is the automobile industry, receiving its initial momentum from the efforts and genius of Henry Ford, who developed the assembly-line system. There are the Woolworth stores, again the result of the hard work and foresight of one man. There is the communication industry, exemplified by American Telephone and Telegraph, an extraordinary example of private enterprise developing a telephone system so vast and so efficient that it is second to none anywhere.

The security industry has likewise progressed and grown under the private-enterprise system, at the same time that it has rendered its services to the people of this country and to investors over the world. After spending our entire business careers in the industry, we can say without qualifications that it has a great fascination, that it provides opportunity for advancement and service, and affords a close and satisfying association with the growth and development of this country.

5 *You as a*

MERCHANT

BY JAMES L. PALMER

PRESIDENT
Marshall Field & Company

JAMES L. PALMER

Born: 1899, Waterboro, Maine

Brown University: A.B., 1919
University of Chicago: A.M., 1923
C.P.A. (Illinois), 1923

World War I: United States Navy
World War II: Special Adviser to the Bureau of the Budget and Office of
   Price Administration (Washington)
   Member President's Reorganization Committee, 1943
   National War Fund: Director, 1944
   Chicago Regional Manpower Advisory Committee
   Chicago Committee for Economic Development: Chairman
   Governor's Committee on Revenue Trends

Member of Faculty, School of Business: University of Chicago, 1922–36
   Professor of Marketing, 1930–36

Business Consultant various corporations, 1925–36

Marshall Field & Company:
   Director Sales Promotion and Research, 1937
   Assistant to the President, 1939
   Vice-president and general operating manager of Chicago stores, 1940
   Vice-president and comptroller of the corporation, 1941
   Vice-president and member of the board of directors, 1943
   Executive Vice-president, 1946

Director:
   Harris Trust & Savings Bank
   International Harvester Company
   General Candy Corporation
   Federal Prison Industries, Inc.
   Chicago Lighthouse for the Blind
   Community Fund of Chicago (President, 1946–49)

Fellow: Brown University

Trustee: Chicago Sunday Evening Club

ONE AFTERNOON, some years ago, my wife called me from the book department in our main store and reported that an elephant was loose among the books. This was a surprising bit of news, even in the department store business. One of our smart promotion people had brought in the elephant to autograph copies of a book, *Eddie, the Elegant Elephant.* The autographing party went off well, but Eddie shied away from the freight elevator on the way out and gave us quite an interesting time for a couple of hours. There were no casualties, but there have been no more elephants in Marshall Field & Company.

The incident of Eddie is merely one example of the excitement and drama of retailing. The unexpected is always happening. There is never a dull moment. Like the gentleman who bought a painting in 1948, then asked for his money back in 1960 because he had taken some art lessons, and with this experience had decided it was not a good painting. Or the day recently when a main water line broke in the toy department and dumped twelve thousand gallons of water in the lingerie department just below. For a day or two we sold very little lingerie. No, you will not lack for excitement in the retail business. Every day, every week, every season brings something new, and often something not anticipated. As a result, the business is ever stimulating, demanding, and challenging.

Almost everyone has had some experience with retailing, for it is literally the main street of American life. Chances are you've been a retailer yourself, a newspaper route, selling lemonade on your front lawn, clerking in a shoe store on Saturdays—all of it to get spending money or help pay your way through school.

The extent to which retailing touches almost everyone is exemplified by our experience here at Field's. Among our distinguished alumni are several former mayors of Chicago; Emily Kimbrough, famous author; Emmett Kelly of the circus; Burt Lancaster and Melvyn Douglas of the movies. We had to fire Emmett for standing on his head to amuse customers, when he should have been selling carpeting. Dorothy Lamour operated an elevator at Field's, before modeling and the movies took her away from us. Yes, almost everyone has worked in retailing somewhere or at some time.

The retail merchandising industry in this country today embraces some two million business establishments, ranging in size from the individually operated corner filling station to such gigantic enterprises as the Great Atlantic & Pacific Tea Company and Sears, Roebuck and Company. Each of these two organizations has an annual sales volume of several billions of dollars.

In retailing, you may find practically any kind of work in which you happen to be interested. You may be an individual proprietor and own and operate your own store. Or you may work for a large retail corporation in any one of an endless number of capacities. Such companies employ merchants, accountants, economists, lawyers, production experts, advertising managers, engineers, transportation experts, doctors, and many other types of specialists.

The term "merchant" is often used in retailing, and men who have achieved great success in building retail enterprises are often termed "great merchants." Among these in the past century are such names as John Wanamaker, George Hartford of A & P, Marshall Field, J. C. Penney, Robert E. Wood of Sears, Roebuck, and numerous others.

A merchant, strictly speaking, is an expert in the buying and selling of merchandise. Many of the famous men of the merchandising world have not been great merchants. They have been great builders of merchandising organizations; they have assembled and developed staffs of great merchants and other types of specialists necessary to the effective functioning of any large retail organization. Among the heads of our best-known retail enterprises you will find merchants, lawyers, army officers, accountants, and even former college professors. It is true, therefore, that no single type of training or background is a requisite for success in retailing.

Retail merchandising is as old as civilization itself. In the beginning of man's history on this planet, trade was the center of life. I recently read a fascinating account of the amber traders of early Europe. They lived in the dawn of recorded times in a land we now call Scandinavia. Excavations in the centuries since they existed show how, following river routes, they spread across the land mass of Europe and touched the faraway civilizations of Asia, Asia Minor, and North Africa.

These bearded men in their fur cloaks traveled with bright bits of amber. They traded with peoples who were not only strangers—not even a language in common—but often were hostile. They had an unfamiliar, new glittering stuff to trade, stuff that went into glamorous decoration—beads, necklaces, bracelets, amulets, belts. They built richer lives for themselves and brought new richness into the lives of others. These early traders were the pioneers of retailing, and after them came the established routes of trade—routes the caravans traveled, routes that later became the river traffic of barges and steamers, the land traffic of railroads and trucks.

Where those trade routes crossed, the early settlements grew. As these settlements grew in size, market places became stationary, and the great cities of trade and commerce sprang from these early beginnings. The histories of these cities dominated the histories of the civilizations that we know—London, Paris, Rome, Athens, Constantinople, Hong Kong, New York, Chicago.

Trade, then, from the earliest times to the present, has been an important part of the bloodstream of economic life, a source of strength to kings and nations, to armies, and to all the peoples of the world. Its history has been filled with romance and adventure: Marco Polo seeking riches in far-off Cathay; the British, French, Spanish, Portuguese, and Italian explorers crossing unknown oceans and continents in their search of gold, spices, or furs.

Hardly less venturesome than these early explorers were the great merchants of the last century and this: J. C. Penney, who came out of Kemmerer, Wyoming, to build one of our great national retail chains; Marshall Field, who went west from New England and arrived penniless in Chicago a hundred years ago to build one of the great names in the department store industry; George Hartford, who in his lifetime built A & P, our largest food chain; Julius Rosenwald and General Robert E. Wood, who in this century built our largest general merchandise retail establishment, Sears, Roebuck and Company.

While great glamour attaches to the names of our early trading explorers, romance and challenge have by no means disappeared from retailing. The adventuresome merchant of today, while not opening up unknown lands, is bringing modern American merchandising methods to countries and continents all over the free world—Mexico, Japan, Australia, South America, and Europe. And at home, he is inventing many new and improved methods of operation in his constant effort to serve the public more efficiently. Sears, in the 1920's, confronted by a dull prospect for its mail-order business, as our country became more and more centralized and urban, invented a new type of department store, usually not located in downtown areas and specializing in things like appliances, hardware, paint, and automobile accessories. Stores of this type have in large part been responsible for that company's amazing success since then. Charles R. Walgreen revolutionized the retail drug business. A & P, which once operated fifteen thousand corner groceries, today operates a much smaller number of supermarkets, serving the public far more efficiently and economically than it formerly did. A generation ago, nothing existed to compare with today's gigantic department store chains: Federated, Associated, Allied, Macy, May, and Gimbel's. Each of these great retail organizations owns and operates twenty or more department stores in various cities throughout the country, many of which were locally and independently owned not so many years ago. Quite a few of these stores still carry their original names, hence their central ownership is not always known to the buying public.

Yes, in the past forty or fifty years, there have been many changes in retailing; and many extraordinary accomplishments by numerous courageous, imaginative, and talented men. Opportunities similar to those which these men seized upon years ago will present themselves in the years ahead, for retailing can never be static. In the future, as in the past, success will come to those most alert, courageous, and imaginative in adapting their operations to the constantly changing public taste, to social trends, and to technological developments.

Should you be interested in retailing as a career, you have a choice of many opportunities. Thanks to the fact that we live in a free society you may, if you wish, start a business of your own. If you have this in mind, you would be wise first to gain some experience in an established enterprise. Even the simplest of retail activities requires a considerable amount of specific knowledge and experience. It is usually folly to risk your effort or capital on a venture you know nothing about. There have been hundreds of thousands of casualties in the retail industry due directly to lack of experience and knowledge. It continues to amaze me, for example, to see how many people fail in retailing because their very first decision, that of selecting a store location, is a poor one. The mortality rate among small merchants has always been very high. The main reason for this is that a great many people enter the field without the necessary skill and training. It is easy to start a store, and it does not require a great amount of capital. Retailing, therefore, attracts many people who think it offers an easy opportunity to make a living and be one's own boss.

So, if you want to start a store of your own, be sure you know something about what you're getting into. Prepare yourself by gaining retail experience. And be sure, too, that you have enough capital. Even though financial requirements are not great, many people fail simply because they run out of money. You should realize, too, that when you're running your own business, you are carrying all the financial risk yourself. There is, on the whole, perhaps more security in working for a sound and established business. But, if you want to start on your own and take the risks, retailing offers that opportunity.

Some young people have a notion that in these times there is no opportunity for one who wants to start a new business. This simply is not true. There are many new names in retailing today, names unheard of ten or fifteen years ago. I have watched with interest, for example, the growth of a garden nursery, started on a small scale about a decade ago, across the highway from one of our important shopping centers. Today, it occupies several acres and offers to the public the widest assortment of garden supplies and merchandise for outdoor living I have seen anywhere. It is without doubt a very profitable enterprise. Its owner knew the nursery business to start with. He then picked a good location, close to a rich market. And he had the courage and imagination to steadily expand his merchandise lines far beyond the point reached by other nurserymen. His knowledge, courage, and enterprise built a successful business from scratch.

Back in 1917, Clarence Saunders of Memphis invented the idea of self-service in food retailing. A giant chain of Piggly Wiggly stores resulted. In due time the distributive pattern changed, and this particular type of small self-service food outlet gradually became obsolete. In the 'thirties, about five great chain-store systems, such as A & P and Kroger, dominated food distribution. These chains still exist, but they have had to modify their methods drastically, opening larger units, offering wider assortments of merchandise, and providing parking facilities. Alongside the chains, during the past fifteen years, thousands of very large supermarkets have sprung up, some individually owned and many taking the form of local chains. Many of these individually owned supermarkets and local chains, operating stores very much like those of the national chains, have been successful. Quite a few, in their efforts to reduce buying costs, have joined co-operative wholesale organizations, which resemble the warehouse structures of the national chains.

Thus, you see, the supermarket, sometimes individually owned, sometimes a part of a local chain, and often a unit in a national chain, dominates retail food distribution today. Nonetheless, hundreds of thousands of small neighborhood food stores, usually individually owned, continue to serve the consuming public.

From this, you can see that change is very much a part of retailing. Self-service altered the grocery store, brought other changes, and finally created the supermarket of today. The point is that in these changes and improvements lie many opportunities.

Almost everywhere in the United States, even in the smaller cities, there are now supermarkets and all kinds of self-service food stores. But this same method of selling has gone further, and the dynamic and ever-changing character of retailing is currently well illustrated by the phenomenal growth of self-service department stores.

Unheard of a few years ago, these establishments have sprung up by the hundreds in cities all over the country. It has been estimated that their sales volume already exceeds $3 billion annually. This self-service movement has been pioneered not by traditional and existing department-store organizations but by individuals more or less new to the industry. These people started out with little more than an idea, that of building inexpensive stores, equipping them with low-cost fixtures, and eliminating a great many costly services, including personal selling. Customers shop in these stores much as they do in a supermarket, selecting their merchandise and paying for it at a checkout desk. They are often able to save money by foregoing the services and conveniences found in traditional department stores. Many of these new self-service stores have been very successful—so successful, in fact, that quite a few established department store, mail-order, and variety-chain organizations have announced plans to enter into the self-service operation. Its strongest appeal, needless to say, is to people in the lower income brackets, who are interested in low prices and are willing to dispense with services.

I have told you about my nurseryman friend, about changes in food retailing, and about the current growth of self-service department stores to establish two simple facts. First, that there continue to be great opportunities in retailing for people who want to work for themselves in businesses which they themselves develop. Second, that retailing continues to be a highly fluid institution, thus creating endless opportunities for people who are

inventive, imaginative, and enterprising. This fact, that there are
unlimited opportunities in retailing, may seem a little puzzling to
young men and women who look about now and seem to see retailing dominated by the great corporate structures: the chain
stores, the mail-order companies, and the great department
stores. Surely, you say, they have solved all the problems of retailing and have left no room for newcomers. This is not true.
Change is still the order of the day in retailing and, in its endless
expansion, there is room and need and a real desire for young
men and young women who have ideas and judgment and the
independence of character to start out and go ahead.

If you do not choose to go into retailing on your own, the
chances are you should seek employment in one or another of the
many corporate structures in the industry. All of these have come
into being in the past century or so. Prior to the Civil War, the so-
called small or independent merchant completely dominated the
retail trade. In fact, he continued to dominate retailing for fifty
years after the war. But early in this century, the chain store, the
mail-order house, and the department store began to assume
prominence.

While many of these organizations were founded in the 1860's
and 70's, they played no important role in our economy until
much later. All had their roots in the Industrial Revolution, the
greatest period of invention in our history, except perhaps the
present. The steam engine, the railroad, the steamship, the telephone and telegraph, and many other inventions, which resulted
in improved production, transportation, and communication, all
emerged during this period. And with them came the growth of
large, modern cities, mass production, and mass merchandising.
Without all these, the great retailing organizations now in existence could not have developed.

The mail-order business, or catalogue selling, was invented to
bring a wide variety of merchandise to people in our sparsely
populated rural areas, which could not support local stores of any
size. As population in these areas increased, the role of the catalogue house became less significant. So these organizations, in

1926, began opening retail stores, building large chain-store systems. They operate over one thousand stores today.

It might be mentioned that chain stores developed, and the system spread over the country, when someone discovered that as transportation and communication methods improved, two or ten or eventually as many as fifteen thousand stores could be operated at a lower cost per unit than could one store.

Department stores became possible only when cities grew large in population. When a single shopping center can be easily reached by five or ten million people, it becomes possible in that center to operate numerous department stores, one or more of which may sell over $100,000,000 of merchandise annually. Thus, Macy's developed, as New York became our largest city; and Marshall Field's, as Chicago became our second largest. At our main store in Chicago, we maintain an inventory of about $40,-000,000, embracing probably one million items of merchandise assembled from all over the free world. The customer who once was confined in her choice to a country general store may now shop under a single roof for any one or more of one million items. The big department store thus performs a unique service for people living in or near cities, similar in nature to that performed by mail-order houses, through catalogues, for country folk. Stores like Field's, Macy's, Hudson's in Detroit, and a few others are, in fact, world famous mainly because of the breadth of choice they offer. In smaller cities, department stores are, of course, smaller, but they perform a service unique in their communities.

Whether you work in one type of large retailing establishment or another, an infinite variety of jobs await you. For example, take my own career. My first job at Field's was to direct its research bureau. Three years later, in 1939, one of my chores as Sales Promotion Manager was the supervision of a physical training course for fashion models. This was interesting work at the time. Two years later, I was Controller of the company, still working with figures, but of a less exhilarating type. And so it goes in any large retail organization.

The principal activities necessary to the running of a large retail business are buying, selling, advertising, design, personnel, accounting, operating, engineering, and real estate. The core activity embraces buying and selling, often known as merchandising. In most department stores, buying and selling are combined under the supervision of the same individual, usually termed a buyer or section manager. Chain stores, on the other hand, usually buy through centralized purchasing departments. Store managers, who have little to do with buying, supervise the selling.

Suppose we take a look now at the heart of department store operation: merchandising. A large department store often has as many as several hundred buyers or section managers. These men and women report to a group of merchandise managers, who in turn usually report to a vice-president and general merchandise manager.

A good buyer must be something of a Jack-of-all-trades. His primary responsibility is the selection of merchandise which appeals to his clientele and can be sold at a profit. He must be an expert in merchandise, whether it be books, gloves, glassware, or furniture. He must know thoroughly and visit frequently the markets in which his merchandise is offered for sale. He must always be on the alert to find new sources of supply. He must be familiar with the tastes of his customers, because failure to buy merchandise fitting these tastes leads only to mark-downs and losses. Particularly in the field of women's fashion, this requires great skill and involves heavy risks, for styles are constantly changing. Millinery bought today, for example, may be obsolete a month from now.

The department-store buyer also has to manage his selling section. He must maintain at all times suitable assortments of merchandise, attractively displayed. He must supervise a staff of salespeople, making sure that these people are properly trained. He must maintain certain records and control the expenses of his department. In brief, the department-store buyer is almost the general manager of his own segment of the business. He, therefore, has to be a very versatile fellow.

Along with their other responsibilities, most buyers do a good deal of traveling. Several of our buyers circle the globe once or twice a year. Our fabric buyer, for example, regularly visits Europe, Thailand, Hong Kong, and Japan. Most of our fashion buyers cover the New York and California markets regularly, and several make trips to Europe. While most of our merchandise is of domestic origin, our buyers are constantly combing world markets in search of products that are new and distinctive: toys from Germany, Italy, and Japan; silks from Thailand; woolens from England; china and glass from all over Europe; and furniture from Scandinavia. There, indeed, is still romance in merchandising, but there also is an element of great public service. But for the retailer with world-wide access to markets, the consumer would indeed be limited in his choice.

You may wonder what one does and how long one takes to become a skilled merchant. Study in a business school or in a school of retailing will help some, but is not a prerequisite. Most of what you learn, you will have to learn on the job. Several years of training are usually necessary before you can claim any reasonable degree of competence. And you will improve as the years go by. Two men in our organization come to mind: one here in Chicago, the other in our London office. Each has been with us about forty years. The one probably knows as much about glassware as any man alive. The other is incredibly expert in British antiques. These men are, therefore, very valuable to us, mainly through long experience in their respective specialties.

Now suppose we talk a bit about the selling aspect of merchandising. Chances are your first job in retailing will be as a salesperson. You may wonder why, after a college career, you should find yourself selling goods behind a counter. The answer is that in no other way can you so quickly and so thoroughly learn about merchandise, about people, and about the gentle art of persuasion. Salesmanship is an art and must be learned by selling. If you expect to be a great merchant someday, you must master this art. You must be skilled in selling, you must know and love merchandise, and you must like to deal with and influence people. Otherwise, you would do well to pursue some other line of endeavor.

There is another good reason why you should have some experience in selling. It will stand you in good stead in any career in which you happen later to find yourself. Whether you are a teacher, a preacher, a lawyer, a mathematician, or an accountant, you will find the ability to influence and persuade others extremely useful.

If you happen not to be interested in selling or in merchandising, retailing provides a myriad of other opportunites. Most large retailers have sizable advertising departments employing copywriters, artists, layout experts, and other specialists. Here, at Field's, we have as one of our vice-presidents a registered architect. He is responsible for the design of our stores, for all window displays, and for all interior display, including the spectacular displays we create during holiday seasons.

In an organization employing tens of thousands of people, a skillful personnel department is a prerequisite. It is responsible for the employment and training functions, supervises salary scales, directs welfare and pension programs, and handles labor relations problems. Nothing is more important to the success of a large retail organization than a competent and loyal staff of employees. Our personnel department carries much of the responsibility for building and maintaining such a staff.

Large retailing organizations also require the services of skilled accountants, engineers, office managers, lawyers, and numerous other specialists. Controllers supervise hundreds of people responsible for the endless detail of record keeping. Engineers install and maintain mechanical equipment: heating, air conditioning, electrical installations, elevators, and escalators. Office managers supervise departments handling customer complaints, mail and telephone orders, and correspondence. Operating superintendents supervise warehouses and delivery systems. And skilled lawyers handle the legal problems which every company has.

To sum up, every large retail operation is multifaceted. It offers a wide variety of job opportunities. A big store is like a big city. It is a community of thousands, working closely with customers and with each other. For the same reason that young people seek big cities, for the variety of experience and the unlimited opportunity to be found in them, so many young people seek out careers in retailing.

Now let's talk about you. Let's talk about the kind of person you are or, to be more pertinent, the kind of person you should be to succeed in retailing. First of all, you should be interested in people. Retailing puts the public just across the counter. You should enjoy meeting people, be curious and eager to serve, if you go into retailing.

You should have a well-developed competitive spirit. Competition is a hallmark of our private-enterprise way of life. And retailing is extremely competitive. You should be eager to get in the thick of the competitive pull and tug, if you want retailing as a career. And you should be ambitious. This goes hand in glove with the competitive way of earning a living. You must want to excel, to get ahead, to be successful in business. You should be alert and interested. You should, if you will forgive an old-fashioned phrase, be a "live wire," energetic, quick, able to get excited.

Retailing affords anything but a quiet life. It is changing, challenging, engaging. You cannot be in it and not be caught up in it. To me, this is all to the good. To you, it may or may not be. Someone once remarked that retailing is a way to grow old quickly or to stay forever young. The kind of person you are, your point of view toward the affairs of the world will determine whether or not you should seek out the strenuous life.

Many young people, probably most, do not really know what they wish to do after leaving school or college. This, to me, indicates that they haven't yet discovered themselves. This was true of me years ago. I started at the age of twenty with the vague idea of someday managing a factory. I operated machines in one for two years and decided this was not my dish. A few years later, and to some extent by chance, I was teaching accounting in a university. A decade after this, I was a business consultant. Twenty-two years out of college, I was a corporation controller. And now I happen to be heading a large merchandising organization. Not a very well-planned career, one might say.

For young people who are uncertain as to their career interests retailing is perhaps a better way than most to remove the uncertainty. I say this because retailing can lead not only to success in and of itself, but because it is an excellent training ground for many other occupations and careers. Retailing is off the diving board and, splash, right into the pool! If you don't know whether you are cut out for a quiet occupation or a challenging and exciting competitive job, you'll find out in a hurry in the retail business.

Your chance for success in retailing can, then, be simply determined. Try it and you'll find out—and soon. Beyond this, you will be gaining valuable experience for the career in which you decide you do have a chance to succeed. But chances are that if you are bright, energetic, and eager for success, retailing will provide the opportunity you are seeking.

We have discussed the challenge of retailing, its emphasis upon the individual, whether it be as customer or as employee, and we have cited its fundamental purpose and its competitive nature. Let's take a look at the rewards it offers.

Most of us, particularly these days, want some measure of economic security. Retailing is often overlooked when people discuss economic stability. But, in good times and bad, well-managed stores survive and prosper. Stores that offer a wide variety of goods in many price lines are especially stable businesses.

Retailing is often not mentioned when people discuss showmanship and excitement. But, as you might suspect from what we've talked about so far, a store is a bazaar, a market place, a fair. It is filled with fun and charged with drama. I can run down the roster of jobs in a big retail organization and find enough glamour, humor, and excitement to satisfy most anyone. Buying trips abroad, fashion showings and expositions, the drama of one holiday shopping season with its bright lights and sentiment—all these are part of the day's work in a department store.

Still, retailing has a reputation for being hard work, serious work, and I don't wish to pass over that. If I were a young person starting out, I'd look for hard work, because it would teach me, sharpen my talents, force me to do my best. Retailing does that.

Retailing is sometimes not regarded as a growth business. This is amusing to me, as I watch the panorama of suburban store development and as I see the main streets of America extending to meet larger populations and growing cities. This is a growth country and retailing, selling right on Main Street, grows right along with it.

Finally, retailers with skill and effort and a capacity for hard work make money. Retailing is a profitable business. And profits, continually making money, are necessary for anyone who wishes to become reasonably well-to-do.

There is one further thought I would like to leave with you. This goes back to our talk about retailing and its place in the world, particularly retailing as a fundamental part of the American way of life. We have seen that competition and freedom of choice make the customer in America the boss of the most prosperous economy that history has seen to date. And in all the massive efforts to serve the American customer—through department stores, mail-order houses, and chain stores—his role and power have not changed. Success in retailing rests not in political or social organization, either the giant state or the vast cooperative, but upon pleasing the individual customer.

This emphasis upon the individual in the market place is uniquely American. And it is important. The continued dominance of individual choice in a massive economy accounts to many for the unusual vigor, the tremendous thrust for growth, and the shattering success of the American way of life.

I say "shattering" and I choose the word carefully. We are told that two giant systems are competing for dominance in the world. History teaches that the American idea, the success of the free-enterprise system, has not only broken old economic patterns but has made it necessary to revise and to adapt new economic and political patterns.

The American free economy with its source of power, the independent customer, continues to be the strongest force for change and progress in history. It has been responsible for the common-market groupings of Europe, for the economic strengthening of all the Americas, North and South, and it is playing a leading role in assisting in the development of new nations in Asia and Africa.

Perhaps because we are so close to it, because we are "it," really, we tend not to see the drive and the direction of our own efforts. But, in this free society that we support, retailing is an integral part. It is not the only part, but it is, with its emphasis upon competition and individual choice, a vital part.

Thus, retailing, to me, should command the attention of young people seeking a place in the world; a place where they can learn and grow, succeed and prosper; a place where their careers will mean something, to themselves and to our society. Retailing is an industry in which you may serve the public, serve our unique economic system, and satisfy, if you will, your own dreams and desires. Its opportunities are legion and its needs are of endless variety. It will continue to cry out for the services of men and women of exceptional intelligence, vigor, courage, and imagination.

_6_ *You as an*

ACCOUNTANT

BY THOMAS G. HIGGINS
Arthur Young & Company

THOMAS G. HIGGINS

Born: Omagh, County Tyrone, Ireland, 1900

Began accounting training with firm of H.B. Brandon & Co., Ireland, 1917
Came to the United States, 1921

Arthur Young & Company in New York, 1921
Senior accountant, 1928
Manager, 1936
General partner, 1938
Member of the Management Committee, 1948
Chairman of the Management Committee, 1954–

New York State Society of Certified Public Accountants:
President, 1959–60
Formerly member of Board of Directors and of various committees
Presently member of Committee on Professional Conduct

American Institute of Certified Public Accountants
Presently:
Member of Council
Member of the Accounting Principles Board
Member of the Trial Board
Formerly:
Member of the Executive Committee
Member of the Committee on Accounting Procedure
Member of the Committee on Professional Ethics

Trustee of Mills College of Education

Past member of the vestry and past senior warden, St. Elizabeth's Church,
Ridgewood, New Jersey

THERE ARE many things to tell you about an accountant and his work, what he does, what he must know, the whole story of his profession. It is an interesting story and I expect, in some ways, it will surprise you. This is because so many people do not know what has happened in the accounting profession. They have no idea what an accountant today is called on to do: how he influences the highest business decisions; plays a decisive part in government; is essential in banking, in all kinds of trade, and in the whole economic workings of the nation. I will do my best to tell you about accounting and about the life of an accountant; but before I get into it, I would like to talk with you for a moment about yourself and your choice of a career.

Let me remind you that picking out your job, deciding on your life work, figuring out what you are going to do with yourself is about as tough an assignment as anybody can come up against. Much of what happens to any man is determined by forces he cannot control, but there is one decision he can make for himself. He can decide what his life work will be, and in making his choice, he will go a long way toward deciding whether or not, throughout all the rest of his days, he will get satisfaction and a feeling of accomplishment from what he is doing. My purpose, in what I intend to write here, is to give you some ideas that may help you make up your mind whether or not you want to have a career in accounting.

I like to see young men go into the accounting profession, *provided they are suited for it,* because I believe, very enthusiastically, that a career in accounting can be an enjoyable, a satisfying, and a remunerative one. Let me make it plain, though,

95

that I will not try to convince you that accounting is necessarily the right field for *you*. You must decide for yourself what your abilities are, where your interests are, and what you yourself really want to be.

Some of the things I will say about accounting may seem elementary to you; this is because I cannot be sure how much knowledge each of you has or how much experience you have had. What I want to do is to make accounting understandable to all of you, whatever your background, to explain what an accountant does, and let you find out something about the kind of life he leads.

First, there are some general terms that need to be defined. We need to understand, in the beginning, what people mean when they speak of a *public* accountant or a *private* accountant. There is an important distinction. You might not like the idea of being a private accountant, but working as a public accountant might suit you well, or vice versa.

To put it as simply as I can, the public accountant works for the public, offering his services to anyone who is reputable, who needs accounting services, and who can pay the fee. The public accountant can begin his practice in one of two ways: he can enter a public accounting firm, hoping to work his way up to become a partner in the firm, or he can begin on his own by opening an office for himself. In this latter case, he is called an "individual practitioner."

The private accountant has nothing directly to do with the public. He is an employee of some business or some agency of government or some institution, and he works entirely for the one organization that employs him. His title can be controller, internal auditor, chief accountant, treasurer.

Many a controller or treasurer of a company began his accounting career in public practice. The public accounting profession has long been a training ground from which corporations often recruit their financial executives.

No matter whether an accountant goes into public practice or accepts a position with some corporation or institution, if he is to rise, he must progressively develop his abilities until he has at least a working knowledge of manufacturing processes, insurance, banking, securities markets, business law, and other fields usually considered outside the accounting specialty.

An accountant, when working for a corporation, either as an executive employed full time by the corporation or as a public accountant called in periodically from the outside, must act as the keeper of the corporate conscience and, on behalf of the stockholders, make sure that the financial statements published by management are fairly prepared and clearly informative. Another of his accounting functions is to help the corporation protect itself against fraud on the part of officers and employees. To do this, he tries to make sure that internal procedures and methods are such that they offer the least possible opportunity for wrong-doing.

Still another of his jobs may be to help run offices efficiently; it is therefore necessary that he be an expert in administrative organization, in the use of mechanical and electronic bookkeeping equipment, and in the flow of paper work. He must also be thoroughly familiar with the rules and regulations of government agencies—the Internal Revenue Service, the Securities and Exchange Commission, Renegotiation Boards, for example—so that he can discuss his clients' (or his employer's) affairs intelligently with them. In fact, far from being an occupation distinguished by monotony and drudgery, merely adding up columns of figures—as unknowing persons sometimes imagine—accounting offers a life of diversity and intellectual challenge hardly equalled by any other profession or occupation.

With background and training such as this, a number of men who began their careers as accountants have risen to the top of American industry. It is commonly known that bankers have become the heads of great businesses. It is known, too, that lawyers have been called to head large companies. Accounting has also been a high road to corporate leadership, but this has been less well recognized.

To cite some examples, there are:

Ernest R. Breech, former Chairman of the Board of Ford Motor Company, is a certified public accountant who made a name for himself in accounting before he was drawn into general management and eventually took on the weighty task of modernizing Ford after the death of its founder.

Frederick G. Donner, Chairman of the Board of General Motors, rose through accounting; as did Harlow H. Curtice, until recently President of General Motors.

Lynn A. Townsend, at Chrysler Corporation, and Gerald L. Phillippe, at General Electric, are accountants who moved into top executive positions.

C. R. Smith, President of American Airlines, came up through accounting. So did Joel Hunter, President of Crucible Steel; Wayne C. Marks, President of General Foods; H. P. Buetow, President of Minnesota Mining & Manufacturing Company; Harold S. Geneen, President of International Telephone and Telegraph Company; F. W. Ackerman, Chairman of The Greyhound Corporation—all these, and there are others.

A good accountant can succeed in either public practice or private employment. To some men, it makes no difference which way they go; others prefer one way above the other. If you decide to go into accounting, either way will be open to you, public or private. It will be for you to decide.

Now that you understand the difference between public accountants and private accountants, we must distinguish between two kinds of public accountants. If you will turn to the yellow pages of the telephone book in your city, you may be surprised by the number of public accountants listed there. You may be puzzled, too, and somewhat confused, by the way they are listed. The main heading may read: "ACCOUNTANTS." Then, there may be two divisions: "PUBLIC ACCOUNTANTS" and "CERTIFIED PUBLIC ACCOUNTANTS."

What is the reason for distinguishing between these two groups? Both of them do the same general type of work. Both care for the accounting needs of their clients. There are, however, important differences.

The requirements to become a "Public Accountant" in some

states are that a man register, pay a fee, and take an examination. In other states, he need only register and pay a fee. In still other states, there are no requirements of any kind, and anybody, without test, proof, or license, can call himself a Public Accountant. Since there are no restrictions in these latter states, a man just assumes the title and begins work.

A person wanting to be a "Certified Public Accountant," on the other hand, must follow a procedure that is national in scope, although it is administered, with some variations, by the states. The basic requirement, necessary for every CPA, is that he shall pass the Uniform Certified Public Accountant Examination. This examination is prepared by the Board of Examiners of the American Institute of Certified Public Accountants (the national organization of CPA's). It is given twice a year on set dates, and the questions, which have been kept under strictest guard, are delivered to the examination halls in armored trucks and the seals broken in the presence of witnesses. While the examination in each state is conducted by the State Board of Accountancy, it is given throughout the nation and begins on the same day in all fifty states, the District of Columbia, Puerto Rico, and the Virgin Islands. The papers, collected and guarded by the State Board of Accountancy, are then sent to New York to be read and graded, except in the case of one state that grades its own papers.

The examination is divided into four parts: Accounting Theory, Accounting Practice, Auditing, and Commercial Law. Two-and-a-half days are required to complete it, and the standards of the American Institute, which usually apply, are rigid. The officials of that organization intend to keep these standards so high that only a completely qualified person can pass the examination and offer himself to the public as a Certified Public Accountant.

Passing the examination is not the only requirement for a CPA, for in most states a candidate must also have a certain amount of education and must spend two or three years gaining experience before he is granted his certificate and can use the title of CPA.

Becoming a CPA does not necessarily make a man a good

accountant, and there are fine accountants who are not CPA's. But being a CPA is a way of achieving a recognized and accepted mark of competence. If a young man decides to make accounting his career—especially if he intends to go into public accounting— I would urge him to plan to become a CPA. In this way, he not only acquires a symbol of competence in accounting; but if he ever wishes to go into an accounting firm, and wants to gain advancement, he will likely be required to be a CPA in order to rise to a supervisory position.

Public accounting, as a recognized profession, is officially about seventy-five years old in this country; but its chief growth has taken less time, almost entirely within the present century. In 1900, there were only about two hundred and fifty Certified Public Accountants in the United States. Today, there are close to seventy-five thousand. Ten years from now, it is estimated that this number will have grown to a hundred thousand or more.

But CPA's, as I have told you, are not the only kind of accountants. If we were to add to the seventy-five thousand CPA's, all the other accountants in the United States—including those in public practice, in industry, in government and in all other activities—the total would come to an accounting work force of perhaps four hundred thousand or even more.

Back in the ancient days of Greece and Rome there were accountants. How much cargo was loaded in the ship? How much was delivered after the ship had sailed to some far-off island? Somebody had to count barrels or bags or pieces. Somebody had to keep the record. This was the origin of the accounting profession.

It was accounting, too, when a cobbler, with an apprentice boy for a helper, keeping his shop in old England, set down the amounts he spent, made a record of what each customer owed, and balanced his books to determine his profits. His accounting was so little and so simple that sometimes, when he was in a hurry, he kept it all in his head. In this casual way, too, accounts were often kept when business was just getting under way in the young United States.

But this way did not continue, because, sometime along in the early 1800's, tremendous changes began to come about in business, in production, in labor, and in management. This was the time that machines began to be generally introduced. These machines could do the work of many men, and with the increasing production and rapidity of output, many of the companies began to find that they could expand. Some of them extended their operations under the very simple organization they already had. Others broke up into departments. They all found that their records became more complex. So, at the time of the Industrial Revolution, companies discovered it was necessary to employ men not only to keep the day-by-day books but also to accumulate and combine reports and to lend assurance to the records. This was really the beginning of the accounting profession as we know it today.

Later, as companies continued to grow, expanding not only into departments but also into separate plants, a system of absentee ownership developed. The days of the cobbler keeping his shop, watching over every detail, and knowing the whereabouts of every penny, were ending. Instead, a man now might own a plant in Manchester, another plant in Liverpool, and still another in London. He could not possibly oversee his entire operation, and he became more and more dependent on his accountant. The accountant became the man who watched over the entire operation of the business, by supervising the records and reports, constantly searching through them, frequently compiling figures from them, and always showing his findings to the owner, so that he could know how his business was going and what his prospects for future profits seemed to be.

The increasingly complicated systems of accounting, inspired by multiple operations of growing companies and by absentee ownership, became even more established as British capital flowed to the United States in greater amounts and extended its holdings in American business. The careful Englishmen and the canny Scots took no chances; they sent capable accountants to America (for at that time there was no accounting profession here) to watch over their investments and report on their safety.

In time, it was perfectly natural that some of these accountants, wanting to increase their earnings, should start reporting on more than one investment and reporting to more than one investor. In this way they began to serve the public, both in England and the United States, offering their services to anyone who needed them and could pay for them. They became public accountants.

It was not until 1896, however, that the designation "Certified Public Accountant" first was used. (Before that, in England, the designation "Chartered Accountant" was used, as it still is.) In that year, the State of New York passed the nation's first public accountancy law. Later, other states enacted similar legislation, with the result that the term "CPA" is now nationally understood and has an accepted meaning in all the states.

In the development of the accounting profession, the first income tax law, enacted in 1913, played an important part, because after this the services of the independent public accountant were increasingly in demand. Four years later, in 1917, the wartime excess profits tax became law, and accountants were needed even more. Then, in 1933 and 1934, with the passing of the Securities Act and the Securities Exchange Act, and with more rigid accounting requirements by the New York Stock Exchange, the usefulness and value of the accountant in the American economy were firmly established. With the passing of the securities acts, the Federal law required all corporations offering to sell securities (above a stated minimum) to the public—provided there was to be interstate trading in the securities—to have their books audited, at the time of the offering and afterward annually, by independent public accountants.

These events brought a vast increase in accounting work in the tax area and in the field of auditing. The developing demand for accountants and their services was distinctly profitable to the men in the profession, and there were other highly desirable effects. The securities acts, in particular, had put the full weight of government authority behind a need, long felt, for

greater uniformity in financial reporting and for stricter standards
in audits. The added authority and stricter requirements greatly
enhanced the prestige of the accounting profession.

The simple accounting operations common in the early days
of British and American business still are used in small businesses,
such as plumbers' shops, meat markets, and other businesses
with limited stocks and sales. But as a result of the economic
developments I have described, most business in the United
States today is carried on by large corporations that are far too
complex to be operated, or directly supervised, by the people
who own them. Actually, the owners are the stockholders, men
and women scattered over this country and abroad, who entrust
the management of the corporation to directors and officers they
employ.

While owners usually have faith in the manager of their
business, it is the accepted custom that at least once a year,
and sometimes more often, the manager must report on his
stewardship. This report usually is honestly and carefully prepared, and might well be accepted without question, but both
groups—owners and managers—believe it is wise for some outsider to examine the report and the records underlying it. They
want someone with an entirely independent point of view,
associated in no way with either side, to say whether he thinks
the report is proper. This independent person is the CPA; the
process he goes through in making his examination, satisfying
himself that the report is fair and just, is called an *audit*.

Auditing is the best-known function of an accountant. In this
work, he is being called on continually to judge the accuracy
and fairness of financial and economic data presented to him
by corporations and other concerns. There are many reasons for
audits and many kinds of audits, and their importance cannot be
too greatly emphasized; they are the foundation for the public's
acceptance of the whole structure of American business.

When a CPA signs his name to an audit report, it means that
as an independent and impartial agent, he has made a suffi-
ciently broad and objective investigation of the financial state-

ments under audit to warrant risking his professional reputation that they can be relied on. In this assurance, he is acting as an agent and protector of the public, and his personal good name, as well as his professional reputation, depends on the faith that the public can put in his signature.

Time and again, the CPA comes to the difficult place where he must disagree with strong and vigorous men, often those who have urgent incentives to influence him. Oftentimes, these men are his clients—who are paying him his fee—and they are urging him to shift his ground of opinion, or possibly to alter his unfavorable appraisal of their accounting methods. They may be insisting that he change his refusal to approve their financial statements. He must then go to the mat with them, no matter who they may be or how insistent or even distraught, for now he is confronted with a matter of principle. At stake are the fairness and accuracy of the statement itself, and, consequently, the reputation of the client, along with the character and endurance of his business. Also, and of gravest significance, there is the whole tradition of trust that the public has come to put in the signature of a CPA.

In refusing to approve any financial statements about which he has doubts, the CPA is following the rigid code of professional conduct developed and backed by the American Institute, which must be accepted and followed by any practitioner in good standing.

This code forbids an accountant to incorporate, to advertise, to pirate employees or clients from fellow practitioners, to base his fee on the outcome of his work, to have any financial interest in a client's business, to violate the confidence of a client, and, most important of all, ever to express his opinion about a client's financial statements unless he has complied with the profession's generally accepted auditing standards.

Most people are aware that a practicing accountant audits his clients' financial statements and expresses his opinion on them, but there is far more to an accountant's work than this commonly known task of auditing. Among his other responsibilities, he must be at home in all kinds of tax work, because, with taxes increasing and becoming more complicated, he is being called on continually to help his clients with their tax problems. Indeed, the whole area of tax work has become the next largest after auditing.

Taxes represent a considerable part of the cost of doing any business, and they bite deeply into the income of almost every individual. For large corporations, and for some individuals, income taxes alone can amount to millions of dollars each year. The persons concerned are willing to pay whatever taxes are legally required; but in the interest of stockholders, creditors, and other participants, as well as their own interests, they properly want the payments held to the lowest penny the law permits. At the same time, they do not want to violate the law by underpaying their taxes.

One of the most important functions of the CPA is to help his clients prepare correct income-tax returns. This is difficult, because the returns of corporations, and even of individuals, have become so complicated that only someone continually concerned with tax matters, and one constantly watching the latest changes in the tax laws, can understand the requirements and meet them properly.

Not long ago, for instance, the president of a company that never had employed a CPA came to an accounting firm saying that his company was in trouble, threatened by a heavy assessment for unpaid income taxes not reported in an earlier year's tax return. The amount was so large that it would put a dangerous strain on the company's frail cash resources.

The accounting firm's tax specialists investigated and found that the tax return had been inadequately prepared by employees of the company not equipped to handle tax matters. The CPA's went at once to the Internal Revenue Service— which, one should always remember, wants only its legal payment—and persuaded it to delay further action until an amended return could be filed. When the return was properly recast, using the correct treatment of a merger which had been in question, it showed that no additional tax was due. The Internal Revenue Service agreed.

In tax work, as in all the activities of a CPA, an important and fascinating part of his duties is to play a questioning role, always seeking out legitimate ways to help save money (including tax money) for his client. For instance, individual state tax laws differ a great deal. This makes it important for a corporation opening a new plant to choose its location with care. From the standpoint of operations, one state might be preferred; but the CPA, after computing the taxes that might be due in that state and others, may be able to show that some other state is far more desirable in regard to taxes.

There are many and varied tax responsibilities for an accountant. Some CPA's find tax work so interesting that they limit themselves entirely to this field, developing such ability in it that their services are continually and most profitably in demand.

The third most important area of activity for accountants, after auditing and tax work, is "management services."

And exactly what is meant by the term "management services"? It is a broad term, in fact, too broad to be pinned down with any specific definition, but, in general, it means just what it says: services to management of a business, of a government agency, an institution, or some other organization that might need the help that an accountant, or a firm of accountants, can provide.

It is the extent of these services that makes definition impossible, because they can be of any kind. But always they are an answer to some need of management, and almost always they are aimed at helping management increase profits. In management services, accountants will assist in setting company goals (budgeting) or plan a new accounting system or help in personnel problems or perhaps produce the figures to show the wisdom of introducing a new product. This extensive service is based on the fact that accounting firms are made up of men who have had such a variety of experience in their years of auditing and advising that they can face almost any business problem that arises and provide facts and wisdom to help solve it. This is the service that comes under the wide heading of "management services."

You will understand this a little better when I tell you that some of the larger accounting firms have as many as two hundred or more men in their management-services departments, men with years and years of experience in all kinds of business. Such men may be found studying records and finding flaws in work methods—whether for production, sales, or some other aspect of business. These are simple matters for them, and frequently they will go on from there to the most complex problems, involving, for example, the revamping of a whole manufacturing system or the reorganization of an entire governmental agency.

Not long ago, one of the largest companies in an important industry, with a fairly stable sales volume, found itself running into a progressive increase in administrative and clerical costs. The company's auditing firm was called in to investigate, and a study team of management-services consultants, along with selected company employees, took on the assignment. At the outset, the consultants were authorized to define the conditions of the study and to recommend measures that could reduce the company's indirect costs.

Studying the work of each department, the team soon found ways of simplifying existing procedures and eliminating unnecessary paper work and details. Also, a number of activities were found to be compatible, and these were combined, although this meant reassigning responsibilities. Work sampling and time studies were then used to judge the remaining work loads, and to determine just how many employees really were needed.

Throughout the time of the study, management was kept posted regarding the productivity of clerical employees, and the effectiveness of their assignments and use. The employees involved also were told the reasons for the study and what was intended to be accomplished by it. Continuous care was taken to make certain that the teamwork of the consultants from the outside and the executives from inside should be close and agreeable. The changes that resulted from the study have proved successful from every standpoint, and, most important of all, the company has been able to make substantial reductions in its administrative costs and a comfortable addition to its annual profit.

Accountants sometimes help in unusual situations. By way of an example, an accounting firm was recently called in by the lawyers representing a group of defendants in an antitrust case. A suit had been brought by a grain broker who contended that the defendants acted in collusion when they ceased serving as his main source of supply. He claimed that his business had been seriously hurt, and he asked for treble damages.

The accounting firm's assignment was to examine the plaintiff's records, covering a period of six-and-a-half years. They did this, ascertaining his profits derived from the grain brokerage business, and they gained such facts and records that a partner of the firm was able to go into court and withstand the most severe cross-examination.

The most exciting innovations in the history of accounting have been brought about recently through the introduction of electronic equipment. Electronic data processing (EDP) has greatly increased the use and value of financial and economic data, and it is producing a revolution in the whole field of information. The accountant of today cannot continue with only the old pen-and-ink practices or the typewriter and simple adding machine of former times; he must now be thoroughly conversant with the techniques and potentialities of electronic equipment. This equipment, instead of lessening requirements for the accountant's services, as might commonly be supposed, is increasing the demands for the work of the really able accountant. He is constantly being called upon by his clients to advise them on the uses and potentialities of these complex machines and to assist in putting them to profitable use.

As an indication of the changes and advances that have come

about since the times when a lone bookkeeper was all that was needed, performing all the duties required of an accountant, let me tell you of a service recently requested of an accounting firm. This firm was asked by a stock exchange to develop an accounting system, using high-speed electronic equipment, that would relieve member brokerage firms—whose offices are scattered over a wide geographic area—from keeping a mass of very detailed records. After digging into the problem for many months, the firm worked out a plan through which any number of brokerage offices could be connected by teletype with a central office, where an electronic computer was installed. The computer did all the brokers' detailed work for them, ending the pressure of trying to maintain the multiple records. In addition, the computer also found time to record all of the transactions—thousands of stock trades daily—for the stock exchange itself. The aggregate savings for the exchange and its member brokers came to millions of dollars a year.

Working out this system was a challenging undertaking for the accounting firm, but after it was evolved, their job still was far from complete. The firm had to present and explain the plan to members of the exchange, convincing them of its utility. One of the most important tasks for a CPA, or, for that matter, for anybody in any kind of business, is to communicate effectively, to get his idea into the mind of the other man and convince him that it is right.

Earlier, I explained the difference between a public accountant and a private accountant: essentially, the one works for many individuals and companies (his clients), while the other is usually employed by one company or institution. Let us now explore the work of a private accountant a little further.

In most companies, the chief accounting and financial executives are part of top management and play a vital part in the most important aspect of conducting a business: the making of decisions.

Accountants work at the heart of every important step in the business process. They use budgets to help set production, marketing, and profit goals. They furnish facts and figures needed to set selling prices on products. They work up cost and other information needed for labor negotiations and personnel policies. They help arrange for loans and financing. Their analyses are the basis for mergers and other transactions involving the ownership of businesses. As officers and directors, accountants may come to participate in the highest councils of their companies.

You have probably noticed that CPA's, too, can do many of the jobs private accountants do. When CPA's are called on to help a client in one of these ways, they work hand-in-hand with the company's private accountants.

Up to now, I have been writing chiefly about the accountant in business; but since government service rightfully interests so many young people, it should be noted that accountants today are being drawn more and more into government affairs at all levels.

Actually, one of the fastest growing occupational demands in Washington today is for accountants of professional caliber. Already there are about thirty thousand of them working for the federal government; the General Accounting Office alone has two thousand, of whom over four hundred are CPA's. Furthermore, some seven hundred of the FBI's six thousand special agents are accountants.

The need for accountants in government increases as government grows more complex. With the multiplicity of laws, the complication of taxes, and the vast extent of the budget; with the staggering records and figures that confront the government, accountants are being called in more and more.

The necessity for accountants in responsible government positions is obvious—to analyze taxes, consider the budget, determine costs, judge expenditures—and the need for them grows in city, state, and Federal affairs. Also, there is an increasing demand for accountants in such public and quasi-public areas as education, hospitals, and charities. Any young man planning his future, and interested in accountancy, should take into consideration the general area of government and public service.

The correct choice of a career is certainly one of life's most important decisions. Almost everyone feels, at the very core of his being, that life should make sense, that the endeavors to which he devotes his main efforts should seem important to him and to others. Men and women seem happiest when their activities provide the fullest release for their individual abilities, and they all want some measure of achievement and esteem. They want to have—or they want to anticipate—a sense of fulfillment, to feel that they may be producing and creating in the broadest sense of those terms.

It would not be wise to press anyone to enter a career, accounting or any other, if it were not congenial to him. This would be a poor service to him and also to the associates he might join later.

This brings us back to the starting point for every young man. What do I *want* to be? How do I *know* whether or not I am fitted for that career? Could I be an accountant? The American Institute of CPA's has prepared tests, known as "orientation tests," to help young people find out whether they are likely to be successful in accounting, and it might be worth your while to take them. A high-school or college counselor can guide you. The thoughts I am going to give may also help.

Many people think an accountant must be a mathematical wizard, but this is not really so, although he should have some background in mathematics. The study of mathematics helps to develop logical ways of thinking and expression, and is, therefore, useful. In the early days, the practice of accounting did not really require much math beyond arithmetic, but, now, more is needed. For example, a knowledge of statistics is becoming important and, in some highly specialized work in the management services area, calculus is used.

A long time ago, the emphasis in an auditor's work was on checking the mathematical exactness of records; but this has changed radically, and today, while mathematics is required and precision is still essential, the advent of machines and the use of electronics make technical exactness less demanding on the accountant than evidence of his judgment, insight, and understanding of business problems.

High among the attributes that an accountant must have are an orderly mind, a capacity for making independent decisions, and a constant curiosity. The need for integrity and character, which I have mentioned before, must again be stressed. Without these qualities, no man has any place in the accounting profession (or in any other). In the privacy of his work, and in the confidence of his reporting, he may often be pressured to waver and shade, but once he begins such deviations, his work is tainted and his career has started to its end.

Among other requirements of an accountant there is one that I cannot emphasize too much: the ability to express ideas well, or, as I said a while back, to communicate. A CPA deals with people more than he deals with figures, and he must be clear, accurate, and even persuasive in his written and oral reports. He must also be able to defend his position in the inevitable debates, some of them prolonged and severe, with bankers, lawyers, tax authorities, sales managers, manufacturing executives, engineers—and also with the chief executive officers of the corporations he serves.

More than ninety-eight per cent of CPA's are men, but women are gaining in importance in public accounting. Despite the obstacles—pressure of work, demands on time, fear that clients may be prejudiced against woman accountants—a number of women have become successful as senior accountants or individual practitioners, and a few have achieved partnership status in CPA firms. Women accountants now have their own national professional society, the American Woman's Society of Certified Public Accountants.

I think it is right that you should know how you would start your work as a public accountant, what would be expected of you, and how you would advance.

As a new employee of an accounting firm, one of your first duties would be to carry out the elementary requirements of audits. For instance, you might help the accountant in charge of an audit to make sure that the amount of cash in the bank, shown by the financial report of the client, agrees with the record furnished by the bank. You might also help with the client's accounts receivable, finding out whether the amounts shown on the books as due are really collectible claims against customers. You might also work on the testing of inventories.

In the main, during your time as a staff assistant—in effect, an apprentice—part of your work would be dull and monotonous; but the simple fact is that no matter where you start out or what occupation you select—a bank, a manufacturing concern, or whatever—your beginning years will probably be pretty tiresome. Your life as a young bank clerk, for instance, would scarcely be exciting, and your time as a factory or sales trainee would not be very interesting. There is just no getting away from the fact that the beginner in any business does the routine work, and your early life in public accounting would, in this respect, be like that in any other field. But the chances are good that in public accounting you would emerge earlier from the routine phase.

If you showed reasonable ability, you would work under pretty close supervision for about two years. Then, one fine day, one of the partners or managers would call you in, give you a file of audit working papers, and tell you to go out and do your first job alone. Off you would go to a strange client's office, where all the bookkeepers would look at you as if they knew more than you did (they wouldn't, actually), and you would sit yourself down, with terrible misgivings, to make your first audit.

You would probably take more time than you should at it, because you would realize for the first time what a load of responsibility had been laid on your shoulders. You would probably do a lot more checking than you should and, in your preoccupation with details, you would probably miss a few barn doors which would be tartly called to your attention when you reported to your boss with your completed audit. No matter, you would be out of the beginner class at last, and all of a sudden you would find out what a fascinating and tantalizing occupation you had picked. From then on, it would just be a question of improving your techniques and learning how to handle the multiple and varied problems that came your way. Your apprenticeship would be over!

As you became more familiar with auditing procedures, you would move on to more complicated work. Sometime within the first few years, you would begin work in some aspects of income tax. You would also become concerned with pension plans, the evaluation of inventories, intercorporate relationships, problems associated with foreign operations. As your experience and abilities increased, you would turn more and more from the fundamental aspects of the work to dealings that involve people and ideas.

Regardless of the level at which you might happen to be working at any time, your career in public accounting would always be a varied one. One day, you might be concerned with the affairs of a small company that makes nuts and bolts. The next day, you might be considering the problems of some giant corporation whose list of products might fill two or three pages.

In the course of all your work, you would meet a great many people at all levels of business—the directors, the presidents, the controllers, the marketing and production executives, research and engineering heads, personnel directors—and you might find that some of the most interesting of them all would be the clerks in the shipping rooms or the timekeepers in the factory. A part of your training, and your testing, would be your ability to get along with all these people.

As you rose in your profession, you might in time become a partner of your firm, and your work then would be very largely in dealing with people. You would advise presidents and managers, meet with directors and stockholders; and be called on for opinions on matters related not only to accounting but also to finance and business generally.

Now, just a word about the material factors: advancement and compensation. In making your career decision you should not be influenced too much by these, but you should know about them before you choose. Suppose you decide to enter public accounting when you graduate from a college or university. If you are typical, you should be a staff assistant for about three years, and a staff senior for perhaps another three. Then you would become a manager. The next step—admission to partnership in the firm—might be expected between the ages of thirty-three and forty-two.

The rate at which an individual advances through the various grades depends entirely on his ability. Seldom, if ever, is progress influenced by seniority, which so often holds back the ambitious and able younger men in other occupations. Because accounting is growing so fast, men and women of ability are promoted as fast as they demonstrate they are qualified for advancement.

In your early years in public accounting, your compensation would be on a level with—or exceed—compensation in other occupations. At the advanced levels of manager or partner, your compensation would be on a par with that of well-paid business executives and other professional men.

There is a saying among accountants that a CPA, at some time in his career, will make use of every scrap of information he has learned from books or picked up in his living. Doubtless, this is an overstatement, but it serves to emphasize the breadth of knowledge and understanding that an accountant should strive to bring to his profession.

Some men have achieved success as CPA's with relatively limited formal education, but the opportunities to do this are becoming fewer. Not long ago, some distinguished accounting practitioners, along with a group of teachers, studied the education and experience requirements for becoming a CPA and for succeeding in the accounting profession, and they reported that the chief need was for more college and university training.

There was a time when a doctor's training could be had entirely by helping other doctors, and a lawyer learned the law by working in the office of another lawyer; but these apprenticeship days have passed in medicine and law, and they are pretty well gone in accounting. If you wish to enter public accounting, you should plan to graduate from college. Some states already include a college degree in their requirements for granting a CPA certificate; in the not-too-distant future, all states may require it. Most accounting firms require that their young accountants be college graduates.

The real question today is not so much the one college degree, but whether a man who wants to be an accountant should continue in school and do graduate work. The trend certainly is toward the continued work, and I think that the pattern of an ideal education for a CPA might be something like this: As an undergraduate he would concentrate on English, the liberal arts, the humanities, the physical sciences, a foreign language, and philosophy or logic. After receiving his baccalaureate degree, he would then undertake his graduate work and specialize in economics, business management, accounting, auditing, and taxation; he might also intern with an accounting firm. This would lead to a master's degree.

After acquiring the master's degree, the candidate would turn his attention to the CPA examination. He would receive his certificate when he had passed the examination and had met the experience requirements of the state in which he lived.

You will notice, I hope, my particular recommendation for undergraduate studies. It is too often the custom for men intending to become CPA's to major directly in accounting and similar subjects while they are still undergraduates. It should interest them to know that today many of the accounting firms are seeking men who first were graduated in the liberal arts and then later took their accounting courses and special studies in graduate work.

A CPA must be a person of broad interests and varied abilities in order to fulfill the responsibilities that will come to him in his different kinds of work, and also he must be able to get along successfully with all the different people he will deal with. The undergraduate training I am recommending will open his viewpoint, improve his ability to communicate, enhance his reasoning powers—and develop still other abilities needed by any man who intends to succeed as an accountant.

Your choice of a future career will be based on many factors: how you rate your own interests and capabilities, what you want from life, what you want to put *into* your life's work.

I cannot know your personal qualifications, but I can say with certainty that the life of a CPA is interesting and varied, the work is diverse and fascinating, and the financial rewards are all that might reasonably be wanted.

With equal certainty, I can say that CPA's contribute significantly to the business and public life of which they are a part, and their opportunities certainly can be expected to expand. Professional accountants reached their present role on the crest of the Industrial Revolution, first in England and then in America. Now, we see the beginnings of a surging new industrial revolution, world-wide, literally an economic explosion among the less-developed nations of the world.

All this can lead only to more international trade, stronger international economic ties—and, as a consequence, the need to expand the international practice of CPA's. Every new event— technical breakthroughs, ventures into space, globe-girdling commerce, mutual security and aid among nations—requires careful assessing of resources in man power, in money, and in materials. Accountants will always stand in pivotal positions, recording and budgeting the input and outgo of mankind's work.

And CPA's serve in yet another important way. You are aware of the bitter competition between our democratic capitalism and the controlled economy of the Communists. Our free-world way is notable for the free flow of reliable information. And in the areas of business and government, this vital flow takes the form of complete and accurate financial reports and accountability, precisely the domain of the CPA.

If, after a painstaking self-appraisal, you choose to go into accounting, you will have selected a meaningful and gratifying life's work. On the other hand, if you decide on one of the other careers so ably represented by my fellow contributors to this book, let me wish you well. In either event, this opportunity to tell young men and women about the profession of accounting is one I would not want to have missed.

7 _You in a_

CAREER OF

SELLING

BY ROBERT W. WOODRUFF

CHAIRMAN, FINANCE COMMITTEE
The Coca-Cola Company

ROBERT W. WOODRUFF

Born: 1889, Columbus, Georgia

Georgia Military Academy
Emory University

The Coca-Cola Company:
Former President, Chairman of the Board, Chairman of the Executive Committee (Retired, 1955)
Now Chairman of the Finance Committee of the Board of Directors

Director:
The Coca-Cola Company
The Coca-Cola Export Corporation
American Express Company
Metropolitan Life Insurance Company
Southern Railway
Trust Company of Georgia

Member Directors Advisory Council, Morgan Guaranty Trust Company of New York

Trustee:
The Berry Schools
Boys' Clubs of America
Georgia Warm Springs Foundation
The National Foundation
National Fund for Medical Education
National Safety Council
Tuskegee Institute
Other educational and philanthropic institutions

Officer and director of several charitable foundations

PHILOSOPHERS TELL US that the gift without the giver is bare. In a very real sense, this axiom applies to what we call selling. No act of salesmanship is soundly successful unless something of the salesman goes with it. His personal integrity, his belief in himself and his product must be an essential part of each sales agreement, if the company selling and the customer buying are mutually to benefit. The mere act of completing an exchange of goods or a product for an agreed price does not necessarily constitute a successful sale, no matter how much the profit may be, for the real salesman must sell something of himself with each sale.

It is necessary, too, for him to be a believing man, believing in himself and his product. Nor is this all. The salesman needs also to believe that what he sells will help the business of the merchant or company buying it. He cannot really separate himself from his product, even after he has sold it and delivery has been effected. He cannot escape this if he wishes. Since he cannot, the wise salesman accepts this reality as opportunity, as a door to a successful selling career.

The more cynical image of American selling is the so-called fast-buck operator, or the theatrical stereotype of Willy Loman in the stage play, *Death of a Salesman,* or that of the girl-chasing "drummer" of another generation. We will leave the sophisticates with their empty cynicism.

The truth is, the nation properly has an affection for the "drummer" of by-gone years. He is a well-loved legend, a part of our national folklore. He deserves more than passing attention, because his contribution was substantial. If he was picturesque, it was because the obstacles he had to surmount were unusual, requiring not merely enterprise, imagination, and intelligence, but a pair of good legs, a strong back, and a stomach able to digest what could be bought at remote "general" stores. The sales custom in those days was to visit every general store in a state. They could be reached sometimes by an "accommodation" train, which accommodated by stopping at every flag stop. More often than not, however, the out-of-the-way towns could be reached only by horse and buggy. The salesman usually could manage breakfast and dinner (or supper as it then was known) at a county-seat hotel or boarding house. Lunch was had at some general store—most of these stores kept a bowl or so for the use of drummers, and many a sale has been made over a handful of crackers and a bowl of canned tomatoes or sardines and cheese. Old-timers have fond memories of how good Cove oysters tasted, eaten out of the can with a spoon. These salesmen were a part of our economic growing up. They earned the place they have in our hearts.

No one disputes, for example, that it was the distribution of goods from the first machines and handicrafts of the young Republic that stimulated the phenomenal economic growth of the new nation. Some of the biographies of Alexander Hamilton note that he urged the first Congress to consider how Great Britain had spread "her factories and agents over the four quarters of the globe." "Consider," Hamilton said, "Britain's huge and varied pile of manufacturers." He planned to draw skilled labor, tools, and machines from Britain, in order to expand the commerce of the Union formed by adoption of the Constitution—and he planned, too, for "agents," for salesmen.

No historian has truly told the story of the salesman in the rapid development and productive growth of our country. The soldier, the statesman, the pioneer, the Indian fighter have all had their biographers. The salesman played an equally important role. He moved goods along the rivers and the trails. The men who went to the frontier with goods to exchange for furs, the traders who opened trading posts deep in the wilderness—all these were a part of the necessary movement and distribution of consumer goods and products. "Selling" was then, as now, the motive power in our prosperity and growth. All through our history, the large majority of our salesmen have been hard-working, competent, knowledgeable men who have made an invaluable, essential contribution. The stereotypes of stage and fiction remain what they have always been: the exceptions.

We tend to think of the Industrial Revolution in terms of vast new machines, of automation, of mass production and assembly. But nothing happens until a salesman books an order. And distribution does not continue unless the product and the man who sold it produce a profit for the man who bought it. Selling is more than a sale.

In the latter half of the Twentieth Century, selling has become complex and specialized. Economic changes have demanded specialization in many endeavors and the salesman, too, must now have special knowledge and the ability to use it. The old drummer has almost disappeared; instead, we can think of salesmen as ranging the world to sell their goods. All the industrial nations now send their salesmen to far places, and the competition for world markets is more demanding than even the economists could believe a decade ago. Indeed, not until near the beginning of the 1960's did our own economists speak so insistently that they finally made themselves heard: "As a nation, we must sell and export more than we have ever done," they said.

So, in a time of increasing economic competition, the nation is calling on its salesmen. This is nothing new to salesmen. Whenever they travel alone, they represent the country. Sometimes, when they are sent out in groups to represent industry or our government, they are called "trade delegations" or "national sale forces"; but they are just plain salesmen, after all—and that is why you are being told this, why it is being emphasized, so that you can recognize and understand the dignity and the importance that can go with selling. There can be pride and many kinds of satisfaction for you, as well as profit, if you decide to go into a career of selling.

The vast broadening of the scope of selling is not merely in the international field. It permeates our domestic growth as well. For example, all kinds of service jobs are increasing and the service industries are continually discovering new ways to sell their services. They remind us of the variety of our selling, just as the expanding range of retail items underscore its magnitude. Think, for instance, in the range of our selling, of the myriad small items in our dime stores over the country and then compare these small things with the new computors and electronic marvels sold to universities, businesses, and research organizations.

We can better realize the whole drama of selling if we think of the thousands of sales clerks in the huge department stores and the smaller retail shops; of grocery clerks and drug salesmen; of insurance salesmen out selling protection of life and property; of men from newspapers and agencies selling the influence and power of advertising; of men whose job it is to sell automobiles, supplies of all kinds, hardware, soft goods, cosmetics, beverages, heavy machinery, tools—the story is unending. But what we plainly see, here and everywhere around us, is that selling is tied irrevocably into our world of business and into our daily living.

Besides all that we are accustomed to, and have come to expect from selling, there will be the new demands of a changing world, the demands of an expanding economy, and this will mean more responsibilities for salesmen and sales managers. At the beginning of the 1960's, salesmen could be said to be helping to create and maintain employment for almost sixty-eight million people. The future will make even greater demands on salesmen, asking that they assist in creating even more jobs. This significant part in the whole national economy is a part of the rewards in the profession of selling, and a part of the satisfaction for the person who will give himself or herself to it.

Now let us consider some assets that a good salesman must have. A young man or woman seriously considering selling as a career must, first of all, have a genuine interest in other people, their problems, their aspirations and needs. It may not be commonly recognized, but it is the salesman, more than any other person, who sees one particularly intimate side of men and women. It is the salesman who meets the true desires, and also glimpses some of the motivations, of mankind; for what man buys not only shows what he wants at the moment, but it can indicate an incentive that may tell the kind of man he is. He may have a compelling incentive for status—the old-timer spoke of it as a desire to feel important—and he may buy accordingly, sometimes acquiring things for show rather than use. He may be dominated by a desire for bodily comforts, for exaggerated security, for pleasure, romance, an urge to keep up with the Joneses, selfishness, greed—all these emotions are encountered, and must be recognized, by the salesman. But recognition is not enough, the wise and successful salesman must know how to use—and when to ignore and discard—such motivations. Only a person who is sensitive to the problems, and the character, and the needs—beyond any buying needs—of other people can become a truly great salesman.

There are many shelves of books written on the art and science of selling. There are pages of procedures and techniques. It may be possible to reduce them to three rules that seem elemental. They involve three closely related areas of knowledge.

One is so obvious it seems needless to say it. Yet, too many young salesmen neglect it. This rule is to learn all he can about the product or the service he is selling. He should be able to discuss it with confidence and enthusiasm. He knows all about his product. He likes to talk about it. He believes in it. He gives it something of himself.

A second is that the salesman must know and study himself. His personality must be genuine. It cannot be contrived or artificial. The greatest salesmen have all been able to project themselves—it is called selling one's self. A teacher or a sales manager can offer instruction in this, but, finally, it can be done only by the man himself. Only he knows if he really believes in his product and if he can sincerely and happily associate himself with it, believing in it and believing, too, that it will fill the needs of the man or company who is buying it.

A third rule follows naturally out of the previous one. The salesman must study customers, or buyers, as thoroughly as he studies himself. He needs to learn the objectives of each, the personality and motivations of each. He should know what sort of man it is he deals with, whether or not he goes to church, what he reads, what his recreations are, and what others think about him. He should know, too, something about the man's business and his business needs. Will the product be of use and value to him? Will it bring him a profit and help him stay in business? Will he welcome the salesman when he comes back? Unless these questions can be answered favorably, the salesman had better pass up that sale. No sale is a success unless the buyer finds out later that he has bought a good product, and that the salesman is genuinely interested in him and his enterprise. One might say, in the best sense, that a salesman and a customer are two people, each of whom needs what the other has to offer.

Selling has its rules. It also has its philosophy. The art of selling can be narrow or broad. Like any other activity, it can be limited by indifference, either in personality or performance, and by lack of imagination. Either limitation is fatal. The person who selects selling as a career must come to his job with a valid image of it. He must see in it an opportunity for service and a challenge in the imperative job of maintaining the dynamics of the American dream: a free society and a free economy, concerned with the needs of free men everywhere.

There is a deep and abiding philosophy in selling. Those who come to it without this understanding will not be too happy or successful. As with most things in secular life, selling involves the material and the philosophic. One flies across the continent, looking down on the exciting, changing panorama that is America. Or, one drives the far-reaching networks of highways, looking at the changing landscape of city, country, forest, and farm. One sees, for example, the vast fields of wheat and corn in the Midwest, and the mind says: "Someone sold the miraculous machines that will come to harvest, to thresh, and to sack the grain. Someone will sell a portion of it for flour or meal. Bread will be baked and salesmen will sell it. Cereals will be manufactured, packaged, and someone must sell it. Some of the grain will become feed for poultry and livestock, and salesmen will sell the fowls and the animals."

The long freight train roars by—and men dig ore and salesmen sell it somewhere to steel-makers. Rails are made and salesmen sell them. Engines, machines, tools, girders for bridges are produced and salesmen travel over the country selling them. In all the cities, buildings rise on land that is bought and sold, and salesmen sell the steel in the buildings, the stone and the trim. Salesmen sell the brick, the cement, the workmen's tools, the glass windows, the air conditioning, the heating. Always and forever, in industry and commerce, there is, and must be, the salesman.

A salesman—wherever he is, wherever he goes—can always say to himself that one of his profession has been there, that salesmen have a part in the lives of individuals, of cities, and nations. The best salesman is he who sees and feels these things. If he can bring a philosophy to it, if he can say to himself that he and others in his profession are filling the needs of the present and future, that the thousands of men and women who sell make specific contributions that meet needs, large and small, insignificant, imperative—if he can realize all this, he will have more success and a happier, more rewarding life.

These conclusions serve, of course, to bolster the basic rules about knowing one's self, the customer, and the relationship between the two.

The salesman is usually a resilient man, perhaps because he must be. He frequently encounters the word "no." He is no stranger to resistance. Competitive life is not soft and he learns to retreat—without quitting—and to come back with a new approach. The history of American business includes the stories of many men who have been in sales and who have become heads of companies or occupied prominent places in management. This almost certainly comes about because in the give and take of selling, in learning to meet and compete with disappointment and negative forces, salesmen acquire a great deal of knowledge about human nature and what is required to make a company's products acceptable, and a company itself a success.

It is difficult not to slip into platitudes in discussing the attributes and the facets of personality that go to make up a good salesman and sound sales practices. One must speak of integrity, of giving of one's self, of being a friend, of practicing, even in the face of severe competition, the tenets of the Golden Rule. We can comfort ourselves that the eternal verities can be called platitudes, if one wishes to be cynical; but be that as it may, the salesman whose career moves from success to success will be the one who is not afraid to live by the oldest of rules, who learns the meaning of true humility, who works hard, who deals honestly, is dependable, and believes that his job is one of service and meaning. All these qualities are involved in what we call good human relations. They are the intangibles of successful selling.

Some years ago *Forbes* magazine published "A Capsule Course in Human Relations." It was this:

1. The five most important words in the language are:

I AM PROUD OF YOU.

2. The four most important words in the language are:

WHAT IS YOUR OPINION?

3. The three most important words in the language are:

IF YOU PLEASE.

4. The two most important words in the language are:

THANK YOU.

5. The least important word in the language is:

I.

There is truth in this small feature. Any veteran salesman, looking back from retirement, recalls that the smart "operators," the men who made fast-buck deals, those who took and never gave, may have started fast, but they faded along the way. They, perhaps, have provided subjects for short stories, movie scripts, and plays. But they never were what we mean when we speak of a "Salesman." The salesman is a participating citizen, an active member in his community, a man whose integrity, service, and giving of self open doors to him any time he knocks.

It is our job to try and look over the hill ahead of us. It is quite a hill. It will require good eyes, minds, vision, imagination, courage, work, and sacrifice. It will not be easy. The phrase "population explosion" leaps out at us from our newspapers. Our cities seem to expand overnight—as, indeed, they do. New buildings rise as if by magic. Old-timers shake their heads and ask, "Where are all the people coming from?" They like to recall when their cities were, in retrospect, small and comfortable and when they "knew almost every person they met on the street." And this growth of cities, this vast increase in population in all parts of the earth, call for greater production of goods and for men to sell them, for salesmen to play their essential part in the world's economy.

The Cold War with communism, as we know it in the 1960's, seems destined to last for a generation or more, unless, of course, it grows hot. Economists shake their heads and wonder what it will be like when Red China, with almost a billion people, begins to put goods on the market. South America is moving into the current industrial revolution. A map is obsolete on the day it is published. Automation has become a word for sociologists, as well as industrialists and scientists. Space budgets of a billion dollars do not astonish us. Men orbit the earth and talk to us. Revolutions of "rising expectations" occupy our military men and diplomats. Political convulsions shake the world. Yet, man has always experienced these frustrations and challenges in one degree or another.

Some of the mighty forces loose in the world are new, mysterious, and awesome. Man is probing into space to see what is there and what planets he can reach. Not only populations and the total of nations expand—so does the universe, and, in all this expansion, the salesman, we may be sure, will find new demands. He will find it necessary to invent sales techniques to fit all the vast needs of technology of space and earth and to move the thousands of new items that will be needed.

Salesmen of a generation hence likely will look at our methods of today and smile tolerantly, as we do about the drummers of yesterday, driving their hired teams to visit general stores, eating a lunch of sardines from the can while talking to the storekeeper about his wants.

But no matter how complex and technical the world becomes, it cannot move without salesmen. Those who bring to selling a keen desire to make it a career; those who have a strong feeling for humanity and who like to work with people in common endeavor; those who have the assets of personality and a liking for work, and who can give of themselves, will find it rewarding beyond present belief.

These qualities are not only essential to a successful career in selling in the strictly professional sense, they are also indispensable to outstanding achievement in any business, in any profession, or in any field of endeavor. Selling is as broad as the world, and, always, the most important product on sale in every man's life is himself.

8 *You in*

INSURANCE

BY FREDERIC W. ECKER

CHAIRMAN OF THE BOARD

Metropolitan Life Insurance Company

FREDERIC W. ECKER

Born: 1896, Brooklyn, New York

Pomfret School
Harvard: A.B., 1918

United States Infantry, 1918
   Wounded Argonne-Meuse campaign
   Awarded Distinguished Service Cross, French Croix de Guerre

Investment banking, 1919–1922
Bankers Trust Company:
   Sales Manager, Bond Department, 1922–25
Metropolitan Life Insurance Company:
   Assistant treasurer, 1925
   Treasurer, 1931
   Vice-president, 1936
   Director, 1936
   Financial Vice-president, 1944
   Executive Vice-president, 1951
   President, 1953
   Chairman of Board of Directors and Chief Executive Officer, 1959

Lend-Lease Administration, 1942–43
Chairman: Lend-Lease Mission to India, 1943

Institute of Life Insurance:
   Director and formerly chairman
American Life Convention:
   Executive Committee
Life Insurance Association of America:
   Formerly Director
Life Insurance Medical Research Fund:
   Formerly Director
Children's Village, Dobbs Ferry, New York:
   Chairman, Board of Directors
China Medical Board:
   Trustee
Insurance Committee, People-to-People Program:
   Member Executive Committee; formerly chairman
Director: Chase Manhattan Bank
         American Cancer Society
         Health Insurance Association of America
Trustee: Committee for Economic Development
         National Industrial Conference Board
         National Safety Council
Vice-chairman: The S.S. Huebner Foundation for Insurance Education
Vice-president: New York Chamber of Commerce
Member: Joint Administrative Board New York Hospital—Cornell Medical
   Center

So YOU ARE TRYING to decide what your life's work is to be . . .

Most people you talk to probably say, "Well, what would you like to do?" And your unexpressed answer probably is, "If I knew—if I really knew—I wouldn't be here talking to you."

It's perfectly natural that you don't know. Let's start with that understanding and not be bothered about it. Few men, presidents or senators, doctors or ministers, knew from the beginning what they were going to be. How can you be sure about something that you haven't been exposed to? I have met only one young man who knew at an early age what he wanted to do in life. He knew at the age of fourteen that he wanted to be an M.D. He studied medicine and became a very good doctor at that.

In most instances, the best you can do is to find out about different careers, and, somewhere along the way, one or two of them will appeal to you more than the others. You may have to experiment some, trying out jobs before you feel at home in one, and that's all right. Of course, you may find *your* job on the first try; if you do, you are that much ahead.

The important thing is to get into work that interests you, and, preferably, work that has a future. Whenever it interests you and there is something to look forward to, it isn't *work;* it fascinates you to deal with each day's problems as they come up. A part of this fascination is in the job itself, but an even greater part is in your attitude. If you carry out each assignment that comes your way as well as you can, and if you are always trying to learn as you go along, then a lot of work becomes fascinating that otherwise might be humdrum. So much of all this—your work, your future, your entire career—depends on you. I know that you have heard that before and if you want to be blasé about it, you can brush it off; but it is true that *you* will give the answer, far more than the job, as to whether you get along, whether you "succeed." The simple fact is that a man with the right attitude is likely to succeed in almost any job.

I was fortunate, I guess. Outside of a brief period between semesters in my sophomore year at college, when I worked as an office boy, I have worked for only three concerns and have had only two fields of endeavor. I worked for a while in investments and I have worked as an executive for a large life-insurance company. Every day has brought new problems and every day has been interesting.

In telling you a bit about my own experiences, hoping they may be of some help to you in your thinking, I suppose I had better start with college. In college, I took the general run of courses for a Bachelor of Arts degree and without any particular idea as to what I was going to do when I graduated, though in the back of my mind I had a partially formed desire to enter medicine. Then, before my junior year was completed, the United States entered World War I. Like most of my associates, I wanted to get in it, so I left college to enter Officers Training School.

Coming back to this country in 1919, I kept thinking about the medical profession; but after two years absence from the discipline of academic life, my desire for a medical career was apparently not strong enough to move me to undertake the five or six years of additional study required. Like all young men, I wanted to get started, and since my alma mater, in a desire to deal generously with those who had served in the Armed Forces and who had accumulated sufficient academic credits, was prepared to give us what was known as a Bachelor of Arts War degree, I accepted this and entered the business world.

My first job was a clerical one with an investment banking

house, and there I started my career in finance. I spent just enough time in clerical work, including the bookkeeping depart- ment, to know what was involved in the way of long hours of overtime to get statements out in a busy period and to know that my associates were extremely quick and capable in their work. I also found out that they were men with a good sense of humor, which goes a long way in making any job run smoothly.

From this, I went into the sales end of the investment business, where I soon found out that if a man is to be any good in the field of investment counsel, he has so much to learn. Realizing that I needed more basic knowledge of balance sheets and income statements, I took a night course in accounting. After six years of study and work in "the Street," I held a supervisory position in the investment department of one of New York's leading banks.

It was at this time that I was invited by the then President of the Metropolitan Life Insurance Company, Mr. Haley Fiske, to join the Metropolitan as Assistant Treasurer in the Investment Department. I was confronted—as you will be—with one of those decisions which face a man from time to time as he makes his progress in his career. By now, I had many friends in the investment business and I seemed to be doing all right in my job. I was hesitant about making a change, but the prospect of in- vesting large amounts of trustee funds for a life-insurance com- pany appealed to me, as did the fine reputation of the Metropoli- tan and its management, so I made the shift and took up what became my life work in the largest insurance company in the world.

At that time I did not have the vision to see the opportunity that lay ahead of me, and I think that few young men will have a clear perception of their future; but they ought not to worry about this. It was enough for me to know that if I worked hard and did an honest job day by day, at the same time trying to learn more and more about my work, it seemed to pay off.

Incidentally, I have heard some young men say they did not wish to work for a large corporation for fear they would get lost and their efforts would be overlooked. I do not think this viewpoint is valid. Large organizations present greater opportunities and now, more than ever, management of such corporations are on the lookout for capable young men within their ranks. If one is willing to put in the extra hours involved in doing his job in a better-than-average manner, if he is careful about learning from his own mistakes and from the mistakes of others, he need not worry about being overlooked.

But, to get back to our subject. It seems to me that a young man starting out today to choose a career, even though he may not have decided on the particular business which interests him most, will almost surely have certain *objectives* in the back of his mind. Most of us start out with some fundamental concepts as to what we want to do with our lives and what we want to have in our lives, and I suggest that we list some of these things.

One thing that we all want is *satisfaction* in whatever we are doing. And just how does one derive satisfaction? First, let's get this fact settled and out of the way—you don't get it by making money. One's goal in regard to making money is constantly changing, and man must look to something beyond money to give him a feeling of satisfaction.

Actually, satisfaction, in any enduring sense, must lie in the feeling that one is making a worth-while contribution to the betterment of men. It seems to me that those in the ministry must have this sense of satisfaction and, I believe, too, that capable M.D.'s have it. As closely as one can define this feeling in business, it seems to me to come from honorably playing a part in a business that meets a basic need of society and is beneficial to all men.

Which leads me directly to my second point: that, to be satisfied, really at ease with himself, and comfortable in the job he is doing, a man wants to be in a business with high ethical standards.

Third, as I have mentioned before, there is this matter of *interest*. One certainly wants to be in a business that holds interest. And what provides interest? Isn't it a constantly changing set of circumstances within the sphere of one's activities? Isn't it always being confronted with new problems to solve?

One wants diversity in one's work, rather than routine, and wants to be in a situation which has breadth, as we say.

Fourth, every man wants to be in a growing business, one which has plenty of room to expand and in which he himself has room to advance. Advancement has deep meaning for each of us, contributing to our sense of accomplishment, and accomplishment is a part of that satisfaction which we have talked about.

Fifth, while money, as I have said, is not *the* goal—and is a mirage if it is—a man still wants to be in a situation where, if he does his part, he can be confident that he will be able to support a wife and family comfortably. He wants to be able to give his children the opportunity for the best in education, to have at least a few of the luxuries of life, and have something stored up for retirement.

One thing more. It is my belief that American youth is not afraid of competition. This is one of the good results of athletics taught in the atmosphere of good sportsmanship.

Unfortunately, some of the social legislation passed in this country over the years has had the tendency to break down some of the old-fashioned virtues, such as self-reliance, which have built this nation. Some of this legislation has solved the problems of the day for some minor portion of the nation, but at times it may have done so by putting less emphasis on the importance of individual initiative. I am calling attention to this because any man, of whatever age, who intends to achieve his goal must have the fire of initiative in his thinking and in his actions, and he can permit no force or factor, from wherever it may come, to put out or lessen that fire.

Now, let's talk specifically about the insurance business as a possible career for you. Before we start, I should admit that my experience has been with a large life insurance company which covers the field of life insurance, prepaid medical care, and annuities, on an individual and a group basis, and that my experience has not been in the casualty insurance business. However, I feel that what I have to say will, in all probability, fit all lines of insurance.

Just what is "insurance"? This is one definition: "Insurance is the institution by which individuals and businesses transfer the risks of financial losses threatened by life's many hazards." For example, your home burns to the ground. You have been fore-sighted enough to have bought a fire-insurance policy, thus join-ing with thousands of other home-owners in transferring your personal risk to an institution of insurance. Without the co-operative action represented by your having taken this policy, your present and future financial position might be in jeopardy. The eighteenth-century Scottish economist, Adam Smith, said that the insurance business, "by dividing among a great many that loss which would ruin an individual, makes it fall lightly upon the whole society."

I have taken fire insurance as an example, but insurance covers the gamut of hazards. A United States government publication, a bulletin put out by the Department of Labor, gives an example of its range: "People can insure almost anything they consider valuable—from a prized personal possession, such as a rare book or pet, to something upon which earnings depend—a ballet dancer's legs, for example, or a pianist's hands. However, the policies most commonly sold are those which insure life, dwell-ings, business plants, machinery, crops, automobiles, and other valuable possessions. People also pay into insurance plans to pro-vide funds for retirement, sickness or disability, and the educa-tion of children. Insurance enables families to conduct their affairs with the assurance that money will be available in emer-gencies, when it is needed."

This, then, is the prime business of insurance: to provide financial protection against life's hazards.

Insurance does a great deal more, but this will do us for a start.

If you were to make a chart of the insurance business, you would make a column for each of its major branches. One, you would head: "Life Insurance." The other, "Property and Casualty Insurance."

Property and casualty companies handle marine, fire, casualty, and surety protection. Included in the almost endless array of

coverages are automobile insurance and workmen's compensation; insurance against losses due to wind, hailstorms, tornadoes;
also insurance against theft, travel accident, and so on—the list is
very long and varied. Then, too, many companies in this branch
also sell personal-disability policies.

The variety of coverages provided by property and casualty
companies are matched, naturally, by the variety of their claim
payments. These payments range from dissipating the cost and
embarrassment of some relatively small economic problem, such
as that involved when you or one of your friends suffers an
accordion pleat in the family car, to that of absorbing most of the
tremendous loss involved in, let us say, an industrial plant explosion, thereby making it possible for the enterprise to remain
intact, retaining its personnel, and continuing in business.

Life insurance companies provide coverages for the benefit of
individuals, families, and business enterprises in the case of disability, retirement, or death to the insured. Such coverages are
available in many varieties and are planned to match many
special situations, both for the individual and on a "group basis,"
under which an employer makes coverage available for his
employees or under which a creditor insures loans of groups of
debtors—in the case, for example, of bank loans or installment
contracts.

It may surprise you to learn that, year after year, the amount
of benefits paid by life-insurance companies directly to *policyholders themselves* is generally greater than the amount paid to
beneficiaries. For example, in 1961, life-insurance companies in
the United States paid $3.6 billions to beneficiaries after the
insured had died. At the same time, these companies paid $8
billion—twice as much and more—to living policyholders. The
latter payments included health-insurance benefits, matured
endowments, disability payments, annuities, cash values, and
policy dividends.

These amounts paid by life-insurance companies to the living,
and the fact that casualty companies obviously make most of
their payments to living policyholders, may lead you to a clearer
understanding of developments in the insurance business, the

changes that have taken place since earlier days when insurance was looked on by many people as a family aid only at the time of death.

Suppose, now, that we take a look at the beginnings of insurance. Insurance began a good deal earlier than most people know.

Some coverages provided by property and casualty companies go back as far as 1000 B.C., when merchants depended on a marine insurance arrangement which operated under the Rhodian sea law. In those days, the various owners traveled with their goods aboard ship and overloading seemed to be the rule. This was all right in calm weather, but during a storm the overload frequently threatened to sink the ship. The cargo nearest the rail was then thrown overboard. The owner of the cargo thus jettisoned was, by agreement, compensated for its full value, each of the other shippers contributing pro rata to make up its cost.

Fire insurance also has a long and noteworthy history, though it does not go back nearly so far as the marine insurance that I have mentioned. The first fire-insurance company of which we have record was formed in England in 1696, thirty years after the Great London Fire. The organization date was November 12, 1696, and its purpose and philosophy is set forth in the corporate plan: "Contributors for Insuring Houses, Chambers or Rooms from Loss by Fire by Amicable Contribution Within the Cities of London and Westminster and the Liberties Thereof and the Place Thereto Adjoining."

While there is some trace of life insurance as early as the third century, when a man devised what might properly be called the first life-insurance actuarial table, the fact is that modern life insurance is generally conceded to have begun in Great Britain in 1762, with the founding of "The Society of Equitable Insurance on Lives and Survivorships."

This late beginning of life insurance puzzled some wise men of earlier days, and Benjamin Franklin, in particular, worried about the lack of interest in this obviously beneficial form of insurance. "It is a strange anomaly," he wrote, "that people will insure their houses, their ships, their merchandise, and yet neglect to insure their lives, surely the most important of all to their families, and the more subject to loss."

Despite Franklin's belief, and that of other men like him, the life-insurance business did not start its really tremendous growth in the United States until after the middle of the last century, until after the Civil War. Once this growth started, however, it continued unabated to this day.

As an indication of its growth: in 1860, insurance companies reporting to New York State had fifty-six thousand policies in force. Their face value was $163 million. In 1962, the number of individuals in the United States covered by legal-reserve companies was estimated at one hundred and twenty million. The life insurance in force at that time was $635 billion.

The principles on which life insurance is based are very simple, but they are among the great concepts of civilization. They may be explained in this way:

Imagine that the men of the senior class of a large university are gathered for their last get-together as undergraduates on the night before graduation. They are talking of their plans for the future, and prominent in this talk is the desire to get married and build a good life for their families.

Finally, the president of the class suggests that they all return the next year for their first class reunion, at which time each can report on his progress. But someone reminds him that they will not all return, that a few will have passed away. This leads to a discussion of the financial situation of widows, perhaps with a child, and someone suggests that each member agree to chip in and pay these widows $25,000. Since only a very small percentage of the members would die in this first year, the cost to each man would be quite small.

The idea was well received and one member said, "Why limit the agreement to only one year?" So they decided to extend their plan, and to pay this money to the widow whenever a member died. At such modest cost individually, they could give real substance to their class fellowship.

Then a member pointed out that whereas the contribution by

each of them would be quite low for the first few years, it would increase rapidly as the members grew older. He questioned if it would be fair to ask members to contribute year after year until, in their later years, after having paid in their portions for so long, the contributions then became so large that the program would have to be discontinued and the remaining few would not benefit from it.

Someone then suggested that they find an appropriate amount to be contributed each year, by each member, which would be sufficient to pay the family of every member whenever he died— and which would not be increased as the members grew older.

And that, in brief, is the basis on which most personal life insurance is conducted today. The premium for this so-called "level premium" life insurance is computed so that it need not be increased as the person insured becomes older. (Naturally, this premium is somewhat larger than that which provides insurance for one year, then is continuously increased as the insured grows older, which is a form of life insurance known as term insurance.)

All this is very simple, in principle. Everyone in a group pays a small premium which, pooled together, will meet the heavy loss sustained by a few. What a blessing to those few in their hour of need: whether it be the life insurance paid to the widow with young children to educate, or the hospital and medical bills resulting from a serious accident, or even the annuity which provides income in one's years of retirement.

Probably the worst catastrophe that can affect a family is to have the head of the family taken away. One cannot, through monetary means, replace the affection and companionship of a husband or the leadership and example of a good father, but through life insurance one can provide the means of keeping the family together. Such insurance can provide the necessities while the children are growing up, and provide for them in such a way that the widow can spend her time in her most important role— that of mother to her growing children—rather than being forced to take on the role of providing the family income while employing someone else to bring up her children. I have yet to meet a widow who feels that her husband had too much life insurance.

Life insurance is the only medium by which a sizable estate can be made available as soon as the contract is in force—and it is in force with the payment of the first premium. A young man thirty years of age, for example, can assure that $25,000 will be available to his family immediately on his death, provided he puts approximately $43 a month, about $10 a week, into level premium life insurance.

If he were to put aside a monthly amount equivalent to these premiums, and could be assured of compound interest at five per cent, it would take years to build up the equivalent of the insurance, particularly when one takes into account the payment of taxes on the interest or dividends received. Yet with life insurance, he is completely covered for this total sum. Furthermore, in a mutual life-insurance company, he may properly expect to receive dividends which he can use either to add to his insurance at no extra outlay or to reduce the net cost of the insurance.

Now, let's look at something else; let's see the other side of the coin. A part of the premium paid for level premium life insurance (or "permanent life insurance," as it is frequently called to contrast it with term insurance) is set aside to help defray the cost of the insurance in later years. The amount thus reserved (which a life-insurance company must do in accordance with legal requirements) is not left idle in the bank. It is invested, and the interest it earns reduces the cost of insurance and is beneficial to each policyholder, lessening the amount of the premium he must pay. Moreover, the policyholder is not the only one who benefits; these invested funds play an important part in the economy of the entire country.

To me, it is fascinating to consider that savings in the form of individual life-insurance premiums—which, if individually invested, would be too small to have any real impact on the economy—when pooled together provide a major source of all capital necessary for the great expansion which has made the economy of the United States the envy of the world. I suspect the substantial use made of life insurance in the United States and Canada is not unconnected with the high standard of living in these two countries.

In the life-insurance business, when considered as a whole, forty per cent of the funds have been invested in mortgages. Just what does this mean? It means that the funds have helped millions of men and women to own their own homes. They have helped other men to own their farms and to till land that belongs to them. The funds have provided the major portion of the capital needed for new office buildings, new shopping centers, new apartment houses, housing developments, and almost all types of real-estate investments.

Nor is this all. The other sixty per cent, generally speaking, represents loans to government and to business, providing funds to build roads, schoolhouses, and all types of government and business needs. These funds have made possible the expansion of factories and the acquisition of new equipment. They provide the capital necessary for bringing natural gas from the Southwest, where it is in surplus supply, to the North, where it is needed for industrial operations as well as fuel for homes. When additional iron ore has been needed, insurance funds have provided the means to develop the mines. Insurance premiums have helped finance jet planes for the airlines; the expansion of our telephone systems; the building of tankers, radios, television sets—almost everything you can think of in our expanding economy.

At the end of 1961, there were $126 billion of policyholders' funds at work in the economy of our country.

So now we come to you, and the possibility of a career for you in insurance. Just what kind of work would you do in an insurance company? Well, the answer is so varied that it is hard to give. The insurance business is so extensive, and includes so much, that you can hardly name any profession or line of endeavor that is not a part of it.

An alphabetical list of insurance careers, which I recently came upon, suggests that they are from A to X—from advertising, that important branch of public relations, to X-rays, that vital part of an insurance company's array of technical equipment. But, then, I had the notion that if we could classify the care of the experimental animals, which are found in some life-insurance companies' biochemical laboratories, as zoology, we could then say that careers in insurance cover the alphabet from A to Z.

There would be little point in offering you a list of careers in insurance and I will just let you name your own calling, one that best suits your desires and qualifications. Almost surely you will find it, or its near counterpart, in insurance.

If you have a bent for engineering, you will find that casualty companies can use talented men in their programs of plant-, transportation-, and highway-accident prevention. If you have an interest in public-health work, life-insurance companies might make good use of your special education and talents. If you are a biochemist, you might carry on insurance work in the study of ways to lessen or eliminate disease hazards.

There is a place for the lawyer in the insurance field, for policies are contracts that must be legally sound; also, claims must be adjudicated, and there is a seemingly endless variety of insurance matters which need the mind and experience that comes from a legal background. In a similar way, we might emphasize the work of medical men and medical technicians in insurance. Other volumes in this series of books deal extensively with law and medicine as professions, but I shall mention that the insurance business offers excellent fields in which to pursue these two professions.

Besides specific jobs and professions, there are *areas* of work in insurance. Mr. Robert W. Woodruff, in another part of this volume, addresses himself to the general subject of salesmanship; but as a specialized addendum to Mr. Woodruff's fine chapter, I would like to offer a section headed the "Insurance Salesman." (I will follow this first section with others on the Actuary, the Underwriting and Claims Specialists, the Investment Specialist, and the Executive Administrator.)

In the insurance business there are a number of titles for the salesman. Depending on the branch of the business, or nature of the company, he may be called: Agent, Special Agent, General Agent, Sales Representative, or Broker.

Whatever he is called, he is the one who takes the first step in "underwriting": sizing up the insurability of a situation or of a person.

He can afford in many ways to be an "individualist," for in a sense he is an independent businessman whose overhead is almost nonexistent and who can, for all practical purposes, set his own hours of work. (They are frequently long.)

Governed by his own special ability and devotion to his calling, he can to a very real degree decide whether his income is to be $5,000 a year or $50,000. Indeed, I have known some who earned much more, more even than the presidents of their own companies.

He is little affected by areas of recession or by seasonal slumps, for the needs that he meets are constant and he has the added cushion of renewal commissions.

Almost everyone recognizes the need for life insurance, and yet few people buy voluntarily. Whether it is due to the fact that human nature tends to put aside that which is unpleasant—contemplation of death—or whether it is procrastination and the tendency to first satisfy the more pleasurable desires for a new car, a new television set or whatever it may be, the fact is that relatively small amounts of life insurance would be sold were it not for the life-insurance salesman.

I presume that only those close to the situation can really appreciate the deep satisfaction that comes to the salesman who, through his knowledge and persuasiveness, has seen to it that when the husband is taken away, the widow has the wherewithal to continue the education of her children in the manner she and her husband had planned together.

The vocation of an insurance salesman is rapidly approaching the status of a profession, and you will find the insurance salesman frequently collaborating with lawyers and accountants, working out programs of insurance for businessmen in connection with tax, estate, partnership, and other problems. It is a very personal business, dealing intimately with people and their affairs. In recent years, more and more college graduates have been entering this field, and finding in it not only incomes that range from good to excellent but also finding that equally important reward, satisfaction, which comes from carrying out a needed social service.

Everyone, however, is not equipped by nature and training to make a success of insurance selling. I would like to give you a little questionnaire, based upon my own experiences and observations over the years. You check yourself against it, and it may help you determine whether your gifts and background equip you for this particular career.

Is it important to you that your life work makes a substantial contribution to the economic and social needs and well-being of your fellow man and of the community? (This query should be asked first in each of the questionnaires that come later. However, having asked it here, I shall not repeat it.)

Do you like people in all walks of life? Do you talk with them easily, listen sympathetically? Do they seem, on the whole, to like you?

Are you personally well organized? Personally well disciplined?

Do you like chipping away at obstacles when you are convinced that your objective is correct?

Are you self-reliant? Can you work effectively in circumstances in which you are pretty much your own boss?

Would you stand up well in a job that required continued education to keep up with new developments? Insurance companies are noted for the breadth and depth of their training programs. Moreover, in life insurance you could carry on postgraduate studies leading to the CLU (Chartered Life Underwriter) designation. Similarly, in the property and casualty field, you could aim at the professional CPCU (Chartered Property and Casualty Underwriter) designation.

If you can answer "yes" to the questions I have listed, I believe it would be to your interest to look seriously into insurance salesmanship as your life work.

Naturally, you want to know about the personal growth possibilities, if you go into this area. There are many men in insurance selling today who have grown, and continue to grow, within the perimeter of their sales careers. There are many, too, who have been recruited from selling into the management areas of their companies—which, I should tell you, are *always* seeking executive talent. In my own company, all the various executive officers in charge of sales started out as insurance salesmen. More than that, one of our senior vice-presidents started as an insurance salesman, and our president began his career as an agent while he was still attending college.

Maybe you are best fitted to be an Actuary. He is a member of one of the least-crowded of all professions.

In the summer of 1961, even after adding to its rolls the new actuaries who qualified in its spring examinations, the Society of Actuaries had a total membership of fully accredited actuaries (Fellows) of only twelve hundred and two. On the rung just below (Associates), there were only eight hundred and ninety-six. This count included Canadians and a few people from other countries.

These figures may be even more meaningful to you if you consider that in the United States today there are almost fifteen hundred legal reserve life-insurance companies, and that the larger companies retain sizable staffs of actuaries. My own company, for instance, has sixty-five Fellows and fifty Associates. (It is significant that of this number not all are now engaged in actuarial work; many of them have gone on to top administrative posts outside the actuarial division.)

The lack of crowding in this internationally recognized profession is evident also in the casualty field. After the 1961 spring examinations, the Casualty Actuarial Society's new total in Fellows was two hundred and five; the number of Associates was one hundred and seventy-eight. Canadians, too, are included in this list, as are some men who are members of both the Society of Actuaries and of the Casualty Actuarial Society.

The need for qualified actuarial candidates is acute.

It is evident, from the standpoint of elbow room, that the actuarial profession has much to offer the career-seeker. Would it meet your ideas of a satisfying life work? Would your aptitudes qualify you for it? Since we are in such an open area, I think it wise for us to examine the actuary's assignment with special care, then trace the steps that lead to professional status.

Stripped to its fundamentals, the actuary's assignment is: to determine what benefits shall be provided by insurance policies, and to determine what such benefits will cost the policyholder.

In these two assignments there is a responsibility to the policyholder in providing adequate protection at acceptable cost, and a responsibility to the insurance company in keeping it solvent.

To put flesh on the foregoing, suppose we follow the actuarial procedure in greater detail:

The actuary utilizes tables of past experience to determine the probable number of claims that the insurance company must be ready to meet in the future, and the amount of money that must be set aside to meet these claims. Depending on the nature of his company, and on his specialization, he will use as his raw materials the mortality tables, statistics on accidents and sickness, on automobile accidents, on marine hazards, and so on, through the long list of life's hazards.

This may sound entirely statistical, but creative imagination plays an important part in the actuary's work. Rapid changes in science bring new products and new manufacturing processes, and these bring new problems for the actuary in the casualty field. Also, changing patterns of modern living bring new challenges to the actuary in the life-insurance field, and result in new approaches, such as those represented by policies that cover whole families; policies that make adequate insurance possible for the young man starting his career, by affording him lower premiums at an early age; policies that make health insurance protection more readily available for people sixty-five years and over.

The actuary works with the company's lawyers in drafting the language of the policies. A policy, as I have told you, is a contract, and for protection of the policyholder and of the company it must be exact in the promises it contains. The actuary is responsible for this exactness.

He also works with the company's medical department, especially in fixing the rules which affect the selection of risks.

His determination of the amount that the policyholder will pay, called the "premium," will be affected not only by probability, as forecast from past experience, but also by the interest rate to be earned on premiums when invested by his company, as well as by data on the company's cost of doing business. From this, it is evident that the actuary must be continually alert and up-to-date on business conditions in insurance and elsewhere; he must be able to distinguish economic trends and fluctuations; and he must constantly compare forecasts with actual experience. He must be able to do all this in the interest of the security of the policyholders and in the interest of the financial stability of his company.

There is a widely held misconception about the actuary which I should like to mention and correct. The actuary is not primarily a practitioner of advanced mathematics. To end this misconception, let me quote the Mathematical Association of America: "College students majoring in mathematics and considering the actuarial profession as a possible career should bear in mind that it is not primarily a mathematical profession. If a student wants a profession which calls for the application of advanced mathematics, he should not become an actuary. If, on the other hand, he desires a profession in which his early training will be based on mathematics and in which all of his work will require the exercise of reasoning and judgment similar to that used in his study of mathematics, then he should consider the actuarial profession."

As if to confirm the general tenor of this statement, part one of the examination given by the Society of Actuaries is not even in the field of mathematics. It is in language aptitude. The next two parts of the Society's examination are concerned with general mathematics and with special "insurance-gaited" mathematics. (It is possible to take these first three parts of the Society's examinations while one is still in college, and it is to your advantage to do this.)

The ideal college base for an actuarial career is the bachelor's degree with a major in mathematics. It is also wise to take courses in business law, economics, finance, and accounting. But let me point out that one should never neglect the humanities.

During college, it would be well for you to seek summer employment in the actuarial department of an insurance company. To combine experience with study is obviously beneficial, and it follows that you can judge the work and judge yourself in it.

After graduation, provided you have indicated your aptitude and continued your interest, you should find it quite easy to get a job with the actuarial department of an insurance company, for remember that this is a very uncrowded profession. You are now established in the first stage of your career, and you will be engaged for some time in what amounts to postgraduate work. The jobs assigned to you at this time generally will be planned with reference to the several examinations you still must take. Your work will dovetail with these upcoming examinations, and your study at the office and at home will go hand in hand. There will be long periods of after-hours study.

Meanwhile, though, during this postgraduate period, you are progressing, both in terms of income and in position with your company.

How long does it take to dispose of the actuarial examinations? How long does the era of postgraduate work and study continue? There is a very great range here, depending on the student's ability and his success with the examinations. Four years, five years, six years are the usual term—though it has been done in two!

This, then, as I have outlined it in broad terms, is what the actuary does and how he earns his professional status.

Certain qualifications are desirable, some essential, for the actuary, and I suggest that you answer the following questions as an indication of your fitness for the career:

Have you a flair for mathematics? Are you a major in mathematics?

Do you like "problems," like to analyze them and satisfy yourself and others with logical solutions?

Do you pride yourself on your ability to express yourself clearly and convincingly both orally and in writing?

Do you find business, in general, interesting, and, in so far as you have had experience, find especial interest in such fields as law, economics, banking, and finance?

Do you find particular challenge and pleasure in the give-and-take of conference discussion?

Are you willing to devote a considerable amount of "free time" to study during postgraduate years, and continuing study after this, in order to win and maintain a place in a field noted for high prestige and excellent income?

If your answer to most of these questions is "yes," you would do well to explore further the possibilities that might lie in an actuarial career for you.

It would seem almost unnecessary to mention the growth possibilities in actuarial work. From actuarial clerk to chief actuary is a well-marked road. But there are other growth possibilities. In many insurance companies, top and key executive positions outside the actuarial division are held by actuaries. The president of a famous life-insurance company is an actuary. In my own company, our executive vice-president is an actuary. So are a number of senior and key administrative vice-presidents.

The Underwriting and Claims Specialist is at the heartland of insurance operations. Although one does not usually combine discussion of these two careers, the qualifications for them have many similarities and it seems logical to me to consider them together.

We have seen that the first step in the acceptance of an application for insurance is taken by the insurance salesman. He acts as the initial underwriter and is frequently referred to as the field underwriter.

Beyond him, and working in the office of the insurance-company's headquarters, is another underwriter who is sometimes referred to as "Home Office Underwriter." His job is to accept the application, reject it, or impose limiting qualifications. It is his stamp of approval that puts insurance protection into force.

Now let us go immediately to the other end of this operation, to the climax of it, and there we meet the Claims Specialist. His job is to examine, approve, modify, or reject, the claims that are made in conjunction with policies issued by his company. Depending upon company or field, these claims will involve almost every hazard to which business or mankind is subject.

The work represented by these two men, the underwriter and the claims specialist, is basic to insurance operations, for they are responsible for contracting to accept risk and for paying the claim when the risk materializes.

If you consider the complications inherent in life today, you will better realize the complications that enter the work of the underwriter and of the claims specialist. This is particularly true in the property and casualty fields, for the rapid advances in science have imposed special problems. Firms and institutions using radioactive isotopes, for example, offer particularly interesting underwriting problems, complicated not only by the absence of insurance experience in such situations but also, in some cases, by top-secret classifications of the projects themselves.

The unpredictability of human nature also holds problems for the underwriter and the claims specialist. The desire of an applicant to put, and keep, his best foot forward presents special challenges to the underwriter, who must manage to uncover the facts whatever they may be. Sometimes, too, little melodramas will call upon the keen analytical mind of the claims specialist to make sure that the great majority of policyholders are not penalized by the occasional deception of a few.

The ability to recognize and handle problems stemming from the vagaries of human nature is an important qualification in both underwriting and claims work, but there are even more significant parallels in the requirements for work in these two areas. In both fields, the possession of an analytical mind is a primary asset. Also, both call for an ability to examine a variety of facts and statements, to sort them out, and to arrive at judgments that are consistent, reasonable, and unbiased. In the claims field, particularly, a law degree or legal training is a decided asset. In both fields, the study of logic, science, and mathematics is helpful.

The underwriter makes his evaluation from sets of facts that have been developed in research. In the case of life insurance, in determining whether the applicant is a good risk, the underwriter will base his decision on the present health of the applicant, as shown by medical reports or the applicant's statement; on his occupation; on his personal history and habits; on his family history; on his income—all to determine whether the type of insurance applied for is justified and whether he will be able to afford to keep on paying for it.

The claims specialist also makes his decision from facts developed in research. His job is to determine whether the claim submitted meets the specification of the policy on which it is based, and, in the case of a contested claim, he may be required to represent his company in court as a witness.

Obviously, the foundation for success in underwriting and claims work is a thorough, intimate acquaintance with the nature, type, and details of all policies offered by the company. This is especially demanding today in the casualty and property field, because of the constantly changing face of industry.

From the foregoing sketch, we can propose another series of questions, this one to give you a chance to match your aptitudes and qualifications with the requirements in the two areas of underwriting and claims:

Does playing a direct, grass-roots part in the vital social functions of insurance—the creating of insurance protection, the paying of insurance claims—appeal to you?

Are you eager to take on meaningful responsibilities to applicants for insurance, to claimants, and to the insurance company itself, always with the understanding that such responsibilities, if consistently and expertly carried out, will lead to even greater responsibilities and opportunities?

Do you have the knack of assembling and sorting out facts and arriving at decisions based on those facts?

Do you have, or are you planning to acquire, scholastic background in the sciences, in mathematics, or the law—studies that help develop the habit of logical thinking?

Are you willing to expose yourself to on-the-job training—basically the only effective kind of training in these fields—and to supplement this training with postgraduate work in school and in courses sponsored by the insurance institution?

Are you a sympathetic observer of human nature? Can you act effectively in the light of your understanding of human nature?

An affirmative answer to most of these questions would suggest that in the underwriting and claims fields, the points at which the vital role of insurance first comes into being and finally reaches its climax, you might find a real challenge and a very satisfying and well-paid life work.

Now let us move on to other areas in the insurance field and begin with a speech by an officer of a life-insurance company. "Many of you," he said at the company's convention of sales managers, "were able to fly here in 707's and DC8's because life-insurance companies had the courage to bridge the gap [in air transportation development] with financial commitments to airlines, and, indirectly, to airplane manufacturers."

The gap that he referred to was a substantial money problem. The jet age was on the next leaf of the calendar and the manufacturers were ready to get into production. The airlines were eager to offer the service, but where was the money coming from to finance these costly jets?

Several life-insurance companies gave the answer. Approximately a billion dollars of life-insurance funds have helped to finance the major United States airlines' changeover from propeller planes to jets.

Using the example of jets to begin with, let us see, in some detail, how the *investment specialist* helps his insurance company to contribute to the well-being of the policyholder and to the benefit of the total national economy. Also, we will consider this side of the insurance business as a possible life's vocation for you.

First, as I have said, insurance costs each policyholder less because of earnings from investments. In fact, insurance is made possible at acceptable rates only because of investment income.

In the case of life-insurance companies, about 21.5 cents out of every dollar taken in during 1961 came from investment income.

Second, the nation's economy benefits substantially and continuously from insurance investments. Just as insurance funds figured in the coming of the jet age, they have also helped in projects that range from the building of private homes to the construction of commercial atomic plants.

To give you some idea of the breadth of life-insurance company investments, let me reproduce, through the courtesy of The Institute of Life Insurance, a tabulation which shows the portfolio you might be said to have, if your share of life-insurance funds was $1,000:

$243 in home mortgages
$157 in public utility and bonds
$151 in automobile, textile, food, machinery, and other manufacturing industry bonds (including $50 in oil and chemical bonds and $9 in shipping)
$81 in commercial mortgages (including $12 in shopping centers and $3 in churches)
$73 in wholesale, finance, service, and other nonmanufacturing industry bonds (including $7 for conversion to jet planes)
$54 in U.S. government securities
$44 in loans to policyholders
$38 in municipal bonds (including $6 for public schools and $12 for bridges, roads, and tunnels)
$32 in railroad bonds and stocks
$31 in real estate
$25 in farm mortgages
$71 in other investments

Turn your imagination loose on this list, and then consider what a variety of knowledge must be available in an insurance-company's investment department to cope successfully with such investments.

You would be right if you surmised that for "home mortgages," the first entry, skilled real-estate appraisers are needed. You would be right, too, if you dropped toward the end of the list and concluded that a man knowledgeable in agricultural management would be needed.

Going through the entire list, you can visualize the need for specialists in many fields: public utilities, manufacturing, municipal, and many others. The number and variety of specialists would be determined by the size of the insurance company and the breadth of its investment activities.

Obviously, too, the work of the security and mortgage analyst in the investment end of the insurance business is of first importance in evaluating current investments and new issues.

Besides this, think of the knowledge that must go into on-the-spot appraisal of a proposed shopping center. Building costs and business trends must be considered; so must such factors as modern retailing practices, population shifts, convenience of location, traffic flow, and the floor plan and architecture of stores.

There must be comparable on-the-scene surveys of projects proposed by manufacturing companies when they apply for insurance-company financing, and this also generally includes personal contacts with the principals of these companies. The experienced investment specialist of an insurance company will frequently travel widely throughout the United States and Canada to confer with leading executives of prospective debtor companies.

Today, many insurance companies make direct loans to industry, that is, without the investment banker acting as an underwriter, although in many instances he may act as an advisor to the borrower. As a consequence, the investment officer of the insurance company plays a major role in determining the covenants necessary, or desirable, in the contract for the proper protection of the insurance-company's investment. This takes an extremely high quality of experience and technical skill, for each contract is made specifically to fit the situation at hand.

Then, too, besides these larger and more complicated investigations, there are always the careful surveys and investigations when the financing of an individual home is under consideration.

The investment side of insurance, by its very nature, is an uncrowded field and one that offers special satisfaction and good income to the college graduate who possesses the necessary qualifications.

How should one prepare oneself?

In college, he should place emphasis on business management and finance. Economics and accounting are important courses. A postgraduate degree from a business school would be a decided advantage. On-the-job training, during college vacations if possible, is very important.

At this point, let me propose another questionnaire, this one intended to match the possibility of a career in the investment end of insurance with your qualifications and preferences.

Do the operations of business in general have an appeal to you?

Do you, so far as you are now acquainted with the field of economics, find it of considerable interest?

Does the prospect of getting behind the scenes of the operation of the economy of the country appeal to you?

Do you like to keep up-to-date on the advances of science and on their application in products and processes?

Would you like to have the sense of taking a hand in the economic advancement of the country?

Does the prospect of eventual association with business leaders in a great variety of fields all over the country appeal to you?

Do you feel at home with figures and with analyses based on figures?

Do you feel at home in your association with people in your varied meetings with them?

Would you accept the necessity of never-ending study in the field of investments, essential in keeping abreast of economic and political developments at home and abroad?

If your answers to most of these questions are affirmative, and if your preparation in school follows along the lines previously sketched, there may be a satisfying and remunerative career for you as an investment specialist in the insurance world.

The high-sounding title of Executive Administrator is intended as a general one. Its purpose is to encompass board chairmen, presidents, executive vice-presidents, and vice-presidents in charge of major segments of insurance companies. It is intended, also, as an important indication to you; for in your consideration of the lower rungs of any career ladder, you probably have had the top rungs in mind, and you probably have asked, "How high can I climb?"

Progressive insurance companies need top-flight executives, and, to create backlogs of such talent, many insurance companies are recruiting selected college graduates and giving them opportunities to take advanced, on-the-job training courses. Such graduates have the advantage of working successively in various departments and getting the feel of a variety of vocations. Eventually, they are placed in areas best suited to their qualifications and wishes. It may be in work that is uniquely a part of insurance; it may be in any of literally hundreds of other management areas, such as personnel management, business research, public relations, employee communications, and so on. Whatever the post, the man is given the opportunity to learn and to advance.

At this time, it seems to me that two points are especially worthy of re-emphasis: insurance offers the career seeker an almost endless variety of occupations in a business that has successfully weathered depressions and unfavorable world conditions; and insurance offers opportunity for work in a field that continuously serves people, serves business, and serves the nation, both socially and economically. And I say, again, that a sense of service in work makes a difference to a man in the long run.

As I look back over thirty-seven years with my company, I cannot think of a more satisfying business to have been in. I am not suggesting that other businesses do not have high ethical standards; but I am prepared to state that, in my own experience, I have never been asked to take any action, nor have I asked others to take any action, which I did not honestly feel was in the interests of the policyholders.

On numerous occasions when, through changed conditions or for one reason or another, we have had better experience than we had anticipated, the benefit payments to our policyholders have been increased over and above those called for in the contract. This, too, has given me a feeling of satisfaction.

My early experience in the company was in the investment department, and I found that the investigation of investment values, and the purchase thereof, was infinitely more interesting than the sale of securities to others. Investment is a fascinating part of the business, with continuously new situations to be looked into every day. One must keep carefully abreast of what is going on in the financial world—the domestic market particularly—but one also must realize that the foreign situation always has its bearing.

In investing insurance funds, our objective makes it essential to look first to the safety of the principal; next, to gaining the highest return consonant with safety, but with a strong sense also of the public interest. Last year, in our company, we invested at the rate of $7 million every working day. I have often been asked, "How do you find outlets for such sizable sums?" The fact is that we have plenty of choices. It is a matter of picking the best.

During the Great Depression in the 30's, we were often asked if we were not worried. The answer was that we were concerned, but not worried. Naturally, there were some investments in difficulty, but the over-all results worked out very well. The real test of investing comes in boom times, not in a depression. The danger is that in boom times, one will be carried away with the unsound thinking of the time rising from the fact that all companies are doing well. At such a time, it is more difficult to choose between sound investments that will stand up under adversity and the "good weather only" propositions.

There are now some fifteen hundred companies in the life-insurance business alone. Competition is keen—whether in the area of investing, designing new policies, or selling; whether in the application of new medical factors to underwriting or new techniques to management or methods. There is always something new, something to engage one's interest and challenge one's abilities.

Life insurance is so well established that one does not ordinarily think of it as a growth industry; but taking the business as a whole, life insurance in the United States has, on the average, more than doubled every ten years since 1900, and has grown at an even faster rate during the immediate past ten years.

Even with this great growth, life insurance is far from reaching its maturity. Why am I so certain about this? Because the life insurance in force, both personal and group, is equal, on the average, to only eighteen months of personal income. This, surely, is nowhere near adequate protection for the people of our country. Furthermore, our population is growing, and incomes are increasing for the vast majority. The market for life insurance has a very long way to go before even approaching a saturation point.

As I have told you, there are all kinds of openings in the insurance business and all kinds of opportunities for advancement. If you are willing to work, and to look on each day's experience as an opportunity to acquire more knowledge, I sincerely believe that you can find an interesting and a satisfying career in insurance.

If you decide to come into insurance, we will welcome you. If you decide to go elsewhere, all good luck go with you.

Here are some sources for detailed information about careers in insurance:

Institute of Life Insurance
488 Madison Avenue
New York 22, New York

Association of Casualty and Surety Companies
60 John Street
New York 38, New York

National Board of Fire Underwriters
85 John Street
New York 38, New York

Society of Actuaries
208 South LaSalle Street
Chicago 4, Illinois

Casualty Actuarial Society
200 Park Avenue South
New York 16, New York

And any executive of an insurance organization in a field or area that interests you especially should be happy to talk to you.

Some references worth consulting are:

Yale Insurance Lectures (Observations in Insurance History by Holcombe). Tuttle, Morehouse & Taylor Press, 1904.

The Metropolitan Life by Marquis James. Viking Press, 1947.

Casualty Insurance by C. A. Culp. Ronald Press, Third Edition, 1956.

Casualty Insurance Principles by G. F. Michelbacher. McGraw-Hill, 1930–42.

Marine Insurance by W. D. Winter. McGraw-Hill, Third Edition, 1952.

Life Insurance by S. S. Huebner-Kenneth Black, Jr. Appleton-Century-Crofts, Fifth Edition, 1958.

Careers in Life Insurance, Institute for Research. Chicago, 1949.

Do You Fit into This Picture? LIAMA. 1957.

A Career in Life Insurance Sales and Service, Institute of Life Insurance. 1950.

Life Insurance, #81 of Vocational and Professional Monographs, by Mildred F. Stone. 1955.

Professional Opportunities in Mathematics, Mathematical Association of America. 1958.

Field News, Convention Issue, 1960. Metropolitan Life.

Insurance World, 1957, Life, Accident and Sickness.

A Career for You in Insurance. Association of Casualty and Surety Companies/National Board of Fire Underwriters, Third Edition, 1956.

Career Underwriting—A Life Work, LIAMA. 1960.

Careers in Insurance, Daily Princetonian. 1956.

Educational Requirements for Employment of Actuaries, U.S. Department of Labor. 1955.

Let's Look at Life Insurance, Careers for College Graduates, LIAMA. 1949.

Employment Outlook in Insurance Occupations, Bulletin 1215–22, U.S. Department of Labor. 1957.

A Career for You in a Life Insurance Company, Institute of Life Insurance. [No Date.]

Careers in Life Insurance—An Invitation to Youth, Institute of Life Insurance. 1954.

A Career with a Future, Metropolitan Life. [Actuarial Recruiting Folder.]

9 *You in*

ADVERTISING

BY MARION HARPER, JR.

PRESIDENT AND CHAIRMAN OF THE BOARD
Interpublic, Incorporated,

and

CHAIRMAN OF THE BOARD
*American Association of Advertising
Agencies*

MARION HARPER, JR.

Born: 1916, Oklahoma City, Oklahoma

Phillips Academy
Yale: A.B., 1938

McCann-Erickson:
  Trainee, 1939
  Manager Copy Research, 1942–44
  Associate Director Research, 1944–45
  Vice-president in charge of Research and Merchandising, 1945–48
  Director, 1946–
  Assistant to President, 1947–48
  President, 1948–
  Chairman of the Board, 1958–
Interpublic, Inc.:
  President, 1961–
  Chairman of the Board, 1961–

American Association of Advertising Agencies:
  Chairman of the Board
Director: National Outdoor Advertising Bureau
          Franklin Corporation
Formerly Director:
  The Advertising Council
  Advertising Research Foundation
Member: National Distribution Council
        Communication and Public Relations Committee
        Alumni Council Phillips Academy

Distinguished Service Award: Young Men's Board of Trade
Charles Coolidge Parlin Memorial Award
Cruzeiro do Sul

Author: *Getting Results from Advertising*
Contributing author: *Public Relations Handbook*

THE EDITOR OF THIS BOOK might reasonably have stated in the Table of Contents: "Advertising: Since advertising is all around us and since everybody knows about it, it was not felt necessary to include a chapter on it."

One reason that this would be a mistake is that the advertising you see and hear can tell you only a fraction of what advertising is like as a career. It would be like judging medicine as a career on the basis of your last X-ray or prescription, or judging law on the basis of a contract of sale or a summons to court.

Any vocation or profession has many aspects, and in a sense it is more than the sum of its parts. This is true of advertising, especially if you consider what different advertising people do.

Suppose you were to take a tour through a modern advertising agency. On one floor you might see copywriters. You might find that one was a copywriter for publications, another a television commercial writer, another a jingle composer. Others might be a fashion copywriter, an industrial writer, and a sales promotion writer. Each would have a different background and aptitude.

Or perhaps you might see men and women over drawing boards. They might turn out to be art directors specializing in publication advertising or in television, or they might be poster artists, fashion art directors, "live" television commercial producers, or specialists in the selection and arrangement of type for ads and printed pieces.

In other offices, you might be introduced to account executives, who are basically all-around businessmen with a specialized knowledge of advertising, or television programming specialists, with backgrounds in show business.

And in offices where desks and bookcases are piled high with reports and studies, you might find several kinds of research people. Some might be engaged in advertising research, basically, the collection and analysis of data on the effectiveness of advertisements and commercials. You would also see people engaged in market research, the task of measuring the types of people in the market for a product on the basis of field surveys. You would see others involved in psychological research, ascertaining what motives, apparent or hidden, move people toward or away from certain products. Others would be in the field of media, the term used for newspapers, magazines, television and radio stations—the "means" for reaching the public—and these people might be setting up schedules of selected media for a given advertising program.

Elsewhere, you might meet people who are casting for commercials, or organizing a fashion show or a sales meeting.

Still others might be organizing advertising programs for overseas markets, and yet others might be busy in the administration of the agency's business affairs.

This would by no means be a complete tour of an agency's activities. Work would also be going on outside the agency, in the clients' offices and outlets, in television studios, on photography assignments, in libraries, and in surveys of consumers.

All of these people engaged in these activities could be said to be "in advertising." Nevertheless, it is apparent that the work of one individual (let us say, an art buyer) might be as different from the work of another (say, a "motivational" researcher) as the work of a pharmacist is different from a broker.

I should mention, by the way, that for convenience, most of the references in this discussion relate to advertising agencies. Thousands of other people are also very much "in advertising": in the advertising departments of manufacturing, retail, and service organizations; in the promotion departments of newspapers, magazines, television, radio, direct mail, and poster firms.

It is correct to conclude, therefore, that advertising is not one career but many; and already you may visualize how the work of advertising extends over a far broader spectrum than might be suggested by the advertisements we see from day to day.

With all this great diversity, what are some things that the various specialties in advertising have in common? As a prejudiced witness, I would offer these generalizations:

Advertising is a field of virtually unlimited opportunity. It offers a broad field for expression of any one of a wide range of talents—and of one's individual creative capacities. You have the chance of learning throughout a career and pioneering new ways of doing things. There is the endless fascination of seeing how large numbers of people respond to different messages and products. Because of its broad participation in business problems, an advertising career can lead to top echelons of management responsibility and bring compensation above average in general business.

What might be your impressions of the day-to-day work in advertising?

You would clearly have many impressions, but suppose you were to sit in on a conference of a "product group": the people from various parts of an agency concerned with advertising a particular product. Just to list the subjects that might come up would fill a small volume; but you would find yourself ranging over almost all facets of a business from top management policies of expansion to ideas for premiums, from response to a new season's television program to the response to a poster, from the sales record of competing products to results of a sampling program, from announcement of a larger (or smaller) advertising budget to viewing of some new television commercials, from a plan to get better shelf display for the product to results of a taste test—and on and on and on.

Or, if you were to eavesdrop on a hundred other discussions in an agency—between copywriters and art directors, between account executives and TV programming people, between department heads and their colleagues—you might well decide that advertising work is a daily and continuous search for new ideas. Advertising is as stimulating as the minds that take part in it, and, in a sense, even more so, since it makes use of a wider variety of communications skills than is found in almost any other field.

Advertising is celebrated as a business of deadlines, and, in fact, it is. This means—at least on the professional side of the business—that one is required to be creative *on schedule*. There is just so much time for your stream of consciousness to flash with "Eureka," before the inevitable "Where is it?"—before copy must go to the printer or a recommendation must go to the advertiser. This can be tension-making, but it can also be pretty stimulating. It is remarkable how productive you can be, disciplined by deadlines.

But I would be wrong to suggest that advertising people do not have time to review last night's TV special or an opening at some Broadway theater, for needless trips to the water cooler, for second and third summations of their points of view. All this seems an essential prelude before they close their doors and work out their individual solutions at typewriters, drawing boards, in research questionnaires, or whatever.

Again, in our hypothetical tour, what might be your impressions of the people you would meet? Would they be very different from any other business people?

I suppose that like attracts like, and that there are several characteristics that most advertising people share. My own experience is that most advertising people have an inventive turn of mind; they enjoy participation; and they are enthusiastic and enterprising. They are fine prospects for the arts, books, theater, and travel; and, in general, they convey a lively sense of being in the mainstream of contemporary life.

As for other characteristics, some are more profound than their colleagues, some more superficial; some more conformable, some less; some more civic-minded, some not so much; some more concerned with cultural values, some less so. As a matter of fact, I would guess that, in a cross-section, they are just as heterogeneous as people of comparable education and responsibility in other fields.

From this, you may properly conclude that there are not too many generalizations one can make about requirements of personality and aptitude in the newcomer to advertising. A personnel director may respond favorably to enthusiasm, but a candidate of a more subdued type may easily establish greater desirability through strength in other attributes. He may, for example, convey a particular creative flair in ideas, language, or art; or he may give promise of the kind of analytical ability which is needed in developing advertising strategy and plans. Historically, people in advertising—as in many other fields—with a particular gift for persuasion seem to reach higher levels of management and compensation than their less-persuasive colleagues.

Perhaps one characteristic that is generally looked for is a feeling of exhilaration for new ideas, new approaches, fresh impressions. Advertising is in the front lines of business competition, and the novel and different are likely to hold a competitive edge. The familiar and trite, the routine and pedestrian seldom win attention, let alone response.

This emphasis on uncovering the *new* calls for plain hard work and energy. Very few of the important jobs in advertising are on a nine-to-five schedule. (Although round-the-clock work in advertising is often more a matter of legend than experience.)

Let me return to our advertising agency. After you have met some people and seen them at work, it is possible that you might, in a visit with an advertising executive, discuss advertising's role in business and its place in the economy. Let me therefore set down some impressions I have gathered over the years, as well as some beliefs I have about the present and future of advertising.

What is the function of advertising? Why do presidents of companies and their financial committees approve expenditures that total more than $11 billion for advertising in a single year?

Definitions do not make for sparkling reading, but they are nevertheless helpful. Let me suggest one from the viewpoint of business at large: *Advertising is a form of communication which*

a company or institution directs, through paid media, to pro-
spective customers, to people who influence the buying decisions
of others (for example, architects, engineers, designers), and to
opinion leaders (people whose tastes and opinions are valued
by their neighbors). The message of advertising is conditioned by
marketing or communications goals, and by the nature of the
desired audience.

This definition is accurate, but woefully incomplete. The
young person will find that work in advertising is not limited to
advertisements, nor should his thinking about the field be
limited. Especially if he is considering advertising as a field for
career progress, he should understand the environment in which
advertising performs.

He will first discover that advertising is inseparable from
marketing, just as marketing is inseparable from business. One
overlaps the other, and each keeps changing.

There are as many definitions of marketing as there are people
in sales and advertising activities. One that seems to make sense
is that marketing is the process by which a product is designed,
produced, distributed, and sold to a consumer. This is true if
every step in the process is directed toward the final result: the
sale. In this case, the product is conceived, designed, and made
with the eventual consumer clearly in mind. It is packaged for
his convenience; it is priced to his budget; it is placed where he
can best buy it; and it is advertised so as to arouse his interest in
doing so. All this is marketing.

Where does marketing begin and leave off in business? Product
design, for example, was once within the total jurisdiction of
production. Now, it is almost within the total jurisdiction of
marketing.

This has come about because business has become more concerned each year with marketing. Business, today, makes its
major decisions on the basis not of what the *factory* says but
what the *market* says—the market being customers, distributors,
and dealers.

Clearly, this represents an important advance in consumer democracy. Just as we believe government should serve the people's will, so in modern marketing the producer shapes his products and communications to serve the wishes of the consumer. Sales— and other reactions—are the ballots that express the favor or the disfavor of the consumer "electorate."

That is why the producer today has come to regard himself less as a producer and more as a marketer. At the assembly line, he is really a producer; but the hundreds of decisions that he feeds into an assembly line are clearly market decisions.

Advertising merges into marketing, just as marketing merges into production. Advertising is the principal communication tool of marketing.

But what exactly is this communication tool? Is advertising so many words and pictures and sounds? The literal answer is "yes," as soon as they appear in a paid advertising medium. The answer perhaps should be: such words and pictures and sounds *become* advertising when their content and character have been determined by knowledge of the product and its prospects, when they convey a message that has a well-defined objective and is creatively conceived and expressed, when they appear in media that support the company's system of distribution, when they gain access to responsive prospects—all at a cost that makes for profitable sales.

Even as a commentary on a definition, this is highly condensed; but it indicates how quickly any involvement with copy and art intended for paid media at once brings involvement with the basic areas of marketing and distribution.

To paraphrase the previous discussion: where does advertising begin and where does marketing leave off?

Is advertising the communications part of marketing? Yes, but almost all marketing is a communications process. It is raw information, as well as information expressed in a way to persuade. Can we say that advertising is the part of marketing communications which the producer addresses to his market? The answer, of course, is that advertisements and commercials are directed to the market, but they are created, in part, out of communications in the other direction, from the market to the producer. (Research specialists in advertising are constantly asking people questions about the products they prefer, their purchasing habits, the television programs they watch, and many other subjects. All this information is used to help the company produce a better product and advertise it more effectively. More often, however, the market communicates to the producer simply through its choice of purchases, whether of cars, clothes, or can openers.)

Advertising starts with the advertiser and his relationship to his market. Choose any company that comes to mind. It has become the kind of company that it is because, in its own way, it has answered certain questions: "What are our goals as to the kind of business we want to be in, the products we want to make, the share of market we want to achieve, the profit level we look for?" Answers to such questions make one company a Tiffany's; another, a Woolworth's—each eminently successful in its chosen field.

Actually, it would be correct to represent a company as a vessel in motion—and its market as a constantly changing shoreline. And between the two, it would be correct to imagine a fog of greater or lesser density. Also, it would be well to keep in mind that other vessels (competing companies) are in the area. You therefore need a constant flow of questions and answers between vessel and shoreline—between company and market—to decide in what direction you should proceed.

What makes for the best communication from advertiser to the market?

First, a clear knowledge of the changing character of the company, product, and prospect.

The company may appear to be the same from one day to the next, but actually it is not. Its planning and performance, the actions of competitors, the economic environment are all influences for change.

Recent developments in the market have been so dramatic as to justify the phrase "marketing revolution." People are constantly changing as customers, and the ways of reaching them with products and messages are also changing.

New living patterns are replacing old ones through the movement of people between suburbs and cities, through higher income levels, through today's greater leisure. Distribution has been undergoing radical changes, with continuing and wider replacement of sales personnel by self-service and automatic vending, and with the growing influence of large retailers—shopping centers, department-store branches, discount houses, and supermarkets.

All these happenings have brought changes in the relationship of a company and its market. They have required stronger *direct* representation of the advertiser to the consumer. This has placed greater importance on the function of advertising and has helped raise advertising volume by more than four hundred per cent since World War II.

To make this advertising effective has required a more-detailed knowledge of the consumer than ever before. The advertiser has come to recognize not one kind of prospect, but several; that is, markets made up of economic, geographical, and even psychological segments. Different products and different appeals are appropriate for various market segments.

It is clear, then, that a company has many ways of communicating with its markets. First is the product, which is the advertiser's basic message to the market—and advertising, packaging, sales promotion, merchandising, personal selling, and public relations—all of which contribute to the customer's knowledge about the product and, eventually, working together, persuade him to buy.

And there are reverse means of communication, from the market *to* the advertiser. There is marketing research (including psychological research), product research, and media and advertising research—all asking questions of the consumer. Through this multiple transmission of information, the advertiser defines his market, designs his product, and plans his communications.

Marketing communications has a special character. It is not

like the transmitting of temperature readings or a radiation count. It is the sending out of *competitive* messages by all competing companies. The goal of these messages is persuasion; and persuasion is the basic business of marketing, the basic service which the advertising agency renders the advertiser.

If you like, a business today is built on a massive consumer-opinion poll. Reports come to you in sales, as well as in responses from cross-sections of the market. Operating with such a system, do you come up with precisely the right product and precisely the right advertising—and then let business run as if by automation? Of course, it does not work that way. In an economy of competitive enterprise, you must constantly come up with innovations and improvements in your product line and in all your communications.

The relevance of all this to your careers is that the field of marketing—and advertising in particular—needs innovators; needs all kinds of creative talent; needs the kinds of minds that can digest volumes of facts and data, that can see new relationships, and that can devise fresh solutions. Minds like these can see an exciting challenge in persuading large numbers of people, and in studying their changing wants and reactions.

Everyone knows that humanity responds not only to cold facts but to varying arrangements and presentations of facts. The headline writer selects—not the most important element in a story, from the viewpoint of history or culture or progress of the race—but rather what he believes is most vital to most of his readers on a given day. The magazine editor selects a cover which may not be the most "scientific" portrayal of an event, person, or situation; but rather one that communicates to the *whole person*, to the reader's knowledge, reason, and emotions. Advertising is also addressed to the *whole person*. It seeks a response in competition with a thousand other claims for attention, and against the terrible odds of the prospect's inertia. Its creative challenge is to find and express the most effective appeal for the largest audience of prospects.

Advertising is really several languages in one, but I would say it has two basic languages. One is reportorial; the other is the language of imagination.

An advertising department, or an advertising agency, has great need for reportorial skills, for the accurate reporting of a company's marketing goals and requirements, for reporting of the needs and preferences of potential customers, and for newsworthy and accurate reporting of the product to the market. Also, since advertising depends on many individual contributions, reporting skills help each participant to convey his ideas and convictions.

And because persuasion is the goal, advertising also lives on imaginative expression. It must conjure up the product or service in the mind of the prospect in realistic and appealing ways. It must establish a "personal" relationship between the prospect and the soft drink, or the cigarette, or the soap—all in a matter of seconds.

This discussion so far has dealt with advertising as a career for both men and women. What about advertising specifically as a field for women?

Advertising has a great deal to offer women, and women have a great deal to offer advertising.

Most of the shopping in the country is done by women, and women's opinions largely dictate what gets bought and what companies prosper. Girls start playing house at the age of three or four and, at least in a large family, work at it from the age of ten or twelve. They spend many hours every day of their lives thinking about the two thousand to five thousand or so square feet that is their home—and the twenty or fifty square feet of their kitchens. And they are likely to find time every day for at least an oblique thought about their clothes closets and dressing tables.

When you've said house, food, clothes, and cosmetics, you've covered a lot of advertising.

Finally, women should certainly be experts in the language that is persuasive with women—it's their own. They have proved they can sell the utility advantages of a floor cleaner in one breath, and in the next, the glamour appeal of a lipstick.

Of course, through the ages, women have also become experts in the language that is persuasive with men. Many women in advertising have proved effective in preparing advertising for products and services largely bought by men: generators, magazine space, sporting goods.

Women have also distinguished themselves in other areas of an advertising agency: in television programming, research, sales promotion, publicity.

I know of few fields which offer women quite as much latitude as advertising. First, for providing a slot for a woman's talents, and, then, affording lines of promotion from her specialized skills to posts of senior management. She may shift not only from one division to another within an advertising agency but to a number of allied fields. Many women I know have moved comfortably between advertising agencies and broadcasting companies, magazines, women's pages and departments of newspapers, and advertising departments of manufacturers and retail stores. Each experience has added new qualifications.

In mentioning women's opportunities in advertising, I don't mean to suggest that men are excluded from the same opportunities. Unlike French nouns, talents don't seem to have a masculine or feminine gender.

At this point in your visit to the agency, you may be inclined to point out that you have been given a quite different impression of advertising than you had gotten elsewhere.

I have conceded that this is the testimony of a prejudiced witness. At the same time, you should be warned that other witnesses, who are outside the field of advertising, are not necessarily without prejudice. Why should this be so?

For the most part, advertising people are anonymous and perform in the background. This has made the field intriguing as a subject for novels, movies, and social comment. Script writers and commentators have seen advertising as a fertile field for taking the public behind the scenes and giving them "the inside story." But the result has done little to clarify advertising's character as a career.

Of course, we can take for granted that no business looks the same to those who are actually engaged in it as to those outside.

In any event, finding out what advertising is really like calls for going behind a great many images that are romantic, satiric, or simply inaccurate. This is partly a technical matter of fiction writing. When advertising—or for that matter, the newspaper business or law or medicine—is used as a background, the writer usually renders it in a quick, telegraphic way. In the style of the graphic artist or cartoonist, he will select certain features—already in circulation as stereotypes—which will win popular recognition. Sometimes, he may do more than justice to the subject, and sometimes less. As a result, on the basis of popular portrayals of advertising, you might very well have received these contradictory impressions:

"Advertising is a glamorous business" . . . "Advertising is hard work and long hours."

"Advertising demands unusual talents" . . . "A good selling personality will take you far in advertising."

"Advertising helps raise living standards" . . . "Advertising helps raise prices."

"Advertising underwrites the news, public affairs, and entertainment" . . . "Advertising exaggerates and takes liberties with factual truth."

As with almost anything, it is possible to find evidence to support each of these statements. The real point is that in deciding on anything as important as a career, it is desirable to go beyond fiction and judge a field in relation to one's own findings, and in relation to one's own interests and aptitudes. It may be the most important kind of investigation that anyone conducts. One can then base a selection of a career not on hearsay or the notions of a script writer, luncheon speaker, or contributor to an anthology, but on one's own facts and evidence.

For this reason, in considering advertising as a career, it is important for the young person to meet as many people in the field as possible and get firsthand impressions of their work situations, their values, their frustrations, and their satisfactions.

You may next ask: what are some of the rewards of an advertising career?

You have perhaps heard that advertising is a well-paid field, and this is true. Advertising is a first cousin of selling, and, like selling, it is well compensated because in part it contributes to the building of a business. Another reason for this compensation is that creative talent, with training in particular lines of business, tends to be in short supply. This develops competition for high-caliber personnel and "bidding up" of their salary levels.

Money may loom large as a factor in choosing a career, but studies in industrial psychology have found that it isn't the most important incentive later on. For many people in advertising, the work itself is the chief satisfaction. Nothing makes for a more satisfying day than when you have come up with a fresh solution that announces itself as the right solution. It is also pleasing to one's vanity to see an idea take shape and be reproduced millions of times across the country. And you will find it rewarding when the advertising you took part in creating helps a company grow. Then, in a broad perspective, it is satisfying to feel that you have contributed in some small way to the vitality and growth of the country's economy, on which people's welfare both here and abroad depends.

What are some of the frustrations of advertising? It has its share.

Many of your best ideas—they are *obviously* the best—often do not see the light of day. Any one idea may involve large sums of money, and its creator is only one of the persons who can have a voice in its acceptance. Also, if you hunger for fame, advertising isn't too satisfying. Almost all contributions are anonymous.

Another possible negative: You may have heard that advertising is not a field that offers the greatest security. It is true that advertising budgets may be sharply cut and that accounts do shift from one agency to another with the result of sudden unemployment. My impression is that most competent people are usually hired quickly, sometimes at a higher salary level. But the job termination means an interruption of employee benefits and, for some, a hiatus in income. While this fact should be recognized, it should also not be exaggerated. Some accounts stay with agencies for forty and fifty years, and many advertising people remain with their firms for anniversaries of several decades. For those, however, who are allergic to a certain degree of insecurity, I would hesitate to recommend advertising, not only for possible hazards of unemployment but because I feel it requires a spirit of enterprise that inevitably involves risk.

Finally, advertising is conspicuous by nature, and it is an easy target for attack or satire. Much of the attack—like the charge that advertising "manipulates" people—I think is nonsense; but some of it very properly lampoons vulgarities and violations of elementary good taste. It can be discouraging to find yourself associated, even remotely, with things that you yourself have resented or winced over, whatever may be your business or profession.

But I am glad to report that advertising at large has fine popular acceptance; and it is likely to gain more as its place in the economy becomes better understood.

In my own view, while we as a people may not applaud service to the national economy with the same fervor as we recognize other kinds, it is nevertheless true that this economic service is essential in maintaining and advancing our society. One way to judge its value is in terms of other societies whose economies are poorly organized and motivated—and whose people are underfed and ill-housed.

It is realistic, however, to recognize that there are different forms of service, direct and indirect.

You may feel a special pull toward a particular field because it seems to perform an urgent human service. You may wish to become a physician, to be engaged in the art of healing; you may wish to be a farmer, to help feed people; or the generous work of the Salvation Army in relieving personal distress may have particular appeal for you.

Each of these callings is clearly a field of service. What of business or banking or real estate, or advertising and marketing? Among these professions, the act of service is not so conspicuous. If you have a compelling altruism, which requires that you see the results of your service in a personal, face-to-face way, then it would seem apparent that the fields of indirect service—those, for example, that relate to the economy—may not be satisfying to you.

If, on the other hand, you see our national economy—the running of it, the planning for it, the development of it—as a force which builds high living standards and provides the conditions for high cultural standards, then you may have at least indirect feelings of satisfaction in the work of business, and specifically in advertising and marketing.

Most of these comments relate to advertising in the world of today, but for the young person looking forward to a career, the '70s and '80s have far more relevance.

What are advertising's prospects in the future of business and our economy?

The most striking development will be the rapid and dramatic expansion of markets and marketing operations.

Most economists agree that by 1970 the U.S. market will have added one-fifth more consumers, two-fifths greater personal income, and one hundred per cent more discretionary income (the money left over after purchase of food, shelter, clothing, etc.). We can expect many more young consumers (more by half in the fifteen-to-twenty-four age group), and more elder consumers (more by one-fourth in the over-sixty-five age group). In short, the market will expand over-all, and especially at both ends of the age scale.

To keep pace with new marketing opportunities, we can expect by 1970 a doubling of present advertising volume.

Growth curves abroad will rise even more sharply. The likely development of an Atlantic Economic Community, along with Common Markets in Latin America and Asia, as well as the successful example of Europe, will be further stimulants to marketing and advertising. With products crossing national boundaries as never before, many advertising people of the future will have international careers.

Also by 1970 we can expect an upheaval in distribution, brought about by the wider use of automation and electronic data processing. As one measure of its application in business, automation equipment in 1960 reached a sales volume of $6 billion, or more than half of the total spent on new plants and equipment. New methods of information processing will permit far-greater precision in defining markets—and more accurate matching of markets to media.

We can expect greater emphasis on co-ordination of all phases of the total marketing effort—advertising, selling, merchandising, publicity—and greater recognition of the decisive importance of marketing in the success of a business. This trend will have particular significance in business careers. Charles Mortimer, Chairman of the Board of General Foods, Inc., has forecast: "In the next decade or two, more than half of the presidents of American corporations will have come from the marketing, sales and advertising areas."

The continuing need will be for constantly higher levels of creative performance. With educational and cultural levels rising around the world, there will be new discrimination among consumers. The routine and the repetitive in advertising, or any other phase of marketing, will be even more unsatisfactory than they are today.

For all these reasons, advertising's needs for talent will grow at a faster rate than in many other fields. Because it must perform in a more complex marketing world, advertising will place a higher premium on quality in its recruiting, and it will extend a particular welcome to honors students. As today, its future practitioners will come from many backgrounds: from English, economics, and psychology departments; from schools of journalism and schools of business administration.

Should the young person look forward to a brave new world of double-domed supermarkets, helicopter delivery fleets, robot salesmen, and telecasts from the moon? Perhaps not, but there will be developments almost as exciting, and advertising will have its share of them. We can be sure that advertising will offer many satisfactions to those who wish expression of their creative talents to be an important part of their working lives.

10 *You in*

PUBLIC SERVICES

BY FREDERICK R. KAPPEL

CHAIRMAN OF THE BOARD

*American Telephone and Telegraph
Company*

FREDERICK R. KAPPEL

Born: 1902, Albert Lea, Minnesota

University of Minnesota: B.S.E. 1924
Lehigh University: LL.D., 1958
Knox College: LL.D., 1959
Union College: D.C.L., 1959
Ohio Wesleyan University: LL.D., 1960
Rensselaer Polytechnic Institute: D.E., 1961
Columbia University: LL.D., 1962
Williams College: LL.D., 1962

Northwestern Bell Telephone Company:
  Groundman, Equipment and building engineer, Area plant engineer, etc., 1924–36
  Plant operations supervisor, 1937–38
  Assistant Vice-president, 1939–42
  Vice-president in charge of operations, 1942–48
  Director, 1942–48
American Telephone and Telegraph Company:
  Vice-president in charge of Long Lines, 1949
  Vice-president in charge of operations and engineering, 1949–53
  President, 1956–61
  Director, 1956–
  Chairman of the Board, 1961–
Western Electric Company: President and Director: 1954–56

Director: Chase Manhattan Bank
         Metropolitan Life Insurance Company
         General Foods Corporation
Trustee: Tax Foundation, Inc.
         Committee for Economic Development
         Grand Central Art Galleries, Inc.
         The American Heritage Foundation
         The Presbyterian Hospital in the City of New York
         National Safety Council

Board of Governors, The American National Red Cross
Armed Forces Communications and Electronics Association
The Business Council
American Institute of Electrical Engineers
Advisory Council, M.I.T. School of Industrial Management
The Salvation Army Advisory Board of New York City
Telephone Pioneers of America
Board of Directors, Boys' Clubs of America
National Advisory Council, Tuskegee Institute
Business Committee for the National Cultural Center

Author: *Vitality in a Business Enterprise*

L ET ME START by explaining what is meant by "public services" in this chapter heading. A public-service company is one that provides a basic service to the general public: electric power, for instance, gas, transportation by land or by air, telephone or telegraph communications.

Admittedly, this classification is a bit arbitrary, because any number of other businesses also provide service to the public. Banking is a service, for example. So is the corner laundry. So is a shoeshine parlor. Nevertheless, by custom and in ordinary usage, the electric and gas utilities, the communications companies, and the railroads, airlines, and bus lines are commonly referred to as public-service industries. As a group, they constitute a large and important part of the total industry of the country. And the job of all of them is just what you might suppose: to provide good, abundant, dependable, efficient, and satisfactory *service*.

All my working life has been spent in the telephone business, in the Bell System, so most of what I can say to you must be based on that experience. Nevertheless, as we go along here I suggest you keep in mind that the whole reason for existence of any public-service company is precisely what the word says: service. Regardless of differences between one kind of company and another, this is fundamental to all of them. Hence, if the idea of providing service, and seeing what you can do to improve it, does not appeal to you, you may want to skip this chapter.

In my own case, however, I have to say that in thirty-seven years of working at a service job, I have found it fascinating all the way. One reason for this is the endless diversity of things to be done. I shall say more about this in a minute, and try to illustrate a bit from personal experience. First, however, so that you may have the general setting, it may be helpful to outline briefly what the Bell Telephone System is and how it is organized.

The System is a closely linked group of companies headed by the American Telephone and Telegraph Company. Around the country there are twenty-one so-called "operating companies," each providing service within a particular region. Then there is the Long Lines Department of the A. T. & T. Company, which provides the long-distance network interconnecting the regional operating companies, and also furnishes overseas service in co-operation with the people who handle communications in foreign countries.

The Bell System also includes two other organizations. One is the Western Electric Company, which manufactures and supplies communications equipment for the operating companies and Long Lines. The other is Bell Telephone Laboratories. This does scientific research and development work for the whole System. What we have in a nutshell is three-way teamwork between research, manufacture, and operations—and the object of all of it, to repeat, is service to the public.

There are many other communications companies in the United States besides the Bell System companies. They include telegraph companies providing domestic and international services, and more than three thousand telephone companies, large and small. The lines of these telephone companies interconnect with Bell System lines to make possible nationwide service.

Even from such a sketchy outline, you can see that there is a great variety of work going on in the Bell System. The process of research and development keeps turning up new kinds of equipment. Thousands of different components and systems are manufactured, including many new ones each year; in fact, the great majority of all the things now made by Western Electric are of types that did not even exist fifteen years ago. Then, all these devices and systems must be installed to work harmoniously with the equipment already in place, and the old must be constantly modified to function in tune with the new. Moreover, new and improved systems lead to new kinds of service to the public, and the people who provide the service must be constantly preparing themselves to make the most of these new opportunities. With steady technological change, it is necessary for the managers in the business to anticipate the human problems that must be solved, to train men and women for new kinds of jobs, to devise new forms of organization that will be needed, to discern the future needs of customers and shape the marketing effort that will meet them most effectively.

The point here is that in a growing public-service business, backed by sound research and technical development, the atmosphere is dynamic and there is no end of challenge and opportunity. There is room and need for all kinds of talent. The communications business, for example, is based on scientific discovery, technical knowledge, and careful engineering. So the field for technical and engineering abilities is wide open, and will, I think, grow wider in the future. However, it would be a mistake for the young man who has had mainly liberal arts or business training in school to feel that a telephone company, for example, needs only engineers. One of my close associates recently remarked that when he was finishing his course at a liberal arts college and considering what sort of business to enter, he had this impression very strongly, and could hardly believe it when a representative of the Bell System suggested a telephone career. However, he decided to try it and soon enough discovered that there was plenty of interesting work for nonengineering people like himself.

Every customer of a public-service company is an individual who has personal needs and wants, and a business like ours must have people who not only *can* deal with customers in a helpful and understanding way, but sincerely *desire* to do so. Good salesmanship is extremely important and the business has great need for marketing and promotional skills.

In any business, of course, one must get to know what the customer needs. But I might stress particularly here that in providing an essential service like communications, which is used by all other industry, learning how to come up with the right systems and methods for serving other large organizations is a full-time job in itself for many people. To serve a bank with many branches, for example, you really must know how that bank operates, what its particular problems and objectives are, and what you can offer that will provide the best and most efficient communications. To serve a steel company, you must have studied the steel industry and the needs of that company. The same is true in all other fields: insurance, hotels and motels, oil, textiles, aviation, department and chain stores, food processing, automobiles, and shipping, to name a few.

As new developments are made in communications, how can they be applied most effectively in the various branches of industry? And, equally important, as other industries grow and develop and change, what new needs will they have for communications, and are we sharp enough to spot them and find the right answers on our own initiative? This is a matter of endless observation and study, of being intimately acquainted with our customers and constantly on the alert to anticipate their needs.

Besides all this, telephone people must deal with others not only as customers; they must negotiate with town councils and highway authorities, with architects and contractors, with property appraisers and tax collectors and the commissions that regulate telephone rates. They must study population trends and plan future construction. They must estimate costs and revenues. They must program computers and understand the operation of all kinds of business machines. They must bargain with unions. They must raise capital through the sale of stock and bonds. They must handle the company's bank accounts. They must do thousands of different things, only a few of which I have mentioned here.

You may be saying to yourself now that one person can't do all these things; there just aren't enough hours in a lifetime. That may be true, but I think what is important to have in mind is that a man with a reasonable amount of ability and real drive and eagerness to work can accumulate a variety of experience that will surprise him. And it needn't take too long either, provided he is willing to take each job that is given him and do his best. That is the first essential.

When I went to work for the telephone company, right out of

college, there were a number of us together in a training course, and some in the group were used to working while others were not. Also, some of them expected a lot more than a young man with a slide rule and a math book and a B.S. degree had any real right to expect. They were so impatient to use these tools of their trade and be full-fledged engineers right off the bat that they didn't get the respect of the rank and file or of the managers of the business either; whereas there were others who took each job that was given them and saw in it something to learn, something that would help their abilities while doing the job as well as possible. They could see that there were two aspects to any job. One is what you can do for it; the other is what it can do for you.

I am not in favor of a man going more slowly than he is able. But impatience is no substitute for ability. My advice to any young man entering a business is that in the first years (and it depends on the individual how many that will be), if he is smart, he will dedicate himself to the business he has joined, unless he finds that it is the wrong business for him. He will take in stride all the jobs he is given, the drab ones as well as the exciting ones, and recognize that people are watching him. They are not giving him these jobs just to get the jobs done. That is the first consideration, but not the only one. They are also giving him the jobs to grow on, to test his drive and determination, his ability to work with others, his capacity to learn. And all the while, they are accumulating multiple judgments on his capabilities.

If you will go at your work with this understanding, not only will you build up a sense of being sure that you can deliver the goods, because you have had the experience, but also, in later life, you will cherish the associations you have made and you will not want to trade them for anything in the world.

Here is an illustration of how a job assignment can get a man into dealing with people all over the map. About three years or so after I started with the telephone company in Minnesota, I was assigned to work on engineering problems involved in the routing of telephone lines and power lines. How a high-voltage power line is routed in relation to nearby long-distance telephone lines, and the way both the power and telephone systems are designed, can make a lot of difference in the quality of telephone transmission. In those days, the difficulties involved in controlling and minimizing the electrical induction between the lines were among the foremost engineering problems of both industries; and the fact that such problems are routine today is testimony to the effectiveness of research and field work done by many, many people through the years.

Much of my job was to negotiate with the power company people all over the state and work out plans and designs and routes in a way that would be satisfactory to all concerned. Also, in the cities and towns around the state, arrangements had to be made constantly for joint use of the same poles by both the telephone company and the electric companies. This meant dealing with the power-company people and also with municipal officials on all sorts of matters: which company would place the poles in which locations, what rental the other would pay, what contracts should be made with city governments, the provisions for liability, and so on. The job was basically an engineering job, but I soon found out there was a whole lot more to it than engineering. There was also the need for diplomacy and fair dealing, for sound business judgment, for awareness of legal problems and requirements, and understanding of the different points of view of many very different people.

A couple of years later, another assignment unfolded a whole new set of problems. It appeared that in the south half of the city of Minneapolis something was wrong with the quality of transmission. Our customers were complaining, and the regular organization responsible had not been able to find the right answer. I was asked to study the whole situation, get together whatever expert help was needed, and bring about a solution in a hurry. This got me into examination of maintenance practices, into face-to-face relationships with customers, into testing and investigating day and night, and into many different phases of our business, because I had to work with specialists in many places. Also, it got me into personnel problems and methods of organization, for as it turned out, one of the principal needs was for a different form of organization and the replacement of people who were simply not meeting their responsibilities.

I mention these instances merely to help bring out some of the points that seem to me important for a young man to think about.

First, as I have said, in a business like ours a man with drive and ability will find in not too many years that he has gone through a wide range of interesting experiences.

Second, one should take what comes and learn from it. This is how you grow, and your growth is indispensable to both you and the company. A business such as the telephone company—or any business, for that matter—is not just something that is there, for people to come into today and go out of forty years later. It is something we create as we go along, making it constantly different and, we hope, better by the effort we put into it. When the telephone was invented, for example, there wasn't any telephone system or service or business. Every bit of it has been built and developed and modified and improved by generations of people, and we are still learning how to do our job. When you join a business, the attitude to take with you is that you are going to start learning and you are not going to stop, ever. This is what will make you one of the builders of whatever business you enter.

Third, I mentioned earlier that some people I have known were impatient and overanxious to get on with their careers before they were qualified. It isn't good to overrate yourself or pretend to abilities you have not yet acquired. But as you do acquire and strengthen them and feel yourself on firm ground, then, I say, use them with all the courage and independence of mind that you have. Do this no matter how much trouble you think it is going to get you into. Be yourself and express yourself. You probably cannot realize this today, but I can tell you for sure that there are more people up the line in a large organization who are searching for talent than you, concerned for your own progress, will ever imagine. Your ambition to get ahead cannot be any greater than their ambition to find, help develop, and reward the able, imaginative growers, the men who are the learners and the builders, the men who are full-scale individuals and have the courage that goes with their abilities.

This is not to say that every supervisor you may meet along the way will be everything you hope he is. You may get supervision, you may get jobs, that are distasteful. You may bump into situations that strike you as utterly wrong. This happened to me in my very first year. I was working as a telephone cable splicer's helper, and we had been working on a very complicated underground splice. The hour was late, so we temporarily wrapped up the cable to waterproof the opening and sealed the manhole, intending to come back in the morning to finish the job. The next morning I reported for work, but my boss, the cable splicer, did not. He was ill. The only thing that occurred to me was to get the job done. So I drove the truck to the manhole location, uncovered the splice, wrapped it for permanent closure, placed a lead sleeve over it, and wiped the joint with hot solder in the approved fashion. This was a complicated splice. It had five cables at one end and two larger ones at the other. Proud of my accomplishment, I called a dispatcher for the next assignment.

What happened? He chewed me out. Who was I, a helper, to think that I could wipe a cable joint? What authority did I have to step out of line, open a manhole, and do this job? My orders were to go and put the whole thing back the way I found it.

You can imagine the effect this had on me. But I forced myself to swallow it and see what would happen next. For one thing, I had satisfied myself that I could do the job. And years later, I found out that the incident had not been lost in the shuffle. There were people who saw a plus in my wanting to get the job done, and were interested in finding out what more I could do.

Another exasperating early experience was during the work with the power companies and city councils that I have already mentioned. As I said, this called for contact and negotiation with a great many people outside as well as inside of the telephone business. But at one time, while I was doing this work, I had a boss who had a row of buttons on his desk, and all of us who worked for him had buzzers on ours. When he wanted you, he would buzz you. To me, this was about as distasteful as anything that ever happened to me, and I was constantly in trouble with the boss because I would disconnect my buzzer. This I did because I simply could not believe that I could deal effectively with power-company managers, city officials, and other people in to see me, if I had to keep jumping up in response to a buzzer. This was an example of pure bull-headed authority, not good supervision at all, and I must say there was much more of this kind of thing than there should have been. But it seemed to me that during such experience, distasteful as it was, the thing to do was to keep going, do what I thought was right, and fight it out.

The points to emphasize here are these:

First, my experience has been that if you do give your best, and it is worth something, there *will* be people in the organization who will recognize it and jump at it, even if somebody else chews you out along the way or sits back and pushes buzzer buttons.

Second, learning is not merely a process of finding out what you ought to do; it is also a process of learning what not to do. A supervisor who does things wrong can teach you every bit as much as one who does them right. An unhappy or distasteful experience may be tremendously helpful to your personal future, *if only you have the wit to learn from it.* No one will ever learn how to manage a job or a business well if he does not also learn, at the same time, how not to manage it. If you have experiences that try your patience and tempt you to go somewhere else, look on them as bad examples for you to profit from. As you move up, be watchful enough to assure yourself that things of that nature are not repeated in your organization. If you will do this, you will surely find that those above you who are searching for good performance will add this to your credit as a man who can really grow.

In reading this, you may have wondered whether some of these things I have been saying pertain exclusively to work in a public-service business or may have more general application. The truth is, I believe, that one cannot draw a hard and fast line between one kind of business and another. Each will have its distinguishing or unique characteristics, but there are plenty of similarities also. It would be misleading to suggest that a person ought to have one set of attributes for one sort of enterprise and a totally different set for another.

The main distinguishing mark of the public-service organization, as I said at the start, is that it must be dedicated to serving the public well, at every hour of the day and night. This means it must have people who are dedicated to serving other people. Dedication is a rather lofty word, not to be used lightly, and I am quite serious in saying that nothing less will do. While the rewards for first-rate performance need to be adequate, and I believe they are, public-service work is not the field for fortune-hunting or get-rich-quick ambitions. But if one feels instinctively that helping to meet a vital public need would be interesting and exciting, if one is looking for a business in which all manner of talents are meshed and mingled, if one puts ahead of mere fortune-hunting the necessity for a life in which one can be "in character," so to speak, on the job as well as off, then working for a public-service organization may bring great satisfaction. I say this not only because of my own experience, but because I know personally so many people in the Bell System—and in other public service companies—who feel just that way about it.

Let me linger on this just a moment. When I showed a friend of mine in the Bell System the first manuscript of this chapter and asked his comment, he said, "I wish you could put more emphasis on the satisfaction people get from a service job."

"But I thought I had already stressed it," I said, "and I don't want to overdo it; readers may wonder if it is really true."

"Well," he said, "I know it's hard to write about intangibles like this, but just the same, this is important to get across if you possibly can."

He was right, of course. We in the Bell System describe the essence of our business in plain, homely words: "the spirit of service." They are more than words. They are something felt, something to live by; and the effort to live by them does, without question, bring to thousands of men and women great satisfaction and pride.

Through the years, a fairly common notion about the public-service companies has been that they are "regulated" companies, in contrast to other industries which are "competitive." If I were you, I would not overemphasize the importance of this distinction. The fact is that in the last generation, regulation has spread over all industry. Conformance with Federal, state, and local governmental rules affects not only the utilities, the banks, the insurance companies, but manufacturing, retailing, and all other branches of modern business.

At the same time, the idea that the so-called "regulated" industries are not concerned with competition has become more and more fictional. All forms of transportation, for example, compete with each other. Electricity and gas compete for many users, and in the future it appears that both will compete more and more with oil for home heating, to give only one example. In communications, competition is growing in several important areas. For instance, the communications companies are in keen competition with the manufacturers of private microwave radio systems to serve the needs of industry and government. And competition in research, in the development of new and improved communication devices and systems, could hardly be more intense than it is right now.

I do not mean to imply that the old-fashioned distinction between "regulated" and "competitive" has been completely eradicated or will be. The communication companies, the utilities, and the railroads and airlines are more subject to government rules at more points than most other industries. But in no sense are they immune to competition, and in no sense is other business free from regulation. There is no black and white about this; it is a matter of degree. But no one should think that a utility or a telephone company, for instance, has its territory or field or future all staked out in advance, to occupy and develop as it pleases. Nothing could be further from the truth. If you were joining the telephone company tomorrow, for instance, I doubt that it would take you twenty-four hours to realize that you were not only in a service organization, but in a business that must think competitively and act competitively all the way from the design of the tools and instruments it uses to the actual sale of the services and, beyond that, the hour-to-hour and day-to-day giving of service after it has been sold.

Having stressed competition, let me also stress another vitally important characteristic of work in a public-service company. This is the need for close co-operation between people. Here, again, I do not suggest that there is a black-and-white difference between our kind of business and other businesses. Every organization needs people working together. If the chef doesn't cook the meal, the waiter can't serve it. But the emphasis on co-operation and co-ordination in public-service companies is extreme. In transportation, for instance, it would otherwise be impossible to make up a timetable. In communications, when a customer orders a telephone installed, there has to be immediate and ready co-operation between the people who handle the order, the installer who visits the home, the man who assigns the line, the craftsman who connects it in the central office, the information operator who gives calling parties the number, the girl who makes ready the directory listing, and so on and so on.

This is the simplest possible illustration. Everything we do in communications requires co-operation. Remember, each time a person makes a telephone call, across town or across the country, we have to be prepared for him anywhere and all along the line. If there is anything wrong at any point, the call will not go through. And if we make a change in our methods or equipment at any location, we must be sure that what we are doing there will be in harmony with the situation everywhere else. Furthermore, this process of change is continuous. It never stops. This means that all through the organization, everyone must be ready to co-operate with everyone else. Designers in the laboratory, marketing and sales people, construction and maintenance men, engineers and traffic managers, manufacturing superintendents and warehouse supply forces—we all do our work with a keen, quick sense of how our jobs fit in with other people's jobs, to the end that our customers everywhere will get the best and most effectively co-ordinated service we can render. I am not writing about rote and routine, but about a fascinating process of shared responsibility, in which lively individuals give their individual best to achieve a common goal.

These are some of the ways in which I would hope you would look at our kind of business. Now, how about some of the ways we would look at you?

First, of course, we would look at your record. How have you responded so far to the tests that have been put in your way? Is your scholastic performance good? What sort of character have you demonstrated? Have you shown signs of ability to lead?

I might say here, by the way, that in the Bell System we have gone to some trouble to find out whether men who have stood relatively high in their college work have also done relatively well in our business. The answer seems clear that there *is* a broad correlation between high standing in school and good progress in the business. Of course, this does not work out a hundred per cent. However, of the men in the Bell System who had above-average scholastic records, a considerably greater proportion have attained positions of large responsibility, with commensurate salaries, than is the case with the men who were in the lower ranks in college. No one should read this statement as meaning that many men who perhaps have not yet found themselves in college will not do well in business. We all know that many have done very well, and I am sure that many more will. Nevertheless, the broad fact is as I have stated it, and if saying it here encourages any readers of this book to step up their efforts in college, so much the better.

I have also mentioned the word "character." It is a tremendously important word. Integrity and high character are the first thing we will look for in you. I know I run some risk in writing about this, for many people are skeptical of the ethical standards of business and some will suspect that I am making a routine bow to good morals. However, I shall take that chance, and you will just have to believe that I mean what I say. If you have any thought of taking part in a public-service business, integrity and high character are the very first essentials, and there can be no misunderstanding about this.

It hardly needs saying that there is much more to character

than just the avoidance of sin, large or small. Character is something positive, not negative. Let me try to explain this in terms of what it means to have the responsibility for a large share of the country's communications.

Suppose the next hurricane knocks out a hundred thousand telephones. What is the responsibility of telephone people? To restore service, of course. But when and at whose convenience? Clearly, the responsibility is to get the service working again at the earliest possible time. But again, what are the factors that will determine "the earliest possible time"? Does the company have supplies ready against the emergency? Are its tools and trucks in good order? Do its men know what to do? In short, how well prepared are we?

We could be relatively unprepared or moderately well prepared or beautifully prepared. And in these preparations, any number of technical developments and human skills will be involved. But behind those, there is something else. I mean the *will* to have made ourselves prepared, the *awareness* that we had a responsibility to discharge, the *determination* that we would equip ourselves with all the skills and materials and methods that would be needed.

When you get right down to it, this is really an ethical matter, not a matter of avoiding wrongs, but of wanting and proceeding on your own volition to do what is positively and constructively right. To put it in the language I have already used, the kind of character you have decides absolutely what kind of service you will give, and excellence of service without excellence of character is something utterly impossible.

To go on a bit further, let us say that those hundred thousand telephones are restored in good fast time. Does this end our ethical responsibility? Not if you accept the concept of character that I am trying to state. For there must be some things that we could have done better. There must be some characteristics of our physical facilities that we could improve, to make them more sturdy. There must be some methods we could sharpen up. In other words, what did this experience teach us? What have we learned? How can we make ourselves *better* prepared?

This is the ethical challenge, the challenge to character. I am aware, of course, that a business like ours has a legal as well as an ethical responsibility to render good service to the public. But it takes more than law to produce quality. Regulation from without cannot bring about excellence. Excellence must come from within.

I have used an emergency situation to help illustrate my thought. But it is obvious that one does not put on character when the wind blows and shed it when the sun comes out. The same principle that applies to preparing for emergencies applies also to preparing for everything else. What can we do to improve not only emergency performance but every day performance? What effort do we make to foresee? What goals do we set for ourselves? And having set them, do we then do all we can to attain them and at the same time look beyond them to establish new ones?

This is the desirable principle of action, and it is only out of the constant application of some such principle, it seems to me, that a great business can continue to make progress and remain a great business. Opposing it is the common human tendency to accept things as they are and do things in the same old way because that is the way they have always been done. Clearly, we must make discriminating use of all that our predecessors have learned and taught us. However, if we let old knowledge and established customs lock us in, then that is the end of progress. Therefore, when I say a business like ours looks for men of character, I mean also that we are looking for a quality of vitality, of enthusiasm, of self-starting energy; a quality that causes men to *want* to set goals for themselves and their business, and do their utmost to reach them.

One hears much these days of "management development programs." We have them in the Bell System and I think they are useful. But to men in college who are contemplating their future careers, it seems important to stress several points.

First, many men seem to have the idea that business life will be something like a continuation of college life. This is not correct. At college, the principal effort of the faculty and the deans is to contribute to your education. That is the very goal and purpose of the school. But the main goal of a business will not be to carry on your education. The main goal of a business necessarily is to get its work done well, now and in the future. If you do not realize this before you join the business, you are in for a bit of a shock when you do.

Second, most of your education in business will come from the work you do on the job, not from training courses. There is no substitute for experience, and it is a mistake to think that training courses by themselves can equip you to grow in responsibility.

Third, and most important, all that any educational process can do for you—in college or out, on the job or off—is help you develop yourself, for the only development that can occur in any person is *self-development*. If a man is not a self-starter and a self-developer, he is not very likely to grow in stature, no matter how much training he gets. I hope, therefore, that you will not let the prevalence of "management development" efforts lead you into the error of thinking that somebody else can bring about your growth. No one can do it except you yourself.

I put this stress on self-development because it is the self-developer, above all, that business needs and wants. Look at it this way. In what I was saying earlier about the ethical character of a business, its drive to prepare itself for its responsibilities, its determination to foresee, to develop better methods, to improve performance—in all this, we are really considering *the ability of the business as a whole to develop itself*. It is the self-development of the business that we need. This is the very guts and heart of business enterprise. But a self-developing business without self-developing people is impossible to conceive of. There can be no such thing.

One further specific point about public-service companies needs emphasis. They are vitally important to the nation's defense. So much of all industry—steel, mining, oil, textiles, chemicals, agriculture, and others—deeply shares defense responsibilities that I do not wish to give the impression of singling out the role of public services in building military strength. Nevertheless, the man who joins a communications or transport or power company should do so with awareness that the needs of defense are a never-ending concern. This goes far beyond the direct service that is rendered every day to the military. In the communications business, for example, we are constantly engaged in strengthening our facilities and improving our techniques, to make ever more certain of our ability to provide essential service without interruption in a national emergency. This is not a matter of making preparations for this or that from time to time. It is something we are doing all the time. It is never out of our minds. It is a way of life.

To sum up, in conclusion, I believe careers in public-service enterprises offer great opportunities for accomplishment and satisfaction to able, energetic men. There is a wide diversity of interesting, important work in an atmosphere of constant change. Many different talents are needed. In the Bell System, for instance, are physicists and mathematicians, engineers and accountants, writers and architects, economists and statisticians, sales representatives and managers, market analysts and safety experts, local and district and division managers of maintenance and construction forces, purchasing agents and manufacturing superintendents, men in charge of telephone business offices and of the central offices where calls are handled, men who meet the communication needs of large industry and government—I cannot begin to give you the full picture. Much more important than any enumeration, however, is the fact that to the able man, the way is open for a wide range of experience to grow on, and the whole Bell System is his opportunity. Not everyone will be president, of course. But there are dozens of positions of top responsibility, any number of very large responsibility—and promotions are made from the ranks.

To stress again a few key thoughts: Your life will be highly competitive. Your sense of dedication to goals of good and improving service will need to be real. You will have to understand the necessity of sound financial management, for, in order to attain its service objectives, the business must succeed as a business and meet with distinction its obligations to investors. You will mix patience with drive and learn from mistakes—your own as well as those of others. Above all, you will bring your full strength of character with you, be always yourself, and be always preparing yourself to do what is right, as well as do more than merely what you are required to do.

With such attributes, a man should do well in any career he may choose. If he chooses a career in a public-service company, I am confident he will achieve much for the benefit of his community and country, and live a useful, satisfying life.

11 *You Can Start a*

BUSINESS OF

YOUR OWN

BY HERMAN W. LAY

CHAIRMAN, EXECUTIVE COMMITTEE
Frito-Lay, Incorporated

HERMAN W. LAY

Born: 1909, Charlotte, North Carolina

Furman University, 1926–28
Business School
Correspondence courses

Farm work, 1929–30
Salesman, 1930–32
Independent food distributor, 1932–39
Founded H.W. Lay & Company, Inc., 1939
President and Chairman H.W. Lay & Company, Inc., 1939–61
President, Frito-Lay, Inc., 1961–September, 1962
Chairman of Executive Committee and Chief Executive Officer, Frito-Lay, Inc., September 1962–

Director: Third National Bank of Nashville, Tennessee
First National Bank in Dallas, Texas
Various other corporations

Member: Planning Council
President's Professional Association
Advisory Council
Board of Trustees Furman University
Chief Executives' Forum

MOST YOUNG PEOPLE, I suppose, at sometime in their lives think about starting a business of their own. Now and then, you meet a young man who knows from the beginning what he is going to do: be a lawyer, be a doctor; but I expect that most of them shop around, and sooner or later they probably consider business. Probably, too, a good many of them think about a business of their own. I am not suggesting it or advising it, because each man has to make up his own mind about his career; but I would like to talk to those who want to go into business, and seriously want a business of their own.

In the beginning, let's establish that I will have little to say about the theories of business. I want to talk some about my own business, because, of course, I know the *details* of it better than any other; but I believe that a man who knows his own business has a pretty good idea of all business and all business practice. Also, I will be calling on the advice given me through the years by older, more-experienced men. Maybe, I can partly pay the debt I owe them by passing on to you some of the things they taught me.

I remember an old ball player I knew when I was a boy. He wasn't the best ball player and he hadn't made any records, but he had worked his way up through the minors and had played a little big-league ball—even stayed on Connie Mack's team for three years. We kids would get around and ask him about baseball, and he would start telling us about the old Athletics with Home-run Baker on third, telling about Ty Cobb and his whirlwind slide and you better get out of his way. Sooner or later, he would get around to himself, what he had done, the time he made a winning hit, the time he struck out. We didn't think he was bragging, that was just the best way he knew to tell us his story of baseball. The best way I know to tell you about starting a business of your own is to tell you how I started mine.

But before I do that, I want to impress you with one fact—and impress it so hard that you will never forget it, hoping that you will set your sights on it now, while you are young, and will start living by it. What I did in my business, starting out with just about nothing, has been done in America over and over again. And the most important fact is this: *it is being done today.* You hear men moan about taxes and government controls; you hear them bemoan foreign competition and wonder what the unions are going to demand next. Sure, this can be worrisome. Sure, it can be a burden; but it is all a part of this remarkable, magnificent Capitalist system that we live in, operate our business in, and most of us prosper in. You young men standing back a little, wondering about business, and particularly about a business of your own—you can come on in, carry the taxes, face the controls, meet foreign competition, and go just as far as your own brains and your imagination and your energy can carry you. Unless you are greedy and want all the money in the world, you can make enough, and more than enough, to live on and be satisfied with.

Now, let's get back to this business of mine. I don't want to be dramatic or set the stage for a punch line, but the simple truth is that I started in business thirty years ago with a potato. That was it—a potato! During 1961, our business totaled about $50,-000,000 and still chiefly out of potatoes. I was a country boy from South Carolina. I didn't finish college. Don't tell me what can't be done in this country! Don't you listen to these "can't" people, when they grumble and say it's not like the good old days. For my part, I can't imagine any better day than right now—unless it's tomorrow.

So let's go back to 1932, when I was getting started. And something else: when I am talking about *my* getting started, about *my* business, I'm talking about young fellows in Texas and Topeka, in Spokane or wherever in this country they may open a shop or a store or a plant or start selling whatever their products may be. All of us are the same; all are Americans getting started, getting going.

Well, I was twenty-two years old in 1932, and I had a Model-A Ford that was four years old. I had a few dollars in my pocket and I was ready, like most young fellows my age, to take on the world. But the world, I found out, wasn't ready for me. We were in the midst of the worst depression in our history and I kept looking for a job, but I got nothing. I advertised and I wrote letters. I wrote two hundred letters, and the only answer I got was "Sorry." When you are twenty-two and ambitious, you want to get going, get climbing. Finding out that nobody wants you, nobody needs you, can turn the world into a frightening place. Even now, I remember that feeling.

I wasn't afraid in the same way that the Depression made so many afraid; those in the long, dismal bread lines, the Salvation Army soup kitchens, the ragged, defeated men that moved in waves with each passing freight train, looking for any job in exchange for a meal at the back door. I had a place to stay and I could have found *some* kind of job, but that didn't satisfy me. I wanted a particular kind: I wanted to sell.

My love of selling came to me early, from the best salesman I ever knew. You might call him a drummer, but a drummer in the grand fashion. He was my dad, and he sold in a time when a salesman knew his territory better than he knew his home town. He knew every hotel desk clerk by his first name and usually had a favorite room in each hotel. Often, he carried the news ahead of the newspaper, and he was as welcome a sight as the mailman. I can still see him sitting on the front porch of a South Carolina farmhouse on one of those hot, dusty afternoons, in his galluses with his shirtsleeves rolled up and his tie loose, drinking lemonade, and gradually, always gradually, working around to his favorite topic, the advantage of horsepower over horses. He sold heavy farm machinery in a time when the horse was still holding its own, and he did it with finesse and ease; he did it softly and with care; and it was a pleasure to watch him sell, because most of all he did it well.

He was selling something else, too; he was selling the farmers of the South the idea that they had to pull the crown off King Cotton's head and plant other crops, to diversify their crops and save their land. He was one of the first to preach this gospel, and he preached it wherever he went: the South had to rid itself of its cross of cotton. I suppose there is something of the preacher in every salesman, his fervor and his enthusiasm, and one reason my father was such a salesman was that he was the most enthusiastic person I ever knew, and what he was selling was always the best.

I learned three things about salesmanship from watching my dad sell: The salesman must know his product well. He must have faith in it. He must have a kind of self-confidence, unobtrusive but sincere, that makes other people feel his faith. It is forty years since my father was drumming through South Carolina, spreading the gospel of mechanization and diversification, but selling has not changed much since then. It still takes brains; it takes looking ahead, energy, a real love of selling, and, most of all, it takes enthusiasm. A lot of young men have energy and a good many have brains, but I can thank my father for the enthusiasm he instilled in me to sell. I guess that was why, during the Depression, when any job was worth having, I kept on looking for a selling job.

Yet, late in the summer of 1932, when I finally got my break, I almost missed it. I had heard that The Barrett Potato Chip Company of Atlanta was looking for a route salesman and I went in and talked with them. But I couldn't see any future in potato chips and food snacks, and I walked out. I wanted to be a salesman, all right, but the idea of driving a truck from store to store selling potato chips wasn't my idea of a job. It just wasn't "good enough" for me.

After a week, and I hadn't found anything to do, I went back to see the Barrett Company again. The job was gone, of course, but they said that they would take me on as an extra salesman, a kind of helper. So I worked at it, and I worked at it hard, selling and making deliveries, and I liked it. I found out that you

can like just about any job, if you work at it. It's when you loaf
and slouch that you begin beefing about the job being no darn
good.

The Barrett Company had a small branch office in Nashville,
Tennessee, and things weren't going so well there. They needed a
man who had an automobile, and, hearing about my Model-A,
they called me in and offered me the distributorship in Nashville. I would get a weekly allotment of potato chips and a
weekly cash allowance. There was no salary, just the advance
against whatever commissions I earned on sales. The territory
would be in northern Tennessee and southern Kentucky, including the city of Nashville, and I jumped at the independence
it offered, the chance to get started on my own.

In Nashville, I lived with my aunt, where my sister had lived
since our mother's death. My income was $100 a month—
$23.08 a week—which wasn't much, even during a depression,
particularly since out of it I had to pay my automobile and
travel expenses. Living with my aunt and giving her just a little
enabled me to get by.

Inexperienced, confident, paying little attention to details and
seldom stopping to find out where I stood, I thought I was
doing fine—and this is part of what I mean about having so
much to learn in business. You take things for granted when you
first start out and you live day by day. You don't think to look
into the corners or behind things and see what is really going on.
For instance, I didn't look around in our warehouse.

The warehouse where we stored the potato chips—for which I
was responsible—was on a street in Nashville called Produce
Row, where the farmers brought fresh vegetables and fruit.
The warehouse, old and poorly lighted, was across the street
from the city dump, where there were rats by the thousands.
Whenever they wanted a tidbit, they sauntered over and went
to work on my potato chips. I knew they were doing it, because
sometimes I would glimpse them, gray shadows disappearing,
and I could hear the ripping of the paper bags and the chips
snapping. But it didn't bother me too much. Rats! They couldn't

eat a lot. Then one day the company told me to take an inventory. And I found out! I learned just what my loss had been to those rats.

At the same time, I discovered that the company had made an honest error in billing me, a small error, but on my income nearly disastrous. I can still remember the night I sat down and painfully prepared a report to the company on the shortages, both from the rats and the error. The next morning, discouraged and miserable, I set out on my hundred-and-fifty-mile swing, doubting if I could ever land enough business to offset my losses.

My customers were roadstands, grocery stores, filling stations, soda shops, and anywhere else that sold potato chips—or might sell them—even schools and hospitals. It was common to work on until late at night, sometimes making the last call well past midnight. Usually, I worked the retail grocers during the day, then caught the drug stores in the early evening, and finished up at roadstands and restaurants after everything else had closed.

To make the swing of one hundred and fifty miles usually took a day and a half or two days, and in December, in northern Tennessee and in Kentucky, it could be cold. Car heaters weren't what they are today and I would drape a blanket over my legs as I drove. The roads snaked around hills, the double-s curves following each other, and the last fifty miles from Clarksville to Nashville always seemed the longest. On cold nights, the closer I got to home the heavier my foot got, and frequently I took those curves at high speed in the gray hours before dawn.

So it was that I was ripping up the highway from Clarksville well past midnight one cold December night. There had been a drizzle earlier in the evening, but now the stars were out and I hunched over the wheel. At one curve, the road cut through an old-fashioned covered bridge. I had been through there many times before and I started into the curve; then I touched my brakes, but they didn't hold. The road was covered with ice. I roared into that bridge and tore out two-by-fours for half its length, until the car hit a steel beam and spun around.

When I came to, I was staring out over the hood at a cold, black night. I could hear the river swishing quietly past the bridge pilings down below. The car was balanced on the edge of the bridge, its rear wheels out in space. I crawled out as carefully as I could and sat down on the bridge, my head roaring. How long I sat there, shivering against the wind, I don't know. Finally, though, a man came along and took me into town. The next morning I got a wrecker and we went out and towed my car back to Clarksville.

Many a person has been in an automobile wreck and there would be no point in my telling about this one except for what I learned from it about business. Taking care of a business when everything is running smoothly is nothing to be proud of. It's when trouble comes that you find out whether you're a businessman or not. In business you have got to be ready for *anything*. It's as if you were boxing a man and doing all right, when suddenly, and from nowhere you ever expected or even heard of, here comes a *third* fist to knock you out. That's the way it is in business, and if you can't take care of the unexpected, if you don't have some reserve and quick adaptability, you can get knocked flat.

What kind of thing am I talking about? I don't know. It might be anything. A fire. A flood. A mechanical failure. The death of a partner. An error in addition. An incorrect estimate. A lawsuit. It can be your fault, as it was my short-sightedness about the inventory, or it can be one of those things that just happen. But whatever it is, it can put you out of business in a hurry if you aren't prepared to meet it and keep going.

Mine? Rats and a slick road. Two days later, I was back in Nashville with the threat of bankruptcy facing me. The damage to the car and the loss to the rats totaled $165. With my income and my thin margin of profit, it might as well have been a million. It meant the difference between my being in business or being bankrupt and out of a job.

I told the Barrett Company that I was getting the territory started, and I told them of my losses and my problems. If they turned me out, they would have to close the territory and lose everything or start a new man and lose money until he learned our customers and the route. I asked them to lend me enough to take care of me and my losses. They saw that I had learned something, was a better businessman for it, and they let me have the money to cover my inventory and the damages to the car. I was to pay it back at $4 a week.

So I started out again, this time with a weekly allowance of $19.08. I was making less money, but I was traveling with what I had learned. My carelessness about the inventory, about the slick road had taught me something. From now on, I was watching out for a third fist. I had to watch out, too, for every penny I spent, for a meal, for anything. I learned that a man can live on next to nothing if he has to.

For the next six months it was get out and go, meet my customers, talk, sell, hand over the merchandise, and go again. I was in debt, and in some ways I was in trouble—the left door of my automobile had been so smashed in the wreck that it wouldn't fit and I had to throw it away and drive with a chain across the opening—but I had a job and a territory of my own. I kept telling myself that it was *my* territory and *my* business. This sense of independence kept me working. Out in the morning and on the road, all day, half the night, sleep where I was, and go again.

That was the way it was, and the way it kept on being until, at the end of the year, my territory had expanded and my profits were climbing. Nothing big, but they were going up. Then, one day I realized that I was doing all the business I could by myself, but there was still more business to be had in the territory. Slowly, almost frightening me, came the idea that I needed a helper. However, I had learned some lessons and I checked into everything, finding out and testing every fact until I finally decided that I really did need a man, a salesman. It wasn't so very long before I needed still another man, this one a warehouseman who doubled as a bookkeeper.

Things were breaking for me and my luck was good. There is always a bit of what we call "luck" in any business venture, I suppose. Sometimes there can be a stroke of such blind luck that a man is suddenly made rich or suddenly boosted far along toward success. But let me suggest something to you, and suggest it as strong as I can: don't you put a penny's faith in luck. It will trick you. You may have a barrelful of luck tomorrow. If so—fine. But don't expect it, and, most of all, don't sit around waiting for it.

Actually, when it comes down to the long record and the hard facts, *you* are your own luck. What we ordinarily call luck may really be a bit of chance, all right, really something unprepared for and unexpected, but usually there is more to it than that. I think that it is partly *intuition*, which is a kind of thinking that goes on when we aren't aware of it, when we aren't consciously working at our thinking. I believe, too, that it is a sense of *timeliness* that you develop and that tells you *when* to make your move. A person may say that the man who opened a new territory last year, established a market for his product, and caught the crest of the sales was "lucky." The man who waited a year and had to take what was left was "unlucky." I don't believe a word of that.

A man makes his success by the decisions that he himself makes and by when he makes them. I was fortunate in going to work for Barrett; but before I did, I had to decide to go back there and ask them for a job, then decide to take the one they gave me. It was a break for me that they offered me the distributor's job in Nashville, but I had to decide to take it. It was another break that they lent me the money when I was in trouble, but don't forget that I had to decide how to present my case to them and convince them. There is always "luck," if you want to call it that, and always a lot of "if's"; but in the end, whether or not you succeed and get where you want to go will depend on the decisions that *you* make. There will be many little decisions and there will be big ones, and it is your average on how you decide, right or wrong, that will determine whether you go up or down. In the long run, in the final judgment of you and your business, this factor of chance will have mighty little to do with it. You can bet your last nickel that there is no "lucky" way, no short, slick, fast-buck way to *permanent* success in business.

Sometimes I wonder how I got started in business. Probably it was back in 1920, when I was ten years old and we were living in Greenville, South Carolina. Our house was across the street from the old Sally League ball park and I started my first business venture on the front lawn, a piano box set up as a soft drink stand. My price for drinks was a nickel, five cents less than inside the park, and the knothole gang bought from me and some of the people, entering and leaving the park, bought from me.

I started a bank account and bought a bicycle. I began carrying a newspaper route, hired some helpers for the soft-drink stand, and was doing fine until the ball park moved to another part of town and that ended my soft-drink business. But I followed the park and this time I went inside, getting a job as a hawker from the concessionaire. It wasn't *what* you sold at the park but *how* you sold it. It was your "spiel" that built up your business. Mine went like this:

> HEY! Get your nicely roasted, nicely toasted,
> California sun-dried,
> Long-eared, double-jointed
> P-e-a-NUTS!
> Five a bag . . .

It was a real screecher, and I expect that some people bought from me just to get me to move on. But I built up customers until, before the summer was over, I was selling peanuts like an auctioneer receiving bids: a couple of fingers raised, a nod of the head, a wink—each meant another bag of goobers sold. It was hot and dusty and hard on the feet, but it was *selling*, and I loved every minute of it. I started out at the ball park, when I was a boy, in the small-snack business. Now, forty years later, I am still in the snack food business.

This love of selling, and of the snack business, led me to make the mistake of breaking off my education. In 1928, I was beginning my sophomore year at Furman University, at just about the time the Democratic National Convention was to be held in Houston, Texas. This was it! Without making serious investigations, without finding out the facts, a friend and I set out for Houston with everything we had—I cleaned out my savings account—and we bought the ice-cream concession at a small hotel. We had $100, which paid the concession fee and bought a supply of ice cream.

The parade route was to go by the hotel, right by our stand. The automobile and pedestrian route also was to go by our stand. We would get the huge parade crowd and the steady flow of pedestrians going to and from the hall. We were all set to make a killing.

There turned out to be one difficulty. At the last minute, they changed the parade route. They changed the route of the automobiles and pedestrians. But we couldn't change our concession stand. So we stood there, day after day, our arms folded, our ice boxes packed with melting ice cream, while a few blocks away the happy crowd nominated Al Smith, "The Happy Warrior."

This was my first lesson in failure. I had acted too fast. The old-timers in the ice-cream business had set up their stands nearer the convention hall, where changes couldn't hurt them. They knew. I had only guessed. It was a good lesson in marketing, and I dejectedly left immediately thereafter for the wheat fields to follow the harvest on up into Canada.

Since leaving the university in my sophomore year, I have many times realized the mistake I made. A lot of young fellows get impatient, feel that college is a waste of time, and drop out. This is likely to cost them dearly in the years to come. I have tried hard to make up for what I lost, attending lecture courses, taking correspondence courses, following selected readings. I still work at it, and feel so strongly about this that we encourage and support men in our company to attend selected seminars and training courses that will improve their business and professional knowledge and abilities. However, I must say to you, particularly you who are in college, or are debating going to college,

that the training you get in later years is not the same as that
you get when you are in college. In college, when you are young,
it's not just the books but the whole foundation that you put
together and that you build on for the rest of your life.

When I quit the university, an education was needed. Today,
it is almost essential. Everything is so fast now that time itself is a
commodity, and success or failure often is measured in minutes
and hours rather than sales and inventories. With things moving
so fast and business so complicated, a man needs all the help
he can get in making decisions. The management of a business,
large or small, calls for the most solid preparation, both from
formal education and experience; and a man simply cannot
know too much as he undertakes to judge buying habits, select
processing methods, and make use of the engineering and
technological advances of our time. It is hard enough for any
businessman just to stay even these days, without having to go
back and try to fill in an educational background.

No matter where you are in your education, no matter how
interested you may be in business, or how impatient you are to
get going, you stay with your education and get it if you can.
Get it before you start in business. Get it while you are starting,
if you must. But get it. When I say this, I don't mean to suggest
that your college education, your diploma, is any stopping point.
In fact, it is little more than a background, a point of view,
a training in how to learn. Your real learning, your greater learning, comes later; and if you think that your graduation from
college is any terminal point, or even a place to pause, then
you may pause there and just stay there. You are just com-
mencing, and it is what you do from "commencement" on that
counts.

Quite frankly, I don't care how much education you have or
how many degrees you have earned, you still can't come into
business and hold your own if you expect to depend *solely* on
your schooling or what you learned from books. Business doesn't
just move; it flies. What you learn from textbooks, the *details*
in textbooks, may be of little use to you by the time you try to
use them. No amount of formal education can make anyone a

profit or pay a dividend, until it is adapted to his particular business and to the demands of his immediate market.

After leaving the university, and after my failure in selling ice cream in Houston, I got first one job and then another, learning a bit from each, until I went to work, as I have told you, as a salesman and distributor of potato chips in Tennessee and Kentucky. The business prospered, even in the Depression, and I hired my first two men. Before long, I added others until, by 1935, there were seven of us.

I also added new products. One was prepackaged popcorn, which we introduced into the South. A short time later, we went into the peanut-butter sandwich business. The snack industry was building up, and buying habits were changing fast. Packaged food snacks were on the counters, close at hand and easy to pick up, at many food stores, drug counters, filling stations, and lunchstands, and, what's more, people were buying them.

Our chief line, though, continued to be potato chips, and I thought we were doing fine until, in 1938, I went to a food distribution convention in Cleveland. There I saw new plants where potato chips were being manufactured in a new way, and there I learned another lesson, or rather had an old lesson confirmed, one that no one can ever learn too well or be told too often—in business, if you aren't on the alert all the time, somebody will come along and get ahead of you. He will make a better product, make it cheaper, cut a fraction off selling cost, develop a fraction faster distribution, figure a fraction onto profits. In business, it is constant and endless competition all the way, the toughest kind, and if you aren't on the lookout and quick to advance, your competition will pass you and leave you back there somewhere, wondering what happened to you and your business and how long you can hold on.

When the potato chip was first produced, it was a fairly uncomplicated item. Today, it is very complicated in its method of production.

The story of the potato chip is said to have begun with an Indian chief at the Moon Lake House in the resort town of Saratoga

Springs, New York, in 1853. His name was Chief George Crum, and history is a little fuzzy about whether he was a real chief or just boasting a bit. At any rate, he was the chef at the hotel, and one evening he was having a hard time quieting one of the leading guests. This gentleman had just returned from Paris, where his palate had been titillated with Parisian dishes, and he was sending back plate after plate of French fries on the grounds that they were soggy and unfit to eat.

Finally, Chief Crum, angry and fed up with this paleface and his snooty palate, sliced a potato into paper-thin slices, threw them into a kettle of boiling fat, sprinkled them with salt, and served them to an absolutely delighted guest. So the potato chip was born! Before the summer was out, "Saratoga Chips" were a regular part of the menu at Moon Lake House, and were being widely introduced elsewhere.

Basically, this method of preparing potato chips continued from its beginning, in 1853, until well into this century. Then, in 1938, in Cleveland, I saw a method that made me know that the old way was done for. A company could no longer succeed if it followed the original way of cooking up a large batch of chips in vegetable oil, packaging them, and cooking up another batch. With the new machinery, the chips were produced in a continuous production line. It was either get into the business in this way or be forced out.

A decision had to be made and my associates and I made it quickly; we would install this new method of manufacturing. We were figuring on how to do it, how to get it started, when I received an offer that was totally unexpected. Sometime before this I had left the Barrett Company, and I was completely surprised when a representative of that firm came to see me and offered me the opportunity to buy the Atlanta and Memphis plants of the company.

"How much cash will it take?" I asked.

"Sixty to a hundred thousand dollars . . ."

"I'll give you my answer tomorrow."

It might as well have been sixty million, but I was being offered my "luck." I made my decision and hurried to the bank, hardly expecting anyone really to listen to me, but I told one of the officers of my opportunity.

"Let them know you are interested," he said.

The bank, however, told me that we must have additional equity capital. I had long before decided never to ask anyone to put money into my company, and I didn't then, and I never have; but the key employees in the company set out to raise what funds they could. Some of my friends and business associates also wanted to participate. The officer of the bank I had talked to became an investor. So did my life-insurance broker, my casualty-insurance broker, the operator of the filling station across the street.

In a month, we raised what we had set out to raise: $5,000 for working capital. The bank lent us $30,000. The Barretts took the remainder in preferred stock. October 2, 1939, the old sign came down and the new one went up: H. W. Lay & Company.

Now I would lie awake at night wondering about the decisions I had made that day, some of them fast, some with a lot of money riding on them. Were they right? Almost immediately we needed additional capital to build a new plant for the continuous-manufacturing process. We made the decision and old and new friends came in, investing in the company; and we built the plant. What next? Where did we stop? Where did we slow down? In business, do you ever stop? Ever slow down?

A man remembers his family and he should remember his health. He takes into account his civic, charitable, and church obligations. But always in his mind is his business, with its endless responsibilities. In his planning and decision-making, his responsibilities extend to the people who work in the plant, to his stockholders, and to his executive associates who helped him start the company and helped him build it. Lying awake is no figure of speech, and that is what you will do if you start a company of your own and make it grow. But be sure and understand this: it isn't all lying awake, wondering a lot and worrying some. There is satisfaction in seeing your company grow and knowing that you are a part of its growth; in seeing the men who have trusted you get the job advancement and the salary increase that they want and have earned. There is a great satisfaction, too, in seeing your stockholders receive the dividends they deserve. It isn't all work and worry in business, not by a long shot; there is pleasure and often there is a great and enduring sense of fulfillment.

Let me give you one touch of advice: put your faith in your company. Give it everything you've got: your thought, your time, your work. And don't be trying to get too much out of it, or even bits out of it, for yourself. The head of a company who is always searching for angles and gimmicks to enrich himself does not always gain permanently what he may seem to profit at the moment. Build your company, and its growth will pay you back. But, you say, you see a way of making ten thousand this year on a quick private deal for yourself. Forget it! Five years from now it may make a million for your company. The company comes before you do, even if you own every share of stock and have total control. Make the welfare of your business your objective, and it will take care of you.

In our company, after we were well started, we kept on with our planning and our figuring. Year after year we kept asking: what next? During the 1950's, we had continued to join with other companies, either through acquisition or merger, in order to increase our operating area and our product line. Then, early in 1961, we began to see what seemed to be next; a merger was concluded with Red Dot Foods, Inc., a Midwestern snack food business. Simultaneously, the business of the Rold Gold Pretzel Company of St. Louis and Los Angeles was purchased. Overnight, our business was almost fifty per cent larger and our area of operations was materially increased. We were growing fast, but we were mindful of advice given us by our elders a long time ago: "It is not how big or how fast you grow but how soundly." It turned out, I am glad to say, that our expansion programs were soundly conceived in the best interests of our customers, our employees, and our stockholders.

Then, finally, late in 1961, we began discussing a merger with another company, the Frito Company of Dallas, Texas. Such a merger would open up vast new areas for our potato chips, and we began talking about a time—we can already envision it— when our potato chips and corn chips will be sold anywhere in the world where there are people to buy them.

This talk of the world, of the whole earth, sounds ambitious— and it is. But the earth is no more impossible now than were Middle Tennessee and Southern Kentucky back in the days when a young fellow could stake his future on a slice of potato or a sack of popcorn or a jar of peanut butter, and any of these could open the door of a new world to him.

Since there were benefits for both companies, the decision for the merger was made. Twenty-five years after H. W. Lay & Company was formed, we joined, in 1961, with the Frito Company (which, incidentally, was founded some thirty years ago on $100 borrowed capital), and we are now Frito-Lay, Inc.

This merger was a big decision for us to make, but every company is continually faced with such decisions, some of them so important that they shape the whole future of the company. Of the innumerable decisions we have had to make, some five or six have been turning points. One was the decision to purchase the Barrett plants in Atlanta and Memphis. A second was the decision to build our own plant, and manufacture chips with the continuous process. A third was to buy another plant in Jacksonville, Florida, paying the creditors 50¢ on a dollar on a nearly bankrupt business, then to come back later, when there was no legal claim on us, and pay the full amount.

Another decision was the renting of an old barn in Greensboro, North Carolina, shortly after World War II, and opening up the whole territory of the Carolinas to our chips. Still another resulted in the building of our present plant in Atlanta. We had been scattered over the city in seven plants, and we needed a great, modern, central plant. How could we build it? How could we finance it? Well, we did finance it, and we went on from there to build our business beyond the dreams that even we, young men and hopeful, would have dared to dream ten years before.

Luck? Call it luck, if you like; but any time you are looking around for your luck in business, be sure also to think and plan and work—and make your decisions with all your intuition and all your care, and make them at the right time.

So what lies ahead for us? For you? For me? It is my most honest belief that there is more ahead for us, for anybody in American business, than at any time in our history. I say this, knowing about the days when they built the railroads across the continent and sent airplanes into the sky. Well, today we are shuttling the oceans as if we were crossing the street, and we are having a closer and closer look at the moon.

This, today, is the earth where we live, and this is the space into which we are moving. Where do you want to build your business? Go ahead. Help yourself.

We are all looking ahead and planning, these days. My old company is now a part of a new company, and I am planning a new business, learning to work with new friends, and beginning to live a new business life. I am the chief executive officer of Frito-Lay, Inc., made up of the two old companies, and their combined income for the 1962 fiscal year was in excess of $145,-000,000. This is a tremendous responsibility, but there is a tremendous future for the new company, and for me.

There is a future, too, equally as important for you, in whatever company you may be starting, even if its plant is in one room, and its income is the few hundred dollars you borrow to get going. Don't let this make any difference to you. Size is nothing but time. Any business is likely to be small in the beginning. Whether it grows with the years depends on how much *you* grow. Don't be impatient. Just work like blazes today, keep looking at tomorrow, and figuring on next week.

_12_ *You Can Work*

WITHIN A

CORPORATION

BY CRAWFORD H. GREENEWALT

CHAIRMAN OF THE BOARD
E.I. du Pont de Nemours & Company

CRAWFORD GREENEWALT

Born: 1902, Cummington, Massachusetts

William Penn Charter School, Philadelphia, Pennsylvania
Massachusetts Institute of Technology:
  B.S. in Chemical Engineering, 1922
D.Sc.: University of Delaware, Northeastern University, Boston University, Philadelphia College Pharmacy and Science
LL.D.: Columbia University, Temple University, Williams College, Kenyon College, Kansas State University
D.S.C.: New York University
L.H.D.: Jefferson Medical College
D.Eng.: Polytechnic Institute of Brooklyn
E.D.: Rensselaer Polytechnic Institute

E.I. du Pont de Nemours & Company:
  Lacquer and Heavy Chemicals Department: Control chemist, 1922
  Central Research Department, Experimental Station, 1924–39
  Grasselli Chemicals Department: Chemical Director, 1942
  Explosives Department: Technical Director, 1943
  Development Department: Assistant Director, 1945
  Pigments Department: Assistant General Manager, 1945
  Vice-president, 1946
  President, 1948–62
  Chairman of the Board, 1962

Director: Equitable Trust Company, 1935–43
          E.I. du Pont de Nemours Company, 1942–
          Christian Securities Company, 1944–
          National Bureau of Economic Research
Trustee: American Museum of Natural History
          National Geographic Society
          Carnegie Institute of Washington
          Kenyon College
Life Member M.I.T. Corporation
Regent Smithsonian Institute
Member: Business Council
         American Institute of Chemical Engineers
         National Academy of Sciences
         American Chemical Society
         President's Commission on National Goals: 1960
         American Philosophical Society

Author: *The Uncommon Man*
        Hummingbirds

UNLESS RECONCILED to a hermit's cave or a desert island, today's generation of young people will find careers and opportunities, both social and professional, within the context of human association. In one way or another, most will become members of organizations, large or small, and many will earn their livings by working for corporations of considerable size. Whether they succeed will be conditioned largely by how well they learn to live within the organizational environment.

A great deal of poppycock has been written about life in an organization, much of it centering on the corporation. Any group activity calls for compromises in which self-interest is tempered by consideration for others. At the same time, it would be a sorry effort indeed unless enlivened and invigorated by individual performances. But all too often, I am afraid, the requirements of good manners and felicitous association are interpreted as a strain upon individual expression. The opposite of this is also true, I am afraid; and personal ambition not infrequently falls victim to the beguilement of group pressures.

People react to the organizational environment in various ways. Most learn, quickly enough, that superficial and extraneous judgments have little to do with the business at hand. Some few respond in angry protest and outraged dignity, managing, meanwhile, to alienate the co-operative support essential to any personal achievement. Others react by assuming that individual initiative has gone the way of the dinosaur, and that refuge lies only in the sanctuary of what is now called "conformity."

The fact is that adjustment requires neither brash self-assertion nor unquestioning compliance. It calls rather for a choice of values which recognizes individual aims and organizational goals as thoroughly compatible, to be achieved with honor both for the individual and the organization.

"Conformity" is, of course, a loose and flabby term, like many which describe abstractions. It is evident that there is confusion between the voluntary conformity of behavior which we call good manners, and the enforced conformity of thought which represents an invasion of personal rights and a brake upon our capacity to follow our own destinies.

In the social area, we bow to conventional standards without loss of self-esteem. In the realm of thought and of ideas, however, we rightfully resist any effort to submerge our personal characteristics into a dull and lifeless composite.

The question is, after all, not qualitative, but quantitative: how much or, better, how little conformity should be tolerated? Jefferson's dictum on the forbearance of ideal government could well be transplanted to this area of human relations. Let us conform as little as is necessary to good manners, pleasant relationships, and the highest use of individual talent.

Conformity in behavior is a human necessity; conformity in patterns of thought a human danger. The Communist "party line" is a fair example of a monolithic unanimity of opinion, even though members could presumably dress as they pleased, grow whiskers, or cultivate bizarre habits. Unfortunately, people have come, in modern times, to mistake one for the other. There is a strong body of opinion which assumes that the conformist is the boy who gets ahead. School boys are now given grades on their "ability to co-operate," presumably on the theory that this will advance their fortunes once they launch their careers. "Co-operation" is, of course, a necessity at any time, but the premium is and always must be on original approaches.

To the extent that it can be said to exist, conformity is not, of course, a characteristic peculiar to business, nor is it uniquely the province of the large group. It may be found in some degree in all organizations of whatever nature or size. I am inclined to think that, man for man, the large business unit represents greater opportunities for individuality and requires less in the way of conformity than other institutions—in government service, say, or in the academic world, or in the military.

I would judge, too, that "conformity" is at least as likely, perhaps more likely, to be present in small groups as large. Adjustment to a given behavior pattern is, after all, just as obligatory in a group of ten as in a group of a thousand, with the important difference that deviations within the smaller group attract far more attention. It is proverbial that small towns will discipline a dissenter far more drastically than the big city would take the trouble to do. By the same token, I venture that conformity is more likely to be found in a small, closely held firm with a dozen employees than in the giant corporation, if only because the range of tolerance in a group of a hundred thousand people must necessarily be wider than in one numbering ten to twelve.

Nevertheless, it seems to be the large business unit which attracts notice in this regard. The belief seems widely prevalent that there is a pattern in such a unit to which the manners, dress, and political views of each candidate for advancement must conform. The general impression has some rather bizarre twists; someone once asked me seriously if it were not true that the Buick had been selected as the official hierarchical automobile because its many grades of size and elegance could be assigned in accordance with rank! Some popular magazines have been airing the curious conviction that the wives of business executives are screened critically as part of the criteria for promotion. A number of novels, movies, and TV shows have sounded the same theme.

I cannot speak for corporations generally, nor for any, specifically, save our own. As for our company, I will say that such notions are sheer nonsense, and I will venture as a guess that the same can be said for most. The superficial symbols, like the gray flannel suit—I don't own one, by the way—actually mean little. Among my most-valued associates, taste in dress covers a pretty broad pattern. The same goes for personal habits, enthusiasms, and, I may say, for automobiles. I could not list offhand the kinds of cars my principal associates drive. One, I know, drives an Opel, since he never fails to proclaim its virtues; another passes me occasionally in a topless Corvette, in which he wears a baseball cap. Perhaps one even has a Buick, grade and model unknown.

As for wives, I can report that among my closest co-workers there are, of course, a number of them whose ladies I have known well for many years. We live in a small town and I remember some when they were on roller skates. There are others of my co-workers whose wives I know well enough to exchange a "How do you do, Mrs. Smith?" "How do you do, Mr. Greenewalt?" There are still others whose marital partners, I regret to say, I have never met at all.

Emphasis on the irrelevant factors of habit and custom, and on the various fictional characteristics, obscure the truth. Actually, the truth itself offers sufficient challenge without inconsequential distractions. Alert and well-managed organizations today are fully aware of the dangers associated with individual submersion. Progress will be made in direct proportion to the intellectual freedom of action given all the men on the team. There is nothing inherent in large organizations which closes the door to high individual performance.

What often distracts us is the fact that modern institutions are less the lengthened shadow of one man, as Emerson saw them, than the conglomerate shadow of many men. Organizations are essentially plural in nature. As the constellation is the ensemble of its stars, a church is the composite of its congregation, an army the total of its ranks and files, so a corporation is the sum of the many talents, skills, and efforts embodied in its people.

The important thing is that each of us do his part and do it as well as he can—doing, as Carlyle says, not what lies dimly at a distance, but what sits clearly at hand. In doing so, we find that there is ample room within our society for individualism, just as there is ample necessity for co-operation. And it is as we learn to distinguish the conformity of behavior from the conformity of thought that we approach the real significance of the term "success."

Success is not a measure of what we are given at birth; it is what we ourselves do with whatever characteristics, either mental or physical, either good or indifferent, with which we are endowed.

Not all are born to reach high places. In physique, intelligence, and good looks, we have certainly not been created equal. Each of us has certain talents and abilities—some of a very high order, some a good average, some perhaps on the poor side. These natural endowments are the tools with which we must live our lives and with which we must build as sound an edifice as we can. If in the years to come we can look ourselves in the eye and say with complete honesty that we have used to the utmost the talents with which we have been endowed, then we will be successful men and women, quite regardless of the stature we assume in the eyes of the world. Conversely, if we fail that examination, we will fail of real success, no matter how high the stature.

Unfortunately, we have fallen victim in recent years to judgments which employ only the universally obvious criteria, often to the neglect of standards much closer to reality. Shakespeare said four hundred years ago that "the world is still deceived with ornament"; today, I sometimes think it is even less attentive to the basic truths. For we take life often at its most superficial, and conclude that achievement can be measured only in terms of applause or wolf whistles or financial compensation. In so doing, we penalize not only those whose accomplishments are beyond the average, but those of lesser qualifications who may well find in their lives only the sober gratification of reaching their full potential.

And to the extent that we apply spurious standards to achievement, we weaken ourselves as a nation. The extraordinarily gifted individual may indeed make contributions of singular importance. We in America owe a great debt to many such individuals—to Franklin, to Washington, to Lincoln, to Eli Whitney. But the gifted few do not make a nation, any more than a few beautiful blooms make a garden. The proportion of outstanding individuals in any nation at any time would probably be fairly constant; the strength of a nation must be determined by the accomplishment of its entire citizenry, at all levels.

The poets and philosophers have admonished us for centuries to set our sights high, to hitch our wagons to a star, to let the reach exceed the grasp. That is all well and good, but too much emphasis on "stars" gives us all too often the feeling that to miss is to fail, when the fact is that failure lies only in complacent contentment. For it is not the reward that supplies the satisfaction, it is the good hard try—win, lose, or draw.

Not long ago someone asked me if our organization would not benefit hugely by the addition of a dozen or so men of genius. Well, of course, no one can overestimate the possibilities inherent in human achievement at the genius level. But in the light of reality, I was moved to reply that our organization would benefit more decisively not by a dozen extraordinary contributions but by a ten per cent increase in efficiency and application diffused through all levels and all ranks of our present personnel. For the difference between an organization of the first rank and one of lesser stamp is seldom great. It was Darwin, I think, who noted that men differ less in the total of their capacities than in the degree to which they use them.

If our company is to be more successful than the enterprises with which we compete, it will not be because we have more men of top-flight ability, but rather because all of our people are distinguished by a small positive increment of devotion, dedication, or determination beyond that of their opposite numbers elsewhere. It is such modest differences in individual achievement, multiplied by many thousands or millions, that distinguish a great company from one that is indifferent; and, with equal truth, a great nation from its weaker neighbor.

The important thing is that we bring into play the full potential of each of us, whatever our capacity. If we, as individuals, count ourselves a failure because we do not reach the pinnacle, or because we are engaged in an effort which, for some reason, we do not regard as worth-while, then our individual capacities decline and with them the strength of our total commitment as a people.

What we feel about others reflects most accurately what we feel about ourselves, and self-diagnosed failure, prompted by acceptance of the foot-race concept of life, often breeds envy and bitterness toward those who pass us in the stretch.

Rational thought and a true sense of appropriateness will demonstrate, I think, that what we call success is relative, that there are compensations and satisfactions to be found at all stages, and that the truly successful person is the one who leaves no plain of his talent unfurrowed, no portion of his potential unfulfilled.

In no area is our need for sensitive perception so acute as in the balance upon which we weigh ourselves and our performance. Alfred North Whitehead, the British philosopher, saw in his long study of historical perspective the applicability of this principle.

"That society flourishes most," he said, "in which men think grandly of their function."

I can find no better advice to a new generation of men than to urge adoption of this precept. Let us think grandly of our function, whatever it may be, at whatever level it is performed. Require of it only that it provide us with maximum opportunity for our efforts.

To be a success, we need only to think grandly of our function and we will think grandly of ourselves. In so doing, we will find rewards for ourselves and progress and greatness for our nation.

13 *A Woman in*

BUSINESS

BY ADELE SIMPSON

PRESIDENT
Adele Simpson, Inc.

ADELE SIMPSON

Born: 1903, New York, New York

P.S. 6, New York City
Wadley High School
Washington Irving High School
Pratt Institute, Brooklyn, 1921

Married Wesley William Simpson, 1930
Children: Jeffrey R.
          Joan Ellen

Designer:
   Ben Gershel: Coat-and-suit manufacturer
   William Bass: Dress manufacturer
   Mary Lee: Dress manufacturer
   Adele Simpson, Inc., 1947

President and Director:
   Adele Simpson, Inc.
Director:
   Wesley Simpson Factors, Inc.

Work displayed:
   Metropolitan Museum, New York, New York
   Brooklyn Museum
   Dallas Museum of Fine Arts

Recipient:
   Neiman-Marcus Fashion Award, 1946
   Coty Fashion Award, 1947
   First National Cotton Council Award, 1953

Member:
   Fashion Group, Inc., New York, New York

THERE IS SO much to tell about women in business that describing the whole range of their careers is impossible, so I decided to tell about my own experiences, not to parade them or display them but because I know them best and they will at least indicate how a woman can have a career in American business today. Where I speak of myself, you can change my name to the names of any number of other women who have built successful careers from banking to broadcasting, from architecture to advertising, and an ever greater number of women who are building such careers at this moment. More and more women are going into business, starting at the absolute bottom, and, some years later, coming out on top. It is their story, from the file clerk to the department-store president, that I would like for you to keep in mind while I write about myself and my own career in fashion.

I was the youngest of five sisters, and twice a year, in the spring and the fall, my mother would buy a bolt of blue serge material. Then she would ask a dressmaker to come in, and, after a week, all the girls would get blue middy blouses and skirts. Each season there would be another bolt of blue serge and all the girls were dressed alike.

As the youngest, I rebelled and decided I wanted to make my own dress. Without technical knowledge, I proceeded to make a dress for myself; one side did not match the other, but that did not matter. I wore it and my sisters were very jealous. I then decided that I would embroider my dresses—all the sisters had been taught dancing, embroidery, and elocution—and with the embroidery on them, the dresses were quite pretty, even though they were cut in rough material and the embroidery design was improvised.

I turned out dresses for my sisters and they were a bit more professional than the first dress I made. Then the girls in the neighborhood all were anxious to have dresses like them. I started making more dresses and even made hats, because I had bits and scraps left over from the clothes I had cut. This was when I was about fourteen or fifteen.

It was at this time that I really started getting interested in clothes. We lived in New York and one of my sisters was a very clever artist who later became one of the outstanding coat and suit designers in America. She was interested in sponsoring and encouraging me. I went to art school first and later to Pratt Institute in Brooklyn, after I had worked for a year and earned enough to pay my tuition. My mother and my father, who was a very fine Fifth Avenue tailor, thought I was ridiculous because I was already earning thirty-five dollars a week at the age of sixteen and that was very good money; so why, they asked, should I give up a perfectly good job to go back to school. But I wanted to learn about clothes technically and I was fortunate to have an encouraging and spontaneous teacher in a day class.

I was fortunate in the evening, too, because I took a draping course offered by a brilliant woman who was the head fitter at one of the big stores on Fifty-seventh Street. She was very French and had real French technique, and I learned about draping from her. Soon I was fascinated with the idea of taking a piece of material and molding it into a dress; it was like sculpturing, like working in clay, and I became completely disinterested in sketching or drawing. I found it wonderful to take a piece of fabric—wool, silk, taffeta, it didn't matter—and mold it into a dress.

About this time the head dress designer at the house where my sister worked became ill and I was given the opportunity of designing, which was the break I had been watching for. My sister made the suits and coats, and I made the dresses to go under them. This was about 1923, and, at this time, there was no mass production; the so-called dress industry was just getting started.

I must be a little technical here for a moment while explaining that the dresses of those days were very complicated—the sleeves, for example, were not actually set into the dress. They were sewn into the corset cover, the lining that went over a woman's corset, and then the top was made so that it hooked together. I couldn't see any reason for this and I decided to make dresses that were simpler, more natural, with the sleeves set into the dress itself. This seems perfectly obvious to all of us now, but it was revolutionary then, and so I got my start. Some women buyers in the stores saw that I was doing something different and creative, and they began to notice me and the clothes I made.

While this was my start as a designer, it never occurred to me to go into business for myself. I just went on working for this same company until my sister got married and left. Then another company, having heard of a young designer who was doing things in a different way, offered me more money than I had ever dreamed of—thirty thousand dollars a year. It was a fortune back in 1928 when taxes were nothing to speak of.

Now at this point—with my making all this money and having no idea what was going to happen to it the next year—I think it is a good place to get away, at least for awhile, from writing about myself and my career, and write about my profession, which is fashion. Learning about fashion is different from learning about anything else, for there is no body of knowledge and no bibliography to guide you, and this is because the very business of fashion is change. Tomorrow's development presupposes today's obsolescence and fashion is new only to take on a new aspect again. Its raw materials, too, forever change, because new looks are made of new stuffs. No matter how much one learns *about* fashion, one never learns *fashion*, because such learning is unending. To play any part in the world of fashion demands the development of an astute sense of what will constitute newness tomorrow, what will be fashion tomorrow: in what direction it lies, where to look for it, how to create it, of what color, shape, material.

Let me say to the girl who is interested in fashion, or interested in anything else that is creative, that she must first saturate herself in beauty until it becomes a part of her, until it is all of her, and she herself is more beautiful than anyone looking at her can possibly see. But even beauty, and the power to translate beauty into creation, is not enough. She must have a disciplined mind. I would like to stop and repeat that: any girl, no matter how artistic or how creative she may be, cannot succeed in business or in the arts or in anything else unless she has a disciplined mind. So often I hear girls chattering away, talking the froth of their impending achievements without the disciplined foundation of accomplishment, and I know that they are immature and in time will realize the embitterment of the failure that they carry within themselves, that they are nurturing as they waste their time in posing and artificial talk. A girl can sail away on a golden galleon of dreams and desires, but eventually, if she is to mold her dreams into substance, she must come back to the yardstick of discipline and the needle of work.

The creative mind and the disciplined mind must continuously work together, if there is to be any form of success in anything. The creative sense must always be strong in its own conviction, able to take an uncharted next step with confidence; and at the same time the sense of discipline must be in command of the techniques to be used, bringing an idea into being and sending it out to its logical commercial destination. To dream is fine, but dreams alone, wandering and uncontrolled, can be futile in business and a girl seeking a career in fashion must quickly and positively learn that fashion, as artistic and creative as it is, must first and last be *business*. Like all business, fashion must make money—plain, ordinary, mundane dollars—in order to survive and grow.

Along with a sense of beauty, there must always be an unfailing sense of the practical. For instance: I have found in the intimacy of a department-store fitting room that no matter how beautiful a dress may be, a woman will have difficulty in absorbing the dress if it has more than one new idea for her. If it is in a *color* that is new to her and a *fabric* that is new to her, then it must be in a shape that is familiar. There must be, for her own security, something that she has owned and worn in her life before. There should also be something about the dress that is familiar both to her husband and to her family; if there isn't, they may look at her and say: "Where did you get that THING?"

In the fashion business, more so than any other, one must be able to lead and to listen, to create and to develop, to excite and to reassure, bearing the compass of new directions and the gyroscope of balance. I can assure you that for those who harness fashion creativity to marketability the rewards are high, the satisfaction intense, and the interest ever-renewing. I can assure you, too, that the way is long, hard, and sometimes frustrating, but always it is stimulating.

I would like to write now for a moment about *world fashion*, and to begin by saying that world fashion is becoming oriented to the West, to the United States in particular, in the common market of world ideas. It is an old-fashioned, out-moded belief that dress fashions come only from Paris. This may have been true in the early 1900's, but with communications as they are now, jet planes shrinking distances—no place unknown, no place remote—we all live in one small world, in fashion as in everything else. Ideas may come from Europe or from India, or a design from an ash tray in Copenhagen, a plate in Lisbon, a tile in Iran. I have seen the color of a mosque—a tower of a mosque at sunset, a certain brilliant blue—and I said: "I must have that color." But in business one must be tenacious about an idea and follow through with it. Anybody can say I would love to have that color or love to make that dress or love to invent some gadget; but unless one wants to do it passionately, and then goes on and *does* it, it never materializes and will just remain in the vacuum of desire and the waste of talk.

Fashion is not only turning to the West, but fashion is already a part of Western democracy. There used to be in fashion the haut monde and exclusive fantasies, but all that is settling down now and is a concept that belongs to the past. That is one of the many things so wonderful about this country; we are democratic in our ideas, and democratic in our fashion and our prices. The idea of class distinction, either in people or clothes, does not exist here. There is no such thing, for instance, as an inferior cotton dress; it is always a good cotton dress and the best you can buy in the world for the money. A woman accustomed to wearing a hundred-and-fifty-dollar dress can buy a six dollar cotton dress, and with her own little accessories or her manner of wearing it can look like a million dollars. Price no longer determines the appearance of a woman, because clothes in our country are democratic, too.

The thought of democracy in our living leads me away from fashion, for the moment, and prompts me to talk very seriously to the girl of Harrisburg or Topeka or San Diego who thinks that she must leave home and go to one city, to New York, if she is to make a success in any business career or to bring her dreams to realization in the arts.

The simple truth is that there is no longer *one* city, in this country or in any other. It used to be that New York was the center of things, the Big Time, but that has changed. Except for the *very* small places, there are few provincial towns in the United States any more. The speed of communications, the constant moving of people, the moving of ideas have broadened the small town thinking and the chances are that a girl's best starting place is at home. But if she is certain that her career is not in her home city, then she might do well to find out about Cleveland and Atlanta and Denver; maybe these cities have a better opportunity for what she wants than she can find in New York. There is nothing magic about New York, and often there is disappointment and heartache. (Yet, even as one writes about the difficulties of living in New York, he can never disregard the advantages of working there. New York is an interesting and stimulating city with the best art, music, theater. One can raise questions about a girl attempting a career in New York—unless she is positive about what she wants, is dedicated and determined; but, in fairness, one can never omit recognition of the city's cultural advantages.)

So many girls say: "But I want to go into one of the so-called glamour professions: the theater, publishing, fashion. Surely, I will have to go to New York."

I don't think so. If a girl wants a job very badly, if she is sincere about it and truthful with herself, she will succeed at the career she plans whether it is in Topeka, Chicago, New Orleans, or wherever it may be. It is the individual and not geography that determines success. The girl who says she would be better off over yonder, somewhere away from home, may only be running away from her own inadequacies.

The idea that fashion opportunities are greater in New York than anywhere else—even that is changing. There is a great fashion market in St. Louis, particularly for Junior clothes. In Dallas, there is a big sportswear market. Manufacturing in Los Angeles is competing with the New York manufacturing market. Chicago, too, is an important clothes center. Boston also has manufacturers making attractive sports and outdoor wear. Fashion no more starts in New York today than it starts in Paris. This—let me say again—is one world, and opportunities for the fashion business are everywhere. We may find some unknown person in Arizona who is making squaw skirts, and her skirts may take the country by storm. It is a worn-out idea that New York is the mecca for starry-eyed girls. If a girl—any girl—has beauty within her, and ability, has a message and is determined to give it, whether it be in fashion or advertising or whatever it may be, she can rid herself of her romantic, excited idea about New York and start her career in her home town. A girl should do an awful lot of research on herself, find out about herself, *and be honest about what she finds,* before she packs her suitcase to head out into the vagueness of New York.

But whether she decides to stay in her home town or to travel, let me say to her that *first,* before all else, she must search her soul to find out what it is that she wants to do; one must feel inside exactly what it is—in other words, it must come from the heart. I could repeat this from now until next week and still not say it often enough. A girl does not succeed by just some frivolous idea that comes off the top of her head. "I would like to go to New York and be a success." You would be surprised how many start out with no more basic idea, no more dictation of the heart, than just that. She wants to be a success! In what? How? Has she asked herself these questions? Can she answer them? If not, what chance does she think she will have in New York or anywhere, starting out blind to the discipline of mind and unaware of the necessity of work? To succeed, wherever it may be, there must be direction and ambition and determination, all blended together in endless work. And there is no point, none whatever, in settling for second best. From ballet dancer to typist, from file clerk to surgeon, a girl has got to plan for the best, and she will get what she wants only by a combination of rosy vision and ditch-digging. If we can't agree on this, that we will settle for nothing below the best, then let's stop. I have no advice for anyone who does anything halfway.

And what can a woman do outside the glamour fields; what can she do in the more prosaic areas of business? *Anything!* The answer is quick—anything. There are difficulties for women, but no limitations. Not long ago I was asked to speak at a symposium held for graduate girls at an upstate New York college where there was a panel of six businesswomen who were asked to speak on "Women in Business." One was an accountant. One was a contractor, a builder. One had a taxicab company in Philadelphia, and she was making a killing because she was smart enough to use a woman's imagination and ideas: she had taught her drivers to be polite at all times and even to hurry around and open the door for their passengers. Of course, the other companies with their tough guys were making all kinds of cracks about it, but she couldn't care less; she was making the money and her drivers were getting extra tips. The finest hotel I know in Europe is the Ritz in Madrid. It is run by a woman, and I am all for women running hotels; they make excellent hotel managers. Women doctors. Women lawyers. Women judges. What job does a girl want? What profession? Pick it out; it is open to her if she has a burning desire to accomplish something.

And whatever it is, whether in business or the professions, a woman in a career needs to face the fact that she *is* a woman. What's more, she can be proud of it, because if she uses her qualities as a woman, her understanding, her energies, her many abilities, she can face any situation and come out not only with an artistic and womanly satisfaction but also with a profit.

In business, she can stand up to any man; I have done it. I can walk into any banker's office, come to the point immediately, with no chatter or charm, and leave with the loan I went in for. The silliest thought that any woman in business can have is to imagine that she is handicapped and to wish that she were a man. I have built a business from just about nothing to a present volume of about five million dollars a year. I design, manufacture, and sell our clothes in some five hundred stores across the country, and I plan the business, make the policies, and nobody can say that I have lost one trace of femininity. This is very important for a woman in business. She must always keep her femininity.

This does not mean for one second that a woman should overlook her advantage of being a woman or fail to cash in on it. I am tiny—four feet, eleven—and with men in business I sometimes make a remark which they say, because I am small, is cute. Maybe it is cute; I don't know whether it is or not, and I don't care so long as they sign the paper and the deal is closed. Because of my size, I get away with a lot.

As a matter of fact, this being a woman, and knowing how to use it, can help you in business, even in transactions with other women. In the first few years of my career I used to go to Europe quite often to see the collections. In those days there were very few women buyers or viewers, mostly men were in the clothing business, and they would go over to see the collections and buy the dresses.

I would go on my own, quite alone, and I would make an appointment with a saleswoman, a French saleswoman in some particular house. Usually the appointment would be for early in the morning, half-past eight or nine, which is very early for the French. So at nine o'clock I would walk into the dressmaking house in Paris, and right behind me would come three good-looking men or two good-looking men—or even *one* good-looking man—and the saleswoman would look at me, look at the men, and who do you think she waited on first?

Of course, I could stand up and say: "Now you look here! I was here first and I am an American and I should be taken care of and I had an appointment." But, being a woman, I realized what was happening, and why shouldn't she take care of these men, and I might just as well face it—one must be feminine and realize, after all, that it is still a man's world (in certain instances).

This happened not once but many times in my business career, because of the men's size and their voices and their attitudes and everything else. Many times they would outtalk me in business deals and in business conferences, but I have learned to sit quietly and hold a right thought—even though at times it might be a little sharp-edged—and eventually things would come through the way I wanted them.

I learned to turn all this into an asset, and after waiting for an opportunity, I would say to the saleswoman: "Look, I know—these men—even though I was here first. I can understand, with your being French and wanting to take care of them, and they are so handsome and I bet they surely wanted to date you."

You know—if you can't lick 'em, join 'em. And pretty soon we two women were figuring on what she would wear when she dated them, and by the time we got around to my business, there wasn't anything she wouldn't do to please me.

Well, now that I think of it, it has been a long time since we left me back there in 1928 making all that money and putting it in the bank and buying stock and seeing myself getting rich. Then the crash of 1929 came, closed the bank, wiped out my stock, and left me with no more money than I had to begin with.

The next year, 1930, I married Wesley Simpson, who was in the textile business. We thought it would be a fine idea to use our experience in business together, and at first it was wonderful, a regular lark; but it wasn't long before the bird began slowly to settle to earth and we started having our difficulties. We would take our business home at night and we were never free from it; it became too much. It grew into a steady conflict of personalities and this is how I understand why so many people in the theater and movies divorce; each one has a personality so distinct that they clash. Just so, my husband is very clever and is full of ideas, but his ideas about business and mine sometimes differed. Finally, we parted in business, each to a separate success. We found that, for us, a career and a business and a home didn't mix. I don't say that they can't mix, but there is apt to be tension in such an arrangement and a woman must be ready to give up a business quickly if a marriage is threatened. Home and family should always come first.

It was after going out of business with my husband that I accepted an offer from a large firm, going to work for them as a designer. By now, though, something had happened to me in my designing, something I had learned, and I was no longer drawing, no longer sketching. Now I was working only with fabrics, and this is the technique I still use today. Occasionally, today, I may make a sketch, but it will be very rough, just a few scratches to indicate what I mean or to remind myself of what I am doing or to keep track of something that I have an idea for; but now, the drawing is only to suggest a silhouette.

I make the first toile myself, of muslin or some other draping material, and drape it on a model or on myself or on a figure, to see how it hangs, what it does, what it suggests. Then I have a cutter cut it, supervising him. The knowledge of cutting is very important, and technical knowledge also is required in order to direct an assistant or a worker in a designing room. After the cutting, I supervise every fitting, and follow through to the finished dress, costume, or suit.

All this is very practical and it is difficult to make this clear to the young people who only dream their dreams and come out with airy ideas and airy drawings; it is hard to make them know that their dreams will soon fade into wonder and puzzlement, into disappointment, when they try to translate them into actual dresses to be worn by smart women who know exactly what they want and demand it. It is all very well to envision a beautiful red chiffon dress floating through the air, and it may look wonderful in a sketch; but if a woman won't buy it and put it on and wear it and be happy in it, then that dress does not function —or, as we say, it does not work. What is more, no store or shop can sell it at a profit.

Not long after I went to work at the large establishment I mentioned a moment ago, I was taken in as a partner. Of course, I was happy, but very soon after this the man who had owned the business had a heart attack and had to retire. So there I was, young, living in an artistic world of creative design, and suddenly having a business on my hands. Besides designing, I now became production manageress, buying supervisor, advertising woman, publicity woman, saleswoman. I had not worked in the fashion business all this time with my eyes shut and I knew at least something about these different departments; but there had always been people to run each department and the head of the firm to supervise them. Now *I* was the head of the firm!

Of course, that was a good many years ago, and I am no longer frightened at the thought of running a big and complex business. In fact, sometimes, now, when I start out in the morning, going to my place of business, I think of myself as a vaudeville actor. You know the fellow I mean: the one who comes out and changes his personality by changing his hat. He puts on a new hat and he is one thing; and he puts on a turban and he is a maharaja; he puts on something else and he is a detective.

This is the way I am all day. The first thing in the morning, when I come in, I supervise the designing room, and there I am wearing an artistic hat, very gay and touched with bright colors. Then I go back and see about the pattern-makers, whether they are getting the right expression into the clothes, and here the hat is already a little less gay and the colors not so bright. Then I supervise production, and look at some of the things that are coming through to be shipped to the stores; after which I go into the piece-goods room to examine the materials that have come in.

By this time I am about to enter my office, and the hat has now become a severe thing, stern in form and meticulous in material, without trace of color; it is now a very business-like hat. In the office there are problems of banking and payrolls and credit and accounts. There are sales people and advertising people and buyers. I am no longer a woman with fingers lingering on a fabric; I am the head of a corporation with ten factories and hundreds of people dependent on me for their living.

Business, for man or woman, should never be only a question of bookkeeping and a return on your money. Business must forever be carried on with consideration for the people to whom you plan to sell. You must always know your public, and clothes must be made for it with perception and understanding. There can be no satisfaction unless, as you design and manufacture, you are thinking about the woman who will wear these garments that you are creating. Unless she enjoys them and loves them while she wears them, you have failed so far as she is concerned, and, on the practical side, if you multiply such personal failures by a number of times, you will find yourself, before long, being forced out of business.

In considering your customers, you constantly ask: Will these clothes fit into the lives of the women for whom they are being made? The sale in the store is incidental; you must think, instead, beyond the sale to the woman who will wear the garment. You must understand this woman and her needs and be so far ahead of her that when she goes into a store wanting a cocktail dress or a dress for a small dinner party, you will have that exact dress waiting there for her, entirely suitable for her and appropriate for the occasion.

I have found that most women are smart in their buying, but sometimes they make mistakes; one must never take advantage of the woman who cannot recognize a dress that is incorrect or inappropriate for her. It is never good business just to have a dress "walk out" of a store. What is good business, and is always important, is to think of what will happen to this dress and how will the woman feel who wears it. You are not in business to sell dresses. You are in business to dress women. There is a big difference in merely selling a dress and in dressing a woman.

In fashion, you not only think of the woman who will wear the clothes you design, but you constantly take into account her changing ways of living and you plan her clothes accordingly. We no longer have maids to fasten us up the back and care for little hooks and snaps—ergo, the zipper!

We no longer live in large houses with large closets. We live in smaller houses with smaller closets, or even apartments, and women now are far more discerning and selective about their buying; they just don't have the space to hang clothes that have no relationship with each other—certainly no space to care for the mistakes that we used to acquire and then put aside in our more extravagant and spacious times. This means, of course, that the designer and manufacturer has to be more careful, far more perceptive in foreseeing exactly what this woman will need for her personal way of life.

Today, weight plays an important part in fashion, influencing the kind of dresses we make and the materials we use. You see a woman go into a store nowadays and she is handed a beautiful dress; but the moment she touches it, she hands it right back. It is too heavy, and whatever else may be right with it, perhaps even perfect for her, it is too heavy and won't fit into her air travel allowance.

There is something else important today about a woman's clothes and this matter of travel. I was in Japan one time, traveling with a most attractive and beautifully dressed Japanese woman. She wore Japanese clothes and was immaculately neat and beautifully dressed. Yet she carried her wardrobe, every bit of it—kimonos, obis, and all accessories for a week—in one large folded handkerchief. I was traveling with suitcases and suitcases, though before I left the United States I believed I had stripped myself to only bleak necessities. On this same trip I went on to India, and there saw an Indian woman put a few saris in a tiny case and head out for a long journey on which she was always fresh and beautiful. So I came back knowing that in order to help the American woman in her new way of living, her increasing desire to travel, I had to build a new quality into her clothes; they had to be foldable and packable.

Before the day of the zipper, we used to pull dresses on over our heads, but this was in the days when we had maids to keep our hair arranged or we ourselves weren't in such a hurry and could just sit before the mirror and primp. Now we are on the go, changing clothes between appointments, and we want our hair to stay arranged; we haven't time to go back to the hairdresser, and, besides, it costs too much to have it done over so often. So, sometime ago, I said it was foolish to keep pulling dresses over our heads, disarranging our hair, and I was the first to make dresses that a woman steps into. Today, a woman can go into a store and try on any of my dresses with a fresh hair-do or even if she is wearing a hat; she has only to step into my garments; and this is because I was thinking of her and her hair-do as I designed her clothes.

You can always tell when you have succeeded and a woman is pleased with what you have done for her. One of my happiest memories is a woman telling me: "I will forever be grateful to you because the first time I wore one of your dresses, the man I wanted to propose to me did propose." She said it had been a very happy marriage, and, even though I had played so small a part in it, what she told me gave me pleasure and some reason for being. With all the problems and heartaches in fashion, and in all other business, there is frequent satisfaction, even joy, and I have found far more happiness in business than disappointment.

Sometimes people say: "You run a business. You make and cut some three hundred and fifty styles a year and provide the money that is necessary to send out these clothes to the stores and bring back a profit. You run a town house near Central Park. You run a country house with thirty-five acres and gardens and lakes. You play the part of a dutiful wife, and, throughout the years that they were young, you watched after your children. How do you do it?"

One hears similar questions asked about other women in business, and the answer, I believe, lies always within the individual woman. And I suspect that in every case the answer for each woman, whatever her career, is in a disciplined and well-organized mind. I run my house almost like I run my business, and I never do anything emotionally. If a servant quits, I don't throw up my hands. If there is a shortage of something, even in the midst of a social occasion, I don't get flustered. One learns to meet a situation, at home or in business. One develops patience and understanding. If I go into my place of business in the morning and see a girl doing something that I don't think she should be doing—if, for instance, she is making a dress in a way I don't think it should be made, I will never go off the deep end and scream at her or scold her at that moment. I wait until the end of the day and then call her in and talk with her, explaining what I think and saying that tomorrow I expect a better job. This is not only the kind way to do it, but it is sensible, for if I had scolded her in the morning, she might just as well have put on her hat and coat and gone home; she would have been ruined for work for the rest of the day. Being a sensitive person, I understand this. Being a businesswoman, I act accordingly.

It occurs to me, at this point, that I may not be directly an-

swering the questions of some women in business. I have been
writing a lot about myself and about my business, but these
women I now have in mind are not the heads of successful enterprises and they don't have servants. Instead, they may have children, who may or may not be in school; and they must get to
work on time, work every day, and punch a clock when they
leave. What about their careers in business?

I would not paint a drab sky rosy, and it would be foolish to
discount their problems and blithely talk about success. Yet I
think that they can manage to rise to executive positions and to
ownership; other women in similar circumstances have done it.
Again, it is a question of discipline—of your mind, your schedule at home and on your job, your plan of study and of advancement, your determination, all of it fitting together into an orderly
and well-thought-out way of life to cope with whatever work and
home situation you have. I would like to remind these women,
and all other women in business, of one important fact: If you
drop your handkerchief, some man nearby may stoop and pick
it up for you. Some man may even hold a door open for you.
But when it comes to business, you are in competition with all
men, and with other women; and unless you yourself plan your
success and carry it out—you yourself working alone and against
whatever competition—you may be completely sure that nobody
else will do it for you. Standing back, waiting for the way to
open for you, while you, a charming lady, pass on through to success—well, you will just keep standing there for the rest of your
days.

This brings up the matter of education. What about a woman's
education for a career in business? And here again we are immediately back to the basic fact: What career does she want?
Does she plan a definite career and intend to work for that goal,
letting nothing stop her? If she wants to be an architect, obviously she must study architecture and all other subjects that go
with this specialized study. If she wants to be a lawyer or a doctor, it is equally obvious what she must study. But if she wants
to go into business, what then? Her course of study may not be
quite so clear. There are any number of business specialties, some
of them included in this book—banking, brokerage, merchandiz-

ing, accountancy, insurance, advertising, public services—and if she is interested in any of these, her studies can be specifically aimed at that goal.

But what about the girl who is not sure of the exact area of business in which she wants to work, though she knows for certain that she wants a place somewhere in the business world? Maybe she thinks that without an exact sense of direction in business she can get along without a college degree, and maybe she could—some years ago; but here again things are changing, and now Ph.D's, a good many of them, are working in large business offices. Phi Beta Kappa keys are common in advertising agencies, publishing houses, the television industry, and newspaper offices. When a girl sails into business with her cargo of desire, she will have a much greater chance of reaching her destination if she has at least one college degree, and two are an advantage. Education, for a man or woman, is a salable commodity today, and the more education you have when you come into the personnel market, the higher the price you can command immediately and the higher the eventual position you are likely to achieve.

Now I think this is the time for us to take notice of one special girl. She is the one who comes into business casually, looking for a job so that she can prowl around, meet men, and get married. I am very careful about hiring a girl and I must always be certain that she is sincere about her work. Of course, I think it is important for her to get married; but if she has nothing more to offer than that she is young, beautiful, and charming, and she expects me to hire her, while she stands on tiptoe looking beyond the business toward men, she is very much mistaken. There would be too much of an investment in her, too much time teaching her the dress business or any other business, and unless she is really serious and intends to be able to cope with both marriage and a career, I think she is apt to be a risk. I suspect that the heads of most other businesses feel the same way. A bright and attractive personality is, of course, an asset; but lighthearted charm, without the foundation of ambition and courage, is a drug on the market, and is quickly pushed aside.

Salaries, of course, are always a problem for women, and,

speaking in generalities, taking into account the overall work situation of women in business today, I don't quite know what can be done about fair and honest salaries. Every now and then somebody tries to get a bill through Congress to equalize salaries for women and men in similar jobs. They may someday pass such a law, but I suspect that personnel departments will manage to get around it. I don't think that women can ever look to business to pay them the salaries they deserve, not so long as business can get them cheaper than men employees.

The answer, I believe, lies in women themselves. Just let a woman make herself so proficient, so indispensable that they can't run the place without her, and they then will pay her the money she earns. Already some women have done it. Dorothy Shaver pulled down a whacking good salary when she was president of Lord & Taylor. Madame Chanel did it decades ago, before the second World War, and then she retired. Recently, however, she came back out of retirement to make another success and a huge salary. If a woman has the talent and the tenacity, the ability to work and the determination to be paid for it, she can get the money. But let me mention something and emphasize it, if I can: wherever you are in business, whether just getting started or already in a good position, don't ever let anything upset you and shake your tenacity, sidetracking you into getting temperamental or into a pout, and causing you to do something silly. Just stay disciplined and tenacious and you will make whatever money is rightfully coming to you. If a woman makes herself indispensable to her company, that fact is sure to be recognized.

I would like to add something else that is especially important. I want to write off, completely and forever, the idea that business is a man's world and that women have to take second place in it. This is a rumor, a masculine canard, fostered by men who live in daily fear as they see capable and energetic women moving into big business. They are also afraid that the truth will leak out and the secret of their own success will become known, that the reason for their being in a high place is that they have surrounded themselves with smart women.

14

New Opportunities in

BUSINESS

BY THOMAS J. WATSON, JR.

CHAIRMAN OF THE BOARD
International Business Machines
Corporation

THOMAS J. WATSON, JR.

Born: 1914, Dayton, Ohio

Brown University: B.A., 1937

Lieutenant Colonel, United States Air Force, 1940–45
  Senior Pilot

International Business Machines Corporation, 1937–45
  President, 1952–61
  Chief Executive Officer, 1956
  Chairman of the Board, 1961

President's Advisory Committee on Labor Management Policy:
  Management Member
National Advisory Council for the Peace Corps:
  Vice-chairman
Bankers Trust Company:
  Director
Time, Inc.:
  Director
Brown University:
  Member of the Corporation
Boy Scouts of America, National Executive Board:
  Vice-president

Trustee:
  American Museum of Natural History
  Air Force Aid Society
  California Institute of Technology
  Thomas Alva Edison Foundation
  Eisenhower Exchange Fellowships, Inc.

A CAREER IS MUCH MORE than a means of making a living. It becomes a part of us as the years go by. It determines how and where we spend much of our time. It determines how we think of ourselves. It affects what others think of us. Most of us find, as we go on in life, that success is measured by more than titles, salaries, and other external marks of success. Our life's work must have a personal meaning, and it must make a contribution to the world we live in. Without these things, any work is too hard or too boring. With them, there is almost nothing we cannot do.

This, I realize, may seem a rather roundabout way to begin a chapter about new opportunities in business. I begin this way because I believe that choosing a career is one of the most difficult decisions we make in life. I would urge any student to go at it deliberately and cautiously. I know, of course, there are many successful men in the world today who were drawn into their careers through chance. But, even when we make the decision early in our lives, there are times when we waver and wonder if we are right.

This question of "job satisfaction" is one which seems to work to the disadvantage of business in the choice of a career. Young people, for example, seem to see an arbitrary division between business and public service or professional careers. Business is looked on merely as a way of making money, as a way of serving one's selfish ends. Government, teaching, and the professions are thought to offer richer personal satisfactions. In my experience, neither idea is necessarily true. Yet, as long as young people have this attitude, business is the loser.

This unflattering view of business got its start many years ago. Charles Dickens' books helped to form it, and generations of writers have kept it alive. The business novel, today, is almost always critical of the corporation. The people's attitudes in such fiction are as predictable as those of the villains and heroes in a Western—and bear about the same relationship to reality.

Historically, however, there were grounds for criticism, and in some instances they probably prevail, even today. For business is a man-made institution, and wherever you find men, you will find some who take unfair advantage of others. But on the whole, there have been vast improvements in the practices and ethics of American business, many of them brought on by the enlightened attitudes of businessmen themselves. Public opinion has speeded the process, with the enactment of the Sherman and Clayton anti-trust laws and other Federal and state statutes. And organized labor has brought its force to bear in redressing some of those historical wrongs. As a result of all these things, business has advanced to a point today where it is a strong and clean force in the daily life of the United States. Reflect for a moment on how the standard of living of the average American has increased in just the last three decades, and you can readily see how powerful a force business has become in the betterment of our lot as citizens of this great country.

Far from degrading people, business has helped lift them up. Business has made it possible for us to satisfy many of our needs and wants. It has helped to free us from much hard labor. It has created leisure and made room for dignity in our lives. And in the case of my own industry, it has enabled us to expand our problem-solving abilities and do things which only a generation ago would have been impossible.

Such a contribution should be quite enough for any group in a society. Today, however, business has an even more important job to do. For American business and the business of Western Europe, as I see it, has a pivotal role in the great contest between the free world and communism.

The Cold War is, to a very large degree, a protracted economic war, in which neither side has decisive natural advantage. Both the Communist and free nations are abundantly endowed with natural resources. Individuals, in terms of native intelligence and abilities, are pretty much alike the world over. Thus, this contest becomes one of organization; the ability of each side to organize its peoples and utilize its resources.

Under our system of government, the organization of people and marshaling of resources is primarily the job of business. If private business fails to do this job as efficiently as the Soviet bureaucrats, then we must inevitably fall behind in economic vitality, world esteem, and, finally, military power. It is no exaggeration to say that business, in the free world, is a front-line Cold War combatant. The methods expert in Detroit and the missile designer in Los Angeles are locked into an impersonal but very real conflict with their counterparts in Moscow and Leningrad.

I am frequently asked how well the Soviets are doing in computers. And I am asked the question by people who see the computer as an important weapon in technological progress and increased industrial production. So we, in IBM, are not left with the feeling that we are standing on the sidelines. On the contrary, we have the satisfaction of knowing that we are directly involved. And I know that my friends in other businesses feel the same way. Everyone in industry in America, whether they are making packaged foods, cigarettes, or missiles, must feel that they are contributing in a substantial way to the community in order to carry on their job with enthusiasm; and, make no mistake, none of us should enter industry in a company in which we do not feel we can be enthusiastic about the product or service which we are manufacturing or rendering.

Business plays a part everywhere in this mighty conflict. The vast aid programs we are undertaking must come, in the final analysis, from wealth created by business. If the world's poor and hungry and illiterate are one day to improve their lot, it will be because our society can continue to produce more than it needs for its own uses. The products we ship abroad to accomplish these aid programs will, in most cases, be supplied by business firms. The technical and organizational methods we export to the developing world are commonly the very same methods that have been created by men and women of business.

Thus, business, as I see it, can put you into the thick of the struggle. It can give you a sense of connection with your times. It can reward you—as nothing else can—with the satisfaction that comes from being a citizen needed in your country and a part of the great test of human will. This, I believe, makes a life worth living and a career in business fully worth-while.

There are many businessmen in the United States today who are no longer motivated by income or prestige; they already have all they want or need. Why, then, do they keep pushing? They do so, I believe, because they value this sense of involvement. They take pride in being a part of what's happening in the world.

Aside from this question of how business fits into the grand design, we should also ask ourselves what has been happening to business in the United States. Times change; trends change, especially business trends. These trends deserve your attention, for they help to point to where employment opportunities may be found in the future.

Two decades make up the whole lifetime of most of the men and women in college today. From the viewpoint of our economy, it is a very short time indeed. Yet in those two decades, in the period since the beginning of World War II, American business has almost completely remade itself.

For example, two vast new industries have been created: aerospace and electronics. The first is one of the nation's largest industrial employers. It accounts for almost a million jobs. The second has given great impetus to all forms of technological advancement. Not yet an industry in 1940, electronics has grown to giant size during the last twenty years. It presently accounts for more than $11 billion annually in manufactured products. Electronics has been rated as one of this century's most important technological developments—on a par, certainly, with the discovery of nuclear energy. It has already had a profound effect on the way we live. And most businessmen believe this is only the beginning.

But a young man looking for opportunity should not overlook the older industries as well. Most of them have expanded enormously—many with new products, new processes, new markets.

Almost half of all industrial sales today, I am told, come from recently developed products.

The petrochemical industry really got its start during World War I, but today that industry is creating some ten thousand newly synthesized products every year. Consumer needs, of course, are always changing, and manufacturers are constantly developing new products to meet that market.

Once again, if I may look to our own industry, we can see how far this change has gone. Twenty years ago, we were producing punched-card equipment and it was mostly used for routine record-keeping. It was not until the early 1950's that electronic computers came into business use. Even at that time, there were a lot of experienced people who did not believe computers would amount to very much. But they found a market and that market has been growing by leaps and bounds. Vacuum-tube machines gave way to transistorized systems. And these transistorized systems will undoubtedly make way for even more advanced forms of technology. Within the last seven years, computer speeds have increased forty times and memory units are now being built to store up to two hundred and eighty million characters of information.

Today, there are almost no limits on the uses to which data-processing systems can be put. There is scarcely a form of human endeavor in which the computer has not won a highly respected place: in business and industry, in science, engineering, medicine, education, and national defense.

Largly as a result of this mid-century business revolution, our country continues to move forward. In 1940, the sum of all U.S. goods and services amounted to $101 billion. By the start of 1961, we were producing at the rate of approximately $550 billion worth of goods and services.

One result has been an increase in jobs, from 47.5 million in 1940 to 66.5 million today. During the last ten years, we have been adding to them at the rate of seven hundred thousand new jobs each year. This is not enough. Our present rate of unemployment is too high. But the economy is healthy and there is good reason to believe that if we are inventive and resolute in the actions we take, we can overcome this difficult problem.

Along with industrial change, there have come many social advances. Americans are better educated. In your generation, for example, eighteen out of a hundred high-school students are going on to baccalaureate degrees. In my generation, the number was less than half of that.

We hear talk about our affluent society. But it always surprises me to learn how really affluent the average American family has become. In the last ten years, I am told, family purchasing power has gone up almost thirty per cent. Three out of every five families are in the middle-income bracket.

The successes of business have been translated into higher living standards and more leisure for most Americans. Businessmen have helped in this, and they have every reason to take pride in the accomplishment. But there is equally good reason for us to temper this pride with a fair amount of reserve. For, while our country's accomplishments are impressive, its needs are still enormous. There is a lot of work to be done.

Despite the billions we spend on education, there is a nationwide deficit of over a hundred and forty thousand classrooms. An alarming number of our cities are in decline. Some eleven million U.S. dwellings, I am told, are considered substandard. Hospital beds are in short supply. Public transportation has gone downhill. Air and water pollution are creating serious health hazards.

But these domestic needs, however acute, cannot compare to the really desperate levels of need which exist elsewhere in the free world. Of the almost two billion people outside the Sino-Soviet bloc, one and a quarter billion exist on a per capita income of less than $100 a year. Two-thirds of the world's total population suffers from malnutrition. In India, for example, millions die each year without ever having known what it is not to be hungry.

Some might argue that problems like these are government problems. In many instances they are, but business cannot divorce itself from them. What we need to overcome these deficits is a higher level of productivity in the United States and increasing industrialization. Productivity, as I see it, is the business of business. If we are to meet our domestic needs and shoulder our responsibilities abroad, we are going to have to increase that productivity.

There are rich opportunities, I believe, waiting in business for anyone who wants to help take on the job.

All college men and women of today have the good fortune of graduating into a world where almost everyone is optimistic about the economic growth of America. This is a healthy attitude, for optimists have the habit of proving themselves right.

My college class, on the other hand, graduated into the Great Depression. Many of my classmates wondered if the nation would ever recover. A great many of them planned their careers, knowing that things were bad and expecting that conditions might even get worse.

There is one very good reason for the present optimistic view of America's growth. A great technological explosion has erupted in the years since World War II. We may argue as to whether this force is old or new, a continuation of the Industrial Revolution or a new revolution in its own right. There are, however, significant differences between them. Not only have the processes of technological change been accelerated but the pursuit of change, of new knowledge and invention, has become a permanent way of life.

Business and government spending for research and development, as of 1960, has risen to more than $13 billion a year. Six cents out of every dollar of IBM income is invested in research and development, and that investment grows every year. This is true of many businesses. Some people have estimated that, by 1970, business and government spending for research and development will go up to $20 billion or more a year.

Almost overnight, in the early 1950's, industry began to draw on engineers and scientists in increasing numbers. By 1960, more than six hundred thousand engineers were employed by private industry; some twenty-five per cent of them were in research and development. In the 1930's, scientists were rare in industry. Today, half the nation's physicists, half the mathematicians, and three-fourths of its chemists have joined the ranks of business.

From these talented men there has come a steady flow of new products, new processes, and—in some instances—whole new industrial complexes. Industry has learned once and for all that investment in research is a necessary investment in the future. The pipeline on new products, new processes begins in the lab. There is no way of telling what may come out the other end. But experience has shown that we gain a great deal more from new products than we put into research.

Equally important, the time gap between the laboratory idea and the ultimate user in being whittled down. The Department of Defense is working hard to reduce the ten-to-eleven-year lead time, now required to design and produce a new weapons system, to four or five years. Nondefense industries are doing the same thing. As of 1950, it took ten years for a major new product to go from the drawing board to the market. Today, the cycle is down to from six to eight years. Experts say this trend will continue.

Moreover, we now find in the market a kind of built-in willingness to try what is new. As a result, we have before us not only an era of new ideas but an era of rather quick conversion of these ideas into products. In addition, we see willingness on the part of consumers and industry to change their buying and production habits.

This situation has no precedent in business history. It means that your opportunities not only exist but they are expanding. It gives good reason for the business optimism that prevails among today's youth. I, too, am convinced that the vast job ahead for business will be accomplished, and well within your lifetime.

Just because the economy is growing does not mean that every business firm or industry will grow along with it. There are tides in business. Obviously, if one can, it is better to swim with a tide than against one.

An industry becomes a growth industry because it meets the needs of its times. Some companies do this better than others. The reason, I've always felt, why some move ahead faster is that their managers develop a sensitivity to historical trends. They are able to see long-term needs. And they believe in their own vision. My father was such a man.

I remember very well an evening in 1923 when my father told us at dinner that he was changing the name of the Computing-Tabulating-Recording Company to International Business Machines. I was nine at the time, and thought this a pretty big name for something that didn't impress me very much. But he, like most business leaders, could perceive trends where others could see only events. When my father died in 1956, IBM was doing business in eighty-three nations abroad.

Growth industries, as businessmen view them, are those whose sales increase more than the average for all industry. *Fortune* magazine has predicted a gain of sixty per cent for all industry during the 1960's. As *Fortune* sees it, four industries will set the pace: electronics with a gain of two hundred and fifty per cent; chemicals, two hundred and twenty-five per cent; machinery and aluminum, one hundred per cent each. The data-processing industry, which was listed under electronics, was given an estimated three hundred per cent gain.

Aerospace, one of the liveliest of all growth industries, was not included, inasmuch as sales forecasts are related in the long run to world events. With the increasing emphasis on space exploration, aerospace expenditures, exclusive of military requirements, may go to $20 or $25 billion during the 1960's.

For the college-educated man or woman, such growth is less important than the *kind* of career opportunities a growth industry can offer. For example, in IBM we anticipate a possible slowdown in the rate at which some jobs will open up. Automated procedures are taking hold in the manufacture of computers and their components. But at the same time, we foresee a marked increase in those jobs which call for technical, professional, managerial, and sales skills. Nor is our experience unique. The same trend, I'm told, is in the wind for many of the more advanced technological industries.

White-collar workers in the United States now number some 28.5 million persons. By 1970, they are expected to increase to thirty-seven million. Within this white-collar category, the groups that are expected to grow most rapidly are the professional, technical, and kindred workers.

Within these groups, engineering may well continue to offer the greatest opportunities. More and more engineers are becoming engineer-businessmen. They are in demand for sales, and they are in constant demand for managerial positions. We see this in our own industry. Engineers and scientists are coming out of the plants and labs to take commanding positions in sales, service, and management.

What preparation will be required of the man and woman who wants to take advantage of these broad new opportunities in business?

Certainly, there will always be a need for the broadly trained, the man and woman with a liberal-arts background. But with the emphasis on technology, there is clearly a pressing need for scientifically trained man power in business and industry. Some observers have estimated that our country will need 1.7 million scientifically trained men and women by 1980. Between 1980 and 2000, that number will have to be doubled again.

If present educational trends continue, we shall go into 1980 with less than half the number we need. And by the year 2000, we shall be able to fill only one technical job in every three.

To date, there has been a great deal of talk about this shortage, but not nearly enough has been done about it. Those of you who are preparing yourselves with some background in science should have exceptional opportunities. Science may demand more work on the part of the student, but this sterner type of preparation is absolutely necessary if we are to sustain our present rate of technological growth.

Today, the scientifically trained have wide opportunities.

Thousands are going into sales in the more technically advanced companies. Great numbers transfer to managerial positions, especially in science-based companies. A forty-year survey of MIT engineering graduates showed that fifty per cent were in jobs other than engineering. Twenty per cent, or one in every five, was in management.

We see this movement in a company like IBM. Ten years ago our sales and management staffs consisted almost entirely of men with business and liberal-arts educations. Today, we are experiencing a substantial shift of scientifically trained people into management.

This does not necessarily mean that there is a shrinkage in business opportunity for the young man or woman educated in business and the liberal arts. The man or woman who is educated in the humanities often brings to business a healthy awareness of some of the faults and the shortcomings of business. He has learned enough of history to know that institutions must change if they are to prevail. And he develops the habit of looking at business to see how the institution can be improved; how it can be made to serve the requirements of the society in which it exists. This kind of critical thinking is just as necessary to business as the scientifically trained innovator. It compels us to ask ourselves where we are going. As long as there are men who will look critically at business in this light, we have reason for believing that business will adapt itself to change and establish its right to survive.

But a liberal-arts or business education today, if it is to be useful, must not exclude the hard sciences. For, as I see it, the student—however broad his outlook may be—who insists on shunning all forms of science is foolishly delimiting his opportunities in business if he wishes to make business a career. Science plays too large a role in business for him to ignore it. James T. Killian pointed this out recently when he said, ". . . science has become one of the essential elements in any liberal education for modern living."

Another point, as important as any I can make: no student today will retire from the same world into which he graduates.

To keep up with change, he is going to have to keep up with learning. The time has long passed when a man can say that he has mastered his profession, close the books, and learn nothing more.

The nature of change has always been unpredictable. In today's technological world, it has become more unpredictable than ever. The rather orderly rungs of yesterday's career ladders may not exist tomorrow. A new technology mastered today in school may be obsolete by another not yet discovered. Such things do not happen overnight. But it is vital that young people beginning their careers recognize that they do happen. The only way to accommodate to these shifts is through constant learning. To get ahead in business—and to stay ahead over the long run—a young man must be prepared to accept uninterrupted education as a necessary way of life.

It won't be easy; but it can be fun, for out of it there comes a great sense of adventure in racing to keep up with the times. That is one of the stimulating things about business. Tomorrow can never be like yesterday.

In all businesses, we try to predict what may happen in the next ten or twenty years. But in most cases, we are really only projecting current trends. This becomes difficult, for trends frequently wander off course. Political events affect them. Social changes may alter them. Technological improvements may completely upset them.

Consequently, we may be able to plan our business life only in a broad sense. What we must not do is to make the mistake of assuming that because some present trends are promising, they will always be so.

I think there are sound reasons for believing that the 1960's will turn out as well as some of the optimistic predictions. Most businessmen are doing their planning on that assumption. But let us not forget that any number of things might happen to upset these estimates.

For one thing, if we were to permit ourselves to be outdistanced by the Soviet Union in economic growth, we would find our country declining in prestige and power.

Or, if we were to pursue a policy of trade restriction, we might ultimately find ourselves in a trade war with Western Europe. This could lead to a breakup in the NATO alliance.

Or, if we were to neglect our social responsibilities by putting up with a second-rate system of education and a persistent high level of unemployment, we might then undermine the structure of our whole system.

If a young man wants to be a good businessman, he must also learn to take an active part in community and public affairs. For, as I see it, business is but a means to an end, rather than an end in itself. It exists to help people supply their wants, to achieve better and fuller lives. It is to these ends that we must direct our energies, for unless all citizens have the opportunity to achieve those things for themselves, we all share to some degree in the failure.

If businessmen are sometimes thought to be self-centered, there is some truth in the belief. As in every profession, there are errants in business, men who put self-interest before everything else. Fortunately, however, they are few and their numbers are declining. The modern businessman looks upon business as a public institution, one which must be valued by the public if it is to endure. He respects public needs and he is aware of the responsibilities of business in the life of the nation. These are the things that give him his sense of values and make his career in business worth-while.

This, then, is the environment you can expect to find in most American business today. It is rich in challenge, in opportunity, in reward. There is important work to be done, for those who choose new opportunities in business.